The DATE DUE Age

—— | VOLUME 9 | ——

Other titles in the
World History by Era series:

WORLD HISTORY BY ERA

The Nuclear Age

VOLUME 9

Terry O'Neill, *Book Editor*

Daniel Leone, *President*
Bonnie Szumski, *Publisher*
Scott Barbour, *Managing Editor*

Greenhaven Press, Inc., San Diego, California

Library of Congress Cataloging-in-Publication Data

The nuclear age / Terry O'Neill, book editor.
    p. cm. — (World history by era; vol. 9)
    Includes bibliographical references and index.
    ISBN 0-7377-0770-4 (pbk. : alk. paper) —
ISBN 0-7377-0771-2 (lib. bdg. : alk. paper)
    1. Nuclear weapons. 2. World Politics—1945– 3. Beat
generation. 4. Nuclear arms control. 5. National liberation
movements—History—20th century. 6. United States—
Military policy. 7. Nonviolence—History—20th century.
I. O'Neill, Terry, 1944– II. Series.

D840 .N82 2002
909.82'5—dc21   2001040847

Cover inset photo credits (from left):
Corel Professional Photos; Photodisc; Corel Professional
Photos; Corel Professional Photos; Planet Art; Digital Stock;
Photodisc
Main cover photo credit: © CORBIS. Atomic Shell Explosion.
The mushroom cloud from "Grable," the first nuclear
artillery shell, part of Operation UPSHOT-KNOTHOLE. The
artillery piece used to fire the nuclear shell weighed 85 tons.
Digital Stock, 90
Library of Congress, 45, 56, 114, 205, 216
National Archives, 123

CONTENTS

Chapter 1: 1945–1949

1. The Atomic Age Begins
The *Enola Gay*'s tail gunner describes his experience
in the plane that dropped the atomic bomb on
Hiroshima.

2. The Atom Bomb: A Survivor's Story
An eleventh-grade boy recalls what it was like when
the atomic bomb dropped on Hiroshima.

3. The Iron Curtain
England's prime minister warns an American audience of the dangers of Soviet aggression.

4. The Truman Doctrine: The United States Will Support Nations Threatened by Aggressors
The U.S. president tells Congress that the nation must
support others that are threatened by aggressors.

5. India's Independence Day
A reporter describes the atmosphere in New Delhi on
the day India became independent.

6. The Transistor
The development of the transistor made way for all
kinds of powerful, miniature technology.

Chapter 2: 1950–1959

Chapter 3: 1960–1969

FOREWORD

The late 1980s were a time of dramatic events worldwide. Tragedies such as the explosions of the space shuttle *Challenger* and the Chernobyl nuclear power plant shocked the world out of its complacent belief that humankind had mastered nature and firmly controlled its technological creations. In U.S. politics, scandal rocked the White House when several high-ranking officials in the Ronald Reagan administration were convicted of selling arms to Iran and aiding the Nicaraguan Contra rebels. In global politics, U.S. president Ronald Reagan and Soviet president Mikhail Gorbachev signed a landmark treaty banning intermediate-range nuclear forces, marking the beginning of an era of arms control. In several parts of the world—including Beijing, China, the West Bank and Gaza Strip, and several nations of Eastern Europe—people rose up to resist oppressive governments, with varying degrees of success. In American culture, crack cocaine and inner-city poverty contributed to the development of a new and controversial music genre: gangsta rap.

Many of these events were unrelated to one another except for the fact that they occurred at about the same time. Others were linked to global developments. Greenhaven Press's World History by Era series provides students with a unique tool for examining global history in a way that allows them to appreciate the seemingly random occurrences as well as the general trends of human progress. This series divides world history—from the time of ancient Greece and Rome to the end of the second millennium—into ten discrete periods. Each volume then presents a collection of both primary and secondary documents that describe the major events of the period in chronological order. This structure provides students with a snapshot of events occurring simultaneously in all parts of the world. The reader can then see the connections between events in far-flung corners of the world. For example, the Palestinian uprising (*Intifada*) of December 1987 was near in time—if not in character and location—to similar protests in Beijing, China; Berlin, Germany; Prague, Czechoslovakia; and Bucharest, Romania. While these events were different in many ways, they all involved ordinary citizens striving for self-autonomy and democracy against governments that were attempting to impose strict controls on their civil liberties. By making the connections between these events, students can see that they comprised a global movement for democracy and human rights that profoundly impacted social and political systems worldwide.

Each volume in this series offers features to enhance students' understanding of the era of world history under discussion. An introductory essay provides an overview of the period, supplying essential context for the readings that follow. An annotated table of contents highlights the main point of each selection. A more in-depth introduction precedes each document, placing it in its particular historical context and offering biographical information about the author. A thorough chronology and index allow students to quickly reference specific events and dates. Finally, a bibliography opens up additional avenues of research. These features help to make the World History by Era series an extremely valuable tool for students researching the rise and fall of civilizations, social and political revolutions, cultural movements, scientific and technological advancements, and other events that mark the unfolding of human history throughout the world.

INTRODUCTION

We knew the world would not be the same. A few people laughed, a few people cried. Most people were silent.

—American nuclear physicist J. Robert
Oppenheimer, on the first atomic
bomb test at Alamagordo, New Mexico

The Nuclear Era, inaugurated by the explosion of a bomb more devastating than anyone had ever before imagined, was a time of unending conflict and tumult. From the Cold War and the rebellions that ended Western European colonialism to the revolutions in art, music, science, and society, the years between 1945 and 1980 were seldom quiet or tension-free.

THE BOMB

The Nuclear Era can be said to have begun on August 6, 1945, the day that, in essence, ended World War II. On that date, the United States, with the agreement of its two major allies, Russia and England, dropped an atomic bomb on Hiroshima, Japan. Three days later the United States dropped another bomb on Nagasaki. By the next day, Japan had conceded defeat. The war was over and the Nuclear Age had begun.

The atomic bombs dropped on Japan were products of the Manhattan Project, an undertaking involving scientists from the United States, England, and Canada—most from the United States—working together on various aspects of the project. Similar research was being conducted in Germany and Russia, but success was first achieved by the workers on the Manhattan Project.

The atomic bomb was made possible by the scientific discoveries early in the twentieth century about the nature of atoms. By the late 1930s scientists knew that the atoms of certain materials could be processed in such a way as to create massive chain reactions—and devastating explosions. The two primary processes they discovered are fission and fusion. The first atomic bombs— also called nuclear bombs—used heavy metal elements (uranium or plutonium) in a fission process: The heavy metal atoms were bombarded with neutrons, splitting the atoms and releasing energy and more neutrons. (Fusion—an even more powerful process—was the basis of the hydrogen, or thermonuclear, bomb developed a few years later. In the fusion process, hydrogen atoms are squeezed together at high temperatures, again releasing massive amounts of energy.)

The atomic bomb was first tested in Alamogordo, New Mexico, on July 16, 1945, on an isolated desert mesa 120 miles south of Albuquerque. Observers were as close as 10,000 yards—a proximity so dangerous as to be unimaginable today. A blinding flash of white light, a tremendous heat wave, and a deafening roar were followed by a huge ball of fire rising above a mushroom-shaped cloud that extended almost eight miles above the ground. A three-quarter-mile patch of the surrounding desert area was fused into glass. People in Albuquerque saw the flash and felt the aftershock. The tests were deemed a success, and less than a month later the bombs were dropped on Japan.

The devastating effect of the two bombs gave a terrifying hint of what would happen if a nuclear war broke out among nations capable of using similar bombs. With a force of more than fifteen thousand tons of TNT, the first bomb immediately destroyed four square miles of Hiroshima, killing 66,000 people and injuring nearly 70,000 more. The second bomb, with a force of 21,000 tons of TNT, destroyed nearly half of the smaller city's structures, killing 39,000 people and injuring another 25,000. The destruction's immensity, and the knowledge that one group of human beings had done this to another, stunned the people of the world. As nuclear physicist J. Robert Oppenheimer, director of the Los Alamos laboratory during the bomb's development, stated, the bomb "made the prospect of future war unendurable." (Oppenheimer later vainly opposed the development of the even more devastating hydrogen bomb.)

Yet flattening cities and killing and injuring human beings were not even the worst effects of the atomic bomb, as many Hiroshima and Nagasaki survivors discovered when they developed various forms of radiation sickness and cancer in the following years. The atomic bomb and its successor, the hydrogen bomb, sent out immense clouds of radioactive fallout that spread for several hundred miles, killing or sickening plant and animal life and destroying the landscape itself. The radioactivity from this fallout could last for centuries, poisoning and destroying all forms of life.

The people of the world knew for the first time that war was capable of destroying Earth. As President John F. Kennedy noted in a 1961 speech to the United Nations, "Today, every man, woman and child lives under a nuclear sword of Damocles, hanging by the slenderest of threads, capable of being cut at any moment by accident or miscalculation or madness."

This "Damocles sword" was one of the most pervasive influences of the Nuclear Age. People and companies built bomb shelters in or near their homes and businesses, stocking them with huge supplies of canned foods, bottled water, and other supplies. Schools conducted bomb drills. The popular American television variety program *Ed Sullivan's Show of Shows* repeatedly broadcast a short animated film showing people's flesh melting and the green Earth turning to blackened desert. People were afraid of the bomb. Life would never again be the same.

THE COLD WAR

With World War II over, people hoped the world would go back to peacetime calm, but this was not to be. Until 1940, the Soviet Union had been friendly with Nazi Germany. In fact, the two nations had signed a nonaggression pact in 1939 even as Germany was busy sweeping through Scandinavia and Europe, taking territory wherever it could. Then, in 1940, Germany attacked the Ukraine, a part of the Soviet Union, sending in 3 million troops that advanced as far as Leningrad. Stunned and angry, the Soviet Union joined with the Western Allies to fight Hitler. But even during the years the Soviet Union was working with the United States and Great Britain to defeat Germany and Japan, the Western Allies did not quite trust the USSR, and the USSR did not trust them. What they had in common were their enemies. What they did not have in common were their essential belief systems. The United States and Great Britain believed in capitalism and democracy. The Soviet Union believed in a repressive form of communism.

Because of these differences, the Allies found it difficult to agree on peace settlements and monitoring arrangements at the end of the war. For the second time in less than fifty years Germany had stormed into other countries, taking over land and people with a fury that threatened to overwhelm not only the small European nations but also the gigantic Soviet Union. The Ukraine alone lost some 6 million people, with another 2.5 million captured and taken to Germany for slave labor. The majority of these people are thought to have perished either at German hands or during Allied air raids. Another 38 million Europeans, Russians, and Americans died, in addition to the 6 million Jews killed in the Holocaust. Neither the Western Allies nor the USSR wanted to see Germany have the opportunity to do this ever again. But their views on how to ensure this differed. To satisfy all, they ended up dividing supervisory responsibilities rather than sharing them. They split Germany into four sectors, one to be overseen by the USSR, the others by the United States, England, and France.

Almost immediately, the USSR moved into Czechoslovakia and Poland and established Communist rule in these Eastern European nations that bordered the Soviet Union. British prime minister Winston Churchhill declared that "a shadow has fallen on the scenes so lately lighted by the Allied victory. . . . From Stettin in the Baltic to Trieste in the Adriatic, an iron curtain has descended across the Continent." The Allies shuddered and turned their attention to rebuilding the rest of Europe through the U.S.-sponsored European Recovery Plan (also known as the Marshall Plan). Through this plan, the United States provided financial aid to European countries devastated by the war. Participants, however, had to declare their commitment to democracy.

Neither side was eager to engage in war again—particularly under the shadow of the atomic bomb—but they had no reluctance to subvert each other in other ways. Thus, in a 1947 speech, American statesman Bernard Baruch declared that although there might not be an active shooting war going on, "let us not be deceived—we are today in the midst of a cold war." His phrase *Cold War* stuck and became the popular name for the years spanning the next four decades.

Almost from its beginning, the Cold War was essentially polarized between the two largest nations, the United States and the Soviet Union—soon to be known as the superpowers—with other nations participating in varying degrees at different times. As early as 1947 President Harry S. Truman asserted the U.S. intent to support nations in their efforts to maintain or establish democratic independence and combat Soviet and other aggression. The Soviets, on the other hand, were eager to spread the gospel of communism. In addition, the superpowers shared the paranoia that everywhere the other nation gained influence was a potential threat to itself. President Dwight Eisenhower described it thus: "You have a row of dominos set up; you knock over the first one, and what will happen to the last one is that it will go over very quickly." The so-called domino theory seemed a perfect justification for U.S. interventions in whatever way necessary to prevent communist expansion.

Examples include the U.S. support until 1980 of tiny nationalist China, beaten during a Chinese civil war by the formidable Communist forces led by Mao Tse-tung. In 1953 the United States

sent nearly 6 million troops to help South Korea fight against
Communist North Korea. The United States became embroiled
in its most demoralizing war when it had its troops fighting
Communists in South Vietnam from 1965 through 1975. The
United States secretly supported rebels fighting Communist or
Communist-sympathizing leaders in several African and Latin
American countries, including Guatemala and Chile. The United
States secretly plotted to kill Communist or Communist-leaning
leaders in Cuba and Zaire as well as in other countries.

At the same time the USSR sent troops into several Eastern European countries to stomp out democracy movements. It sent
various kinds of aid, including troops, to several African nations.
It blockaded Berlin and built the Berlin Wall. And it periodically
cracked down on its own satellites (Hungary, Poland, and others) to enforce Communist control.

The Cold War tensions deeply affected ordinary citizens. In the
United States, for example, people fell victim to "the red scare,"
a time in the early 1950s when Communists were considered the
equivalent of the devil incarnate. "Better dead than red" was a
popular slogan, and politicians and everyday citizens set about
routing out all suspected Communists.

Wisconsin senator Joseph R. McCarthy made a name for himself when he claimed that Communists were working in the State
Department. Communists were blackballed from many occupa-
tions, and suspected Communists were hounded out of jobs,
schools, and towns. The red scare also seemed to justify U.S. intervention in the politics and wars of many countries. At the
same time, Russia's fear of the United States caused it to intervene in other nations' affairs as well.

THE ARMS RACE

A constant companion of the Cold War was the arms race. The
nuclear bombs that destroyed Hiroshima and Nagasaki were
only the first step in the decades of ever-increasing arms design-
ing, building, and stockpiling. The United States was the first to
have the atomic bomb, but by 1949 the Soviet Union had successfully exploded its first one. This elevated the Cold War to a
new level. Now both of the major powers had similar capacity to
cause worldwide devastation.

Then, in 1952, another nation entered the lethal class: England,
too, had acquired the nuclear bomb. But the United States moved
things a notch higher once again by developing the hydrogen
bomb, which was much more powerful than the atomic bomb.
Within a few more years, France and China had nuclear bombs,
with more countries to follow by the late 1970s.

Even though two bombs had caused enough havoc to end World War II, neither the United States nor the USSR was satisfied with having one or two bombs. They began to stockpile the weapons and to develop new means of deployment and of making smaller, more powerful versions. Eventually, each superpowers' nuclear arsenal contained enough of the weapons to destroy the entire earth several times. U.S. general Omar Bradley's 1948 remark in an Armistice Day speech seemed even truer as the years passed. Bradley said, "The world has achieved brilliance without wisdom, power without conscience. Ours is a world of nuclear giants and ethical infants."

Some effort was made to control the bomb inventories and the ways they were tested, for as was shown in Japan, the bombs left more damage behind than flattened buildings. The world's leaders knew the accidental release or loss of a weapon could be perilous indeed. In 1963 the United States and USSR agreed to the Nuclear Test Ban Treaty, which confined nuclear bomb testing to underground sites and banned them from the atmosphere, in outer space, and underwater. In 1972 the Strategic Arms Limitations Talks (SALT) limited the deployment of antiballistic missiles, weapons designed to destroy incoming intercontinental ballistic missiles (ICBMs) with nuclear warheads (nuclear bombs) before the ICBMs hit their targets. SALT also forbade the building of additional nuclear warheads. In 1979 SALT II set further limitations.

These various agreements (which were also signed by other nations with nuclear capabilties) should have reduced the levels of tension inspired by the massive arms buildups—and, in calmer times, the agreements were, indeed, soothing—but neither superpower was ever confident of the other's honesty.

THE END OF EMPIRE

As if the overwhelming tensions incited by the Cold War and the arms race were not enough, the world underwent many other political and military upheavals during the Nuclear Era as well. In particular, the period saw the end of the Western European empires established during the Industrial Revolution and earlier.

Many countries had colonies, but the primary colony holders were Great Britain (whose colonial empire prior to World War II contained nearly one-fourth of the earth's land surface and population), France, Portugal, Belgium, Germany, Italy, and Spain. These seven nations claimed almost every African country, as well as countries in Asia and elsewhere, as their colonies. Each of the seven treated its colonies somewhat differently. Some ruled their colonies entirely from home, giving the native people no say in their government and often offering little in the way of education or other benefits. Others encouraged native participation in government, provided educational opportunities, and helped create useful infrastructures that would benefit the colonies when they obtained their independence. The ruling country's means of governing often affected how a colony became independent—as most did during the Nuclear Era. (In fact, in Africa alone some fifty new nations emerged during this period, some through violent independence movements and some through voluntary relinquishment by the colonial power.)

There were probably many reasons for the relatively quick end to the European nations' empires, but a primary one was World War II. The war exacted huge costs from Europe, and maintaining colonies, particularly ones that did not want to be colonies any longer, was an expensive business. Some nations could simply no longer afford to keep their colonies, and others no longer had the resources to control rebellious colonies.

Although Africa had the most colonized nations, India's independence—gained from Great Britain in 1947—was key to ending European colonialism. Indians had been trying to achieve independence for decades, and by the time World War II was over, Great Britain was ready to grant it. Britain was one of the colonial rulers that encouraged local participation in government, and India had developed a large Indian bureaucracy. This helped the transition from colony to independent nation go relatively smoothly in the area of self-government, although other problems did occur—the largest being the inability of India's large Muslim and larger Hindu populations to work together. Consequently, instead of merely liberating the colony, Britain divided it into two separate nations—Hindu India and Muslim Pakistan—when it granted independence. Some five hundred thousand people died in the mass migrations that took place as Hindus in Pakistan relocated to India and Muslims in India relocated to Pakistan. Unfortunately, even that did not end the two groups' antagonism. Almost immediately after independence, the two began fighting over the northern border province, Kashmir.

Nevertheless, Britain liberated most of its remaining colonies in the next decade, inviting them to remain connected to the mother country as part of the British Commonwealth, a group of countries, including Britain and former colonies, that maintain close ties and acknowledge the British monarch as the symbolic head of their association.

Not every British liberation went as smoothly as India, however. In Kenya, for example, the Mau Mau, anticolonial Kikuyu tribal members, fought bloody battles against the English beginning in the early 1950s. After many Mau Mau assassinations and acts of sabotage, the British declared a state of emergency in 1953 and sent in thousands of troops to crush the uprising. Within three years, more than eleven thousand rebels and some two thousand colonial loyalists had been killed. Nevertheless, the Mau Mau continued their campaign, and in 1963 Kenya eventually gained its independence.

Britain—and other colonial rulers—did not relinquish every colony. Britain, for instance, gave part of Ireland its independence, but it hung on to Northern Ireland, believing it was not ready to be independent and that it was more tied to England psychologically than southern Ireland. But Northern Ireland was—and remains—a deeply polarized region, split by economy and—especially—by religion. Catholic nationalists want independence and Protestant loyalists want to remain part of Great Britain. Both sides are responsible for countless bombings, murders, and other violence in the name of their cause.

INTERNAL WARFARE

Sovereign countries, too, were subject to the upheavals common to the Nuclear Era. Many countries underwent civil wars or other violent internal conflicts during this period. A prime example is Israel.

For decades, Jewish leaders had been lobbying to gain a Jewish homeland in the Middle East where the Jews had originated. As a result of war with Turkey, the British had a mandate over a country called Palestine. Containing the city of Jerusalem—holy to Christians, Jews, and Muslims—Palestine was a highly desirable location to the Jews. The British had encouraged their immigration there following World War I. But the Jewish immigrants and the Arabs (mostly Muslims) who already lived there were in frequent, deadly conflict.

Following World War II the British agreed to give up the land and to let the United Nations determine how it would be settled. In 1948 the UN divided Palestine into Israel, which was given to the Jews, and Jordan, which was given to the Arabs. Jewish refugees, fleeing the horrors of the Holocaust, flooded into Israel. Native Palestinians moved to Jordan but felt displaced. In addition, a major bone of contention was Jerusalem, now located in Israel.

Immediately after the partition, Arabs attacked Israel in the first of many Arab-Israeli wars. In most cases, Israel gained even more territory in these conflicts, angering not only the Jordanian Arabs but the surrounding Arab countries as well.

In 1964 several Palestinian nationalist groups banded together into the Palestinian Liberation Organization to work toward the dissolution of Israel and the reclamation of Palestine. The two groups continued their battles throughout the Nuclear Era and beyond.

SOCIAL REVOLUTION

While political and military battles were raging around the world, so were battles for social justice, in some cases as violent as the military battles.

South Africa is a prime example. Originally settled by Dutch colonists during the seventeenth century, then going through various periods of being a colony and being a sovereign nation, South Africa gained its final independence following World War I. Of primary importance to the ruling class—the Dutch who had descended from the earliest European settlers in the area— was maintaining the separation of the races. In 1948 the Nationalist Party came into power and formally established apartheid, a complex series of laws that established the ways the races could work and live—as separately as possible. Not only was racial mixing forbidden, but blacks, coloreds (mixed race), and groups such as Indians and Asians had to have passbooks with them at all times. These stated the individual's official race and determined where in the country that person could be at any time. Protest and rebellion began in earnest in the 1970s, at first using the nonviolent techniques made famous by Mahatma Gandhi of India, but in 1960, when the South African government used military might to quell a demonstration in the black community of Sharpeville and ended up killing and injuring dozens of blacks, the antiapartheid protestors also resorted to violence to further their goals. At the end of the Nuclear Era, the two groups were still struggling to find a livable solution.

The United States, too, was rife with social polarization and revolution during this era. Blacks used both peaceful and violent means to achieve equal rights; students and others demonstrated both for and against U.S. involvement in the Vietnam War; women banded together to protest gender discrimination; environmentalists and animal activists often used extreme measures to demonstrate the importance of their cause; domestic terrorists set off bombs in general protest against the government. It is doubtful that ever before or since has the United States seen as much social foment as during the 1960s and the 1970s. Much of this foment resulted in improved social justice through such legislation as the Civil Rights Act, passed in 1968 and requiring equal rights for all citizens, regardless of race or gender, in public accommodations, housing, voting, education, and other areas of American life.

SCIENTIFIC REVOLUTION

Not everyone experienced turmoil and conflict during the Nuclear Era. In the scientific field, many amazing advances occurred. Some of these, such as the laser, came out of the same research being done to improve military weapons or resulted from the Cold War competition. The space race is one example of the latter.

With the development of the atomic bomb, the two superpowers used science to develop more and better ways to deploy the weapon should the need arise. They developed amazing rockets that could be controlled remotely and strike with pinpoint accuracy. These advances in rocketry led scientists to believe that humans could conquer space. The superpowers secretly worked on that goal, and in 1957 the Soviet Union launched the first artificial satellite, *Sputnik I. Sputnik*'s successors managed to launch a dog into space that same year, and it was not long before the Soviets had a person orbiting Earth. The United States raced like mad to catch up. Allowing the Soviets supremacy in space not only hurt U.S. pride but was also viewed as a potential military threat. President John F. Kennedy devoted many resources to the space race and crowed with triumph when Americans landed the first men on the moon. For many years the space race was a deadly competition between the superpowers, but ultimately both countries won when they began to cooperate in the venture to conquer space.

Other examples of the extraordinary leaps of science during the Nuclear Era include the transistor, which made many large electric devices obsolete. With the development of the transistor, which became smaller and smaller over time, ordinary people could use pocket radios and other miniature devices that previously had only been the stuff of science fiction. The gigantic ENIAC computer was developed in 1946 by researchers at the University of Pennsylvania. Before the end of the Nuclear Era, the personal computer was almost within the reach of an ordinary household.

In 1953 scientists first proposed the molecular structure of human DNA, "the building block of life." The first human heart transplant was performed in South Africa in 1967, an operation that changed the face of medicine.

REVOLUTION IN THE POPULAR ARTS

Many changes also occurred in the world of the popular arts during the Nuclear Era. Whether the changes were actually advances was always a matter of debate.

In the early 1950s art, music, film, and theater reflected the early Cold War paranoia and conservatism. But by the mid-1950s rebellion struck, and the popular arts took off in new directions. In music, rock and roll took the field, making teen tastes dominant in determining what and how much sold. Parents decried the music's corrupting influence, but teen dollars kept the music going, and it kept evolving in "dangerous" new directions—from rock inspired by rhythm and blues to the drug-influenced psychedelic music of the 1960s and the punk rock of the 1970s.

In literature, Jack Kerouac and the other Beat writers scandalized the public and the academic world with their free-flowing, antiestablishment, gritty writing.

In the art world, the abstract expressionism style, which had taken over the art world in the 1950s and which portrayed very few recognizable representations of actual objects, gave way to the purely, caricaturishly representational pop art style.

AN ERA OF TENSION, CONFLICT, AND ACHIEVEMENT

It is impossible to touch on every important event of the Nuclear Era in a book of this length. But the editor has made every effort to select articles that provide a perspective on some of the era's major events and movements. The articles include both eyewitness accounts and historians' overviews. A chronology highlights additional events and shows the chronological interweaving of the various events and movements of the era. A bibliography provides many starting points for the reader's further exploration of the Nuclear Era. Together, this volume gives readers a broad perspective on a fascinating period in history.

WORLD HISTORY BY ERA

1945–1949

CHAPTER 1

THE ATOMIC AGE BEGINS

GEORGE R. CARON AND CHARLOTTE E. MEARES

On July 17, 1945, at Los Alamos, New Mexico, as the war in the Pacific dragged on after the war in Europe had ended, the United States secretly tested the world's first atomic bomb. One witness, British scientist Sir Geoffrey Taylor, wrote that from a distance of more than twenty miles, he "looked directly at the ball of fire [through a very dark protective glass lens]. I saw it expand slowly, and begin to rise, growing fainter as it rose. Later it developed into a huge mushroom-shaped cloud, and soon reached a height of 40,000 feet." He adds that though the blast was exactly what scientists had expected, "the whole effect was so staggering that I found it difficult to believe my eyes."[1]

A week later, on July 25, U.S. president Harry S. Truman met with Russian dictator Joseph Stalin and England's Prime Minister Winston Churchill. The three leaders decided that in the interest of saving both Allied and Japanese lives by ending the war, they would challenge Japan to surrender, and if the Asian nation refused, the United States would drop the bomb on Japan. Japan did not surrender, so on August 6, a B-29 bomber passed over Hiroshima and dropped the deadliest cargo a warplane had ever dropped.

Despite massive devastation, Japan still did not surrender; three days later another B-29 dropped an atomic bomb on Nagasaki, which ended the war in the Pacific.

The following account describes the experience of the men in the *Enola Gay*, the plane that dropped the bomb on Hiroshima. George R. Caron was the *Enola Gay*'s tail gunner.

Excerpted from *Fire of a Thousand Suns*, by George R. Caron and Charlotte E. Meares (Westminster, CO: Web Publishing, 1995).

ince the *Enola Gay* would not climb to altitude and pressurize for some time, Caron—as he had gotten into the habit of doing on long flights—came forward to stretch his legs and shoot the breeze with the men in the waist.

The midnight breakfast pancakes had burned out fast and Bob was getting hungry. So were Shumard and Stiborik. As the officers were hoarding Perry's lunches in the nose, Caron crawled through the long tunnel to raid the brown bag before none were left. The mess officer apparently kept the crew's waistlines in mind when he prepared their allotment of half a diagonally cut turkey C-ration sandwich each and an apple or an orange. Caron pushed what remained of the sandwiches and rolly-polly fruit in front of him as he wormed his way back through the tube.

For the past three and a half hours, the exhausted Jake Beser had been napping on the floor at the entrance to the tunnel. Caron, figuring the best way to expedite the movement of food, rolled the apples toward Stiborik. One bounced out of the tunnel and landed on Jake's head.

Jake needed to get up, anyway. Black coffee fought back his numbness and cleared the haze. Shortly, he would monitor Japanese radio for wavelengths that too closely approximated those selected to activate Little Boy's complex proximity fuse. Every time one of the proximity fuse signals bounced back from the earth's surface, it closed another circuit, until a sequence had been completed and the bomb detonated. Just before takeoff, Beser had been given a small piece of rice paper listing the newly designated top secret wavelengths. In the event of capture, the rice paper would end up in his digestive track.

Even in the midst of war, miles above the earth, the physical body still required attention. Caron had hooked his green canvas-covered canteen onto his web belt and brought it forward from the tail with him. He double-checked that he had the right one. The guys were always switching his good water canteen with the old one that he used to take a leak in. Before takeoff, he'd make sure that the right canteen was in the right place.

At 4:25 A.M., Shumard, Stiborik and Beser were teasing him about taking a slug from the wrong canteen when Tibbets' dark, wavy hair broke through the light at their end of the tunnel. He spoke to each of them, then squatted beside his tail gunner.

"Bob, have you figured out what we're doing this morning?"

"Colonel, with all the security you've had us under, I'm afraid to guess."

"It's OK now. We're on our way. You can guess anything you want."

A Physicist's Nightmare

"Is it a chemist's nightmare, Colonel?" he asked, thinking of the superexplosive they were carrying.

"No, not exactly."

The light lit. Lawrence's cyclotron and splitting atoms and a process called fission came off the pages of books and into his imagination.

"Is it a physicist's nightmare?"

"You might call it that."

The five exchanged a few more words, then Tibbets began to wriggle forward through the narrow, padded tunnel. When nothing but his foot stuck out, Caron yanked on it. The gesture was inappropriate between an enlisted man and his commanding officer. But it was too late. Long ago Caron realized Tibbets was no ordinary commander. The Colonel put himself in reverse.

"What's the problem?"

"Colonel, are we splitting atoms this morning?"

Tibbets knew his tail gunner's fascination with physics. The question didn't come as a surprise. "Yep. We sure are." . . .

An hour out of Iwo Jima, the moon arced over the horizon on the *Enola Gay*'s right. From his lonely compartment, Caron watched mesmerized as the silver slivers below connected like the giant sterling links of Neptune's necklace. Finally, the deep blackness between the swells gave way to shimmering pools of liquid dawn. In the narrow cleft near the horizon, the sky blushed, rendering distant stars invisible. As the veil of darkness lifted from the *Enola Gay*, morning light transformed her argentine fuselage to gold.

Stiborik spotted Iwo Jima in his scope. At 5:20 A.M., the three planes were rendezvousing only three minutes past Dutch's calculations. The *Enola Gay* was performing flawlessly. Captain Charles McKnight's *Top Secret* would not be needed. From nine thousand three hundred feet, the *Enola Gay* circled left. *The Great Artiste* and Number 91 slipped smoothly into a loose formation with her, and the three soaring eagles glided back over open ocean.

Parsons and Jeppson steadfastly watched the thirty-inch-high and twenty-inch-wide console panel that monitored Little Boy's vital signs. Umbilical cords linked the bomb's batteries and electrical circuits to the monitor where gauges blinked and dials oscillated. Once the bomb-bay doors opened at thirty-one thousand feet and Little Boy began its fall, the umbilical arming wires would be severed, activating the timing devices within the bomb. . . .

At 7:25 A.M., as the *Enola Gay* was at twenty-six thousand feet and climbing, Caron heard Eatherly's voice on the intercom. Nelson had picked him up at the designated 7314 kilocycles.

"Cloud cover less than three-tenths at all altitudes," Eatherly radioed. "Advice: bomb primary."

A visual drop at Hiroshima now seemed a foregone conclusion. Actually, Tibbets had not anticipated otherwise. Lewis switched off the IFF—Identification, Friend or Foe—and watched for landmarks. The island of Shikoku rose to meet them. Beyond it opened the Inland Sea.

From wind and drift calculations, Dutch Van Kirk reset their compass heading to three hundred forty-four degrees. At landfall, they swung east, their altitude thirty thousand seven hundred feet.

At 8:05 A.M., the navigator announced ten minutes to AP.

Caron tried to wriggle into his flak jacket. It was useless. He put it back on the floor where it might do more good. Unrestrained, he rubbernecked for fighters and black puffs of smoke that signaled flak from antiaircraft batteries on the ground. Nothing. Thank God! In rapid-fire succession, his mind conjured images of Zero shells and flak, connecting with the device harpooned like a mighty whale beneath them.

Antiaircraft fire wasn't what concerned Lewis most. The star center of his high-school football team tackled run-ins head on. They were something he could control. Turbulence was another matter. He had logged enough hours to know that as a land mass heated up—especially one surrounded by water—thermals could become an unpredictable problem. The challenges of the next ten minutes and anticipation of their dangerous dive-turn maneuver brought Lindbergh's counsel clearly to mind. "Watch trim and attitude. Be sure to pick up enough speed in the dive. . . ."

Eatherly's cryptic message had been correct. "Some vagrant winds had cleared a ten-mile hole in the cloud cover," Lewis scratched into his journal. The ill-fated city was bathed in sunlight.

Automatically, Ferebee positioned his damp forehead against the specially designed brace on his M-9B Norden bombsight. He knew the gyroscopically stabilized aiming device that determined correct flight course and bomb release point perhaps better than any bombardier. While bombardiers in other squadrons checked out on the Norden after twenty visual and five radar drops, Ferebee and his fellow 509th bombardiers had honed their eye-hand coordination on thirty bombs a week for eight months, dropping sixty on radar. During test runs over Japan, he had plunked every one of his practice bombs right into the "pickle barrel."

Dutch changed their heading to two hundred sixty-four degrees. At 8:12 A.M., from thirty-one thousand sixty feet, he spotted their initial point sixteen miles from the Aioi Bridge. "IP," he called to Tibbets.

Although Ferebee and Lewis teamed effectively, the bombardier and Tibbets worked as one. They synchronized their instruments.

At 8:13:30 A.M., Tibbets watched an intent Ferebee press his forehead against the sight. "It's all yours," the pilot said. Ferebee made the final adjustments on the Norden, touched the ailerons to maintain his alignment.

THE DROP

"On goggles," Tibbets' voice crackled over the intercom. When he could see nothing with his goggles on, the pilot snapped them back onto his forehead. Lewis quickly wrote in his journal, "There will be a short intermission while we bomb our target." Then he pulled down his protective goggles.

Ferebee had already ruled them out. Colorful frames of Hiroshima began to appear in his viewfinder, like a tinted newsreel in slow motion. The exceedingly handsome officer had nearly made it into big-league baseball. The war had a way of waking people from their dreams. Now, he was aiming for a different sort of goal. He turned on the low-pitched tone signal that alerted the crew they were in the final fifteen seconds of the bomb run. One and two miles behind, respectively, *The Great Artiste* and Number 91 heard the tone. So did the weather planes and the radio operator of *Top Secret* at Iwo Jima.

The bombardier concentrated on his aiming point, the T-shaped Aioi Bridge, that was moving from east to west into the sight's cross hairs. He took a shallow breath and held it. At 8:15:17 A.M., the bomb-bay doors burst open. Released from its menacing hook, Little Boy ripped away from its monitoring cables. The tone stopped.

"Bomb away," Ferebee said loudly, compressing his lungs with release of the words.

Nearly five tons lighter, the *Enola Gay* bolted upward. . . .

THE BLAST

At 8:16 A.M., the last of the complex series of detonation circuits closed within the bomb. Missing its target by eight hundred feet, it released its fury more than a third of a mile above the Shima Clinic.

Forty-three seconds after Little Boy's umbilical ripped away from the *Enola Gay*, the blast's blinding flash reached Caron's eyes. When his vision had been partially restored, he saw nothing outside his right side window but blue sky. Suddenly, an unholy globe of compressed air rose to eye level. Like some protoplasmic substance from a science fiction movie, it threatened to engulf them. Caron was flabbergasted. Before his unintelligible warning reached the crew, it struck with violent force.

What the jolt did to his engines, flight engineer Duzenbury wasn't sure. But it gave him a moment of pause. He was relieved that all instruments indicated normal function.

Almost instantaneously, the ricochet wave rushed toward them. Caron shouted a warning. Four seconds after the first, it bounced the plane.

The bomb did what it had been designed to do: destroy by heat and blast. The subtle secondary consequences of uranium fission, visible only in the coming days and months as changed cell structures, were vastly underestimated and little understood.

Survivors nearest the hypocenter saw only the *pika* (flash). "The light of many suns in one," Lawrence had written of Trinity, yet his description was appropriate for Hiroshima as well. Farther away, others heard the *don* (boom) that they described as "a hundred thunders sounding at once, shaking the earth on its axis." Trinity's awesome roar was the equivalent of only half the Hiroshima *pika-don*. The only thing relevant was an object's distance from the point directly beneath the burst. Like a wheel whose crushing weight converges at the hub, the epicenter collapsed. At the rim, life was meted out by long, fragile spokes. What heat hadn't turned instantly to vapor, the blast and shock wave—potent as a dozen typhoons—smashed to bits.

LIKE BUBBLING MOLASSES

In his cubicle, Caron pointed the cumbersome K-20 camera toward the spectacle outside, but the gun sight and window frames blocked the view. The escape hatch window on his right offered the least obstruction. Quickly, he asked Tibbets to turn the plane just five or ten degrees. Now he could see Hiroshima—or what was left of it (Captain Lewis noted he had just seen a city disappear in front of his eyes). *Airplanes . . . there was an airport and part of a harbor, out beyond the lavalike flow. No . . . it was more like bubbling molasses the way it spread over the city and crept up into the foothills.* Melted earth and steel roiled in the mass of energy that consumed all matter in its path.

"Holy Moses, here it comes," Caron said to no one and everyone. Rapidly, he collected his thoughts and directed his words toward Tibbets. "Colonel, it's coming toward us . . . the head of the cloud is coming toward us." The pilot instantly changed course.

This *had* to mean the end of the war, nineteen-year-old Nelson said aloud when he could finally see for himself. Such raw power could only horrify the enemy into submission.

"A caldron." Shumard associated the boiling action of the cloud, full of all kinds of colors, with an unearthly brew. It sent shivers up his spine. And terrified him. "There's nothing but death in that cloud," he said. Then he thought he heard a voice say, "All the Japanese souls are rising to heaven."

The great whirl of soot, vaporized matter and earth fanned upward, then crowned like a giant umbrella, casting the disconsolate city into shadow. Hiroshima, like Jornada del Muerto, had become a scorched desert.

Caron snapped the shutter until there was no more film to shoot. As Tibbets requested, all the way back to base, Caron kept his eyes on the cloud. When he finally lost sight of it, the *Enola Gay* was an hour and a half south of Hiroshima. The leviathan still hadn't disappeared below the horizon. It had been merely obstructed by high stratus clouds. He informed Dutch. The navigator indicated that the city was three hundred and sixty-three miles behind them. Caron calculated the curvature of earth at that distance was roughly twenty thousand feet. Since the cloud had risen above them when Tibbets leveled off at thirty-one thousand, then, it had apparently attained a height of fifty thousand feet. . . .

A VICTORIOUS HOMECOMING

Twelve hours and thirteen minutes after the *Enola Gay*'s breath-holding takeoff, she received a rousing homecoming from several hundred officers and enlisted men, cheering from the flight line. A ring of tan uniforms closed in behind them on the taxiway. . . .

"The atomic bomb," broadcast [President Harry S.] Truman to millions of Americans who had also been praying for surrender, had been used "against those who attacked us without warning at Pearl Harbor, against those who have starved and beaten and executed American prisoners of war, against those who have abandoned any pretense of obeying international laws of warfare. We shall continue to use it until we completely destroy Japan's power to make war. Only a Japanese surrender will stop us."

NOTE

1. Sir Geoffrey Taylor, "The World's First Atom Bomb Test, Los Alamos, 17 July 1945," in *The Permanent Book of the 20th Century: Eye-Witness Accounts of the Moments That Shaped Our Century*. Ed. Jon E. Lewis. New York: Carroll and Graf, 1994, p. 442.

THE ATOM BOMB: A SURVIVOR'S STORY

Iwao Nakamura

When the United States dropped the atomic bomb on Hiroshima, Japan, on August 6, 1945, it was one of the most devastating acts ever perpetrated on one nation by another. More than one hundred thousand Hiroshima residents died, and the city was reduced to rubble. Three days later, a second bomb was dropped on the city of Nagasaki, finally forcing Japanese surrender and the end of World War II.

The atomic bomb, unlike its precursors, not only destroyed lives and property in an initial explosion; the effects of radiation given off in the blast continued to kill people for many years. People not struck down by the bomb or its resonating shock waves were struck down days, months, or years later by radiation-related illnesses.

The bomb's effects were so harmful that most people wanted to ensure that this weapon would never be used again. Nevertheless, testing of nuclear bombs continued even during peacetime as no nation that could construct a bomb wanted to be vulnerable to another.

The bomb's side effects came to light once again in 1954 when a Japanese vessel was contaminated by radioactive fallout from nuclear tests in the Pacific. This prompted an international anti-bomb campaign. Professor Arata Osada contributed to the anti-bomb efforts by compiling students' accounts of their experiences at or near Hiroshima the day the bomb was dropped. President of Hiroshima University of Humanities and Science and dean of the Hiroshima Higher Normal School when he compiled these accounts six years after the bomb's blast, Osada published the stories of several students of early grade school through high school age.

Iwao Nakamura, the author of the following viewpoint, was in the eleventh-grade when he wrote this account. He was in the fifth grade when the bomb was dropped on Hiroshima. His brief account is typical of those in Osada's book. Like many others, he found that recalling the events of that time was painful, and he describes some of the agony he felt as he saw the devastation around him.

Today, as I begin to write an account of my experiences after five years and several months have passed, the wretched scenes of that time float up before my eyes like phantoms. And as these phantoms appear, I can actually hear the pathetic groans, the screams.

In an instant it became dark as night, Hiroshima on that day. Flames shooting up from wrecked houses as if to illuminate this darkness. Amidst this, children aimlessly wandering about, groaning with pain, their burned faces twitching and bloated like balloons. An old man, skin flaking off like the skin of a potato, trying to get away on weak, unsteady legs, praying as he went. A man frantically calling out the names of his wife and children, both hands to his forehead from which blood trickled down. Just the memory of it makes my blood run cold. This is the real face of war. To those who knew nothing of the pitiful tragedies of Hiroshima's people, the scene would seem like a world of monsters, like Hades itself. A devil called war swept away the precious lives of several hundred thousand citizens of Hiroshima.

I, who cannot forget, was in the fifth year of primary school when it happened. To escape the frequent air raids, I and my sisters had been evacuated to the home of our relatives in the country, but on August 2, I returned to my home at Naka Kakomachi (near the former Prefectural Office) during the summer vacation, to recover from the effects of a summer illness that had left me very weak. At the time, there were five of us living in Hiroshima: my parents, two younger brothers (aged five and two) and myself. I used to drag myself along to the nearby Prefectural Hospital every morning at eight.

It was after eight on August 6 and the midsummer sun was beginning to scorch down on Hiroshima. An all-clear signal had sounded and with relief we sat down for breakfast a little later than usual. Usually by this time, my father had left the house for the office and I would be at the hospital for treatment.

I was just starting on my second bowl of rice. At that moment, a bluish-white ray of light like a magnesium flare hit me in the face, a terrific roar tore at my eardrums and it became so dark I could not see anything. I stood up, dropping my rice bowl and chopsticks. I do not know what happened next or how long I was unconscious. When I came to, I found myself trapped under what seemed like a heavy rock, but my head was free. It was still dark but I finally discovered that I was under a collapsed wall. It was all so sudden that I kept wondering if I was dreaming. I tried very hard to crawl free, but the heavy wall would not budge. A suffocating stench flooded the area and began to choke me. My breathing became short, my ears began to ring, and my heart was pounding as if it were about to burst. 'I can't last much longer,' I said to myself, and then a draft of cold air flowed past me and some light appeared. The taste of that fresh air is something I shall never forget. I breathed it in with all my might. This fresh air and the brighter surroundings gave me renewed vigor and I somehow managed to struggle out from under the wall. Where were my parents? Where were my brothers? I looked around in the dim light and glimpsed the hazy figures of my parents looking for me. I hurried over to them. Their hair was disheveled and their faces pale. When they saw me, they sighed with relief, 'Oh you're safe, you're safe.'

A Street Filled with Flames

Fortunately, my mother and I were unhurt, but blood was streaming from my father's forehead and staining his dirtied shirt bright red. I tore the shirt I was wearing into strips and bandaged his cuts, at the same time looking at the scene around us. Nothing was left of the Hiroshima of a few minutes ago. The houses and buildings had been destroyed and the streets transformed into a black desert, with only the flames from burning buildings giving a lurid illumination to the dark sky over Hiroshima. Flames were already shooting out of the wreckage of the house next door. We couldn't see my two brothers. My mother was in tears as she called their names. My father went frantic as he dug among the collapsed walls and scattered tiles. It must have been by the mercy of God that we were able to rescue my brothers from under the wreckage before the flames reached them. They were not hurt, either. The five of us left our burning home and hurried toward Koi. Around us was a sea of flames. The street was filled with flames and smoke from the burning wreckage of houses and burning power poles which had toppled down blocked our way time after time, almost sending us into the depths of despair. It seems that everyone in the area had already made their escape, for we saw no one but sometimes we heard moans, a sound like a wild beast. I began to shudder as I thought that everyone on earth had perished, leaving only the five of us here in an eerie world of the dead. As we passed Nakajima Primary School area and approached Sumiyoshi Bridge, I saw a damaged water tank in which a number of people had their heads down, drinking. I was so thirsty and attracted by the sight of people that I left my parents' side without thinking, and approached the tank. But when I got near and was able to see into the tank, I gave an involuntary cry and backed away. What I saw reflected in the blood-stained water were the faces of monsters. They had leaned over the side of the tank and died in that position. From the burned shreds of their sailor uniforms, I knew they were schoolgirls, but they had no hair left and their burned faces were crimson with blood; they no longer appeared human. After we came out on the main road and crossed Sumiyoshi Bridge, we finally came across some living human beings—but maybe it would be more correct to say that we met some people from Hell. They were naked and their skin, burned and bloody, was like red rust and their bodies were bloated up like balloons. Nevertheless, since we had not seen any living person on the way, we felt better seeing them and soon joined this group in our attempt to escape from Hiroshima. The houses on both sides of this street, which was several dozen yards wide, were in flames so that we could only move along a strip in the center about three or four yards wide. This narrow passage was covered with seriously burned and injured people, unable to walk, and with dead bodies, leaving hardly any space for us to get through. At places, we were forced to step over them callously, but we apologized in our hearts as we did this. Among them were old people pleading for water, tiny children seeking help, students unconsciously calling for their parents, brothers, and sisters, and there was a mother prostrate on the ground, moaning with pain but with one arm still tightly embracing her dead baby. But how could we help them when we ourselves did not know our own fate?

A SMOLDERING DESERT

When we reached the Koi First Aid Station, we learned that we were among the last to escape from the Sumiyoshi Bridge area. After my father had received some medical treatment, we hurried over Koi Hill to our relatives at Tomo Village in Asa County. When we were crossing the hill late that evening, we could see Hiroshima lying far below, now a mere smoldering desert. After offering a silent prayer for the victims, we descended the hill toward Tomo.

THE IRON CURTAIN

WINSTON S. CHURCHILL

During World War II and the early decades of the nuclear age, England's Prime Minister Winston S. Churchill was one of the world's most influential leaders and an outspoken opponent of Soviet expansion. Although Russia had fought with the Allies during World War II, its actions following the end of the war were disturbing. Churchill saw that Communist Russia was strong and aggressive and if left unchecked could well lead the world into another war. This would be devastating on a human level, and perhaps on a greater level, given that the unholy power of nuclear bombs had been demonstrated.

Churchill believed the answer was for the Western nations, under the auspices of the newly formed United Nations, to band together to counter Russian aggression in Europe, Asia, and in developing postcolonial nations of Africa. Further, Churchill viewed Britain and the United States as most capable of limiting Russian aggression and deterring the nuclear threat.

The following selection is excerpted from Churchill's famous speech presented at Westminster College in Fulton, Missouri, on March 5, 1946. In it, he describes the "shadow" of Russian aggression as an "Iron Curtain" falling over Europe and separating tyrannized from free nations. Although Churchill's Iron Curtain was metaphorical, it became a literal reality in 1961 when the Soviets erected the thirty-mile long, heavily fortified Berlin Wall in occupied East Germany to separate communist East Berlin from democratic West Berlin.

T he United States stands at this time at the pinnacle of world power. It is a solemn moment for the American Democracy. For with primacy in power is also joined an awe-inspiring

Excerpted from *The Second World War: The Gathering Storm*, by Winston S. Churchill. Copyright Winston S. Churchill. Reproduced with permission from Curtis Brown Ltd., London, on behalf of the Estate of Sir Winston S. Churchill.

accountability to the future. If you look around you, you must feel not only the sense of duty done but also you must feel anxiety lest you fall below the level of achievement. Opportunity is here now, clear and shining for both our countries. To reject it or ignore it or fritter it away will bring upon us all the long reproaches of the after-time. It is necessary that constancy of mind, persistency of purpose and the grand simplicity of decision shall guide and rule the conduct of the English-speaking peoples in peace as they did in war. We must, and I believe we shall, prove ourselves equal to this severe requirement.

When American military men approach some serious situation they are wont to write at the head of their directive the words 'overall strategic concept'. There is wisdom in this, as it leads to clarity of thought. What then is the overall strategic concept which we should inscribe today? It is nothing less than the safety and welfare, the freedom and progress, of all the homes and families of all the men and women in all the lands. And here I speak particularly of the myriad cottage or apartment homes where the wage-earner strives amid the accidents and difficulties of life to guard his wife and children from privation and bring the family up in the fear of the Lord, or upon ethical conceptions which often play their potent part.

SHELTER FROM WAR AND TYRANNY

To give security to these countless homes, they must be shielded from the two giant marauders, war and tyranny. We all know the frightful disturbances in which the ordinary family is plunged when the curse of war swoops down upon the breadwinner and those for whom he works and contrives. The awful ruin of Europe, with all its vanished glories, and of large parts of Asia glares us in the eyes. When the designs of wicked men or the aggressive urge of mighty States dissolve over large areas the frame of civilized society, humble folk are confronted with difficulties with which they cannot cope. For them all is distorted, all is broken, even ground to pulp.

When I stand here this quiet afternoon I shudder to visualize what is actually happening to millions now and what is going to happen in this period when famine stalks the earth. None can compute what has been called 'the unestimated sum of human pain'. Our supreme task and duty is to guard the homes of the common people from the horrors and miseries of another war. We are all agreed on that.

Our American military colleagues, after having proclaimed their 'over-all strategic concept' and computed available resources, always proceed to the next step—namely, the method. Here again there is widespread agreement. A world organization has already been erected for the prime purpose of preventing war. UNO [the United Nations Organization], the successor of the League of Nations, with the decisive addition of the United States and all that that means, is already at work. We must make sure that its work is fruitful, that it is a reality and not a sham, that it is a force for action, and not merely a frothing of words, that it is a true temple of peace in which the shields of many nations can some day be hung up, and not merely a cockpit in a Tower of Babel. Before we cast away the solid assurances of national armaments for self-preservation we must be certain that our temple is built, not upon shifting sands or quagmires, but upon the rock. Anyone can see with his eyes open that our path will be difficult and also long, but if we persevere together as we did in the two world wars—though not, alas, in the interval between them—I cannot doubt that we shall achieve our common purpose in the end.

I have, however, a definite and practical purpose to make for action. Courts and magistrates may be set up but they cannot function without sheriffs and constables. The United Nations Organization must immediately begin to be equipped with an international armed force. In such a matter we can only go step by step, but we must begin now. I propose that each of the Powers and States should be invited to delegate a certain number of air squadrons to the service of the world organization. These squadrons would be trained and prepared in their own countries, but would move around in rotation from one country to another. They would wear the uniform of their own countries but with different badges. They would not be required to act against their own nation, but in other respects they would be directed by the world organization. This might be started on a modest scale and would grow as confidence grew. I wished to see this done after the First World War, and I devoutly trust it may be done forthwith.

It would nevertheless be wrong and imprudent to entrust the secret knowledge or experience of the atomic bomb, which the United States, Great Britain and Canada now share, to the world organization, while it is still in its infancy. It would be criminal madness to cast it adrift in this still agitated and un-united world. No one in any country has slept less well in their beds because this knowledge and the method and the raw materials to apply it, are at present largely retained in American hands. I do not believe we should all have slept so soundly had the positions been reversed and if some Communist or neo-Fascist State monopolized for the time being these dread agencies. The fear of them alone might easily have been used to enforce total-

itarian systems upon the free democratic world, with consequences appalling to human imagination. God has willed that
this shall not be and we have at least a breathing space to set our
house in order before this peril has to be encountered: and even
then, if no effort is spared, we should still possess so formidable
a superiority as to impose effective deterrents upon its employment, or threat of employment by others. Ultimately, when the
essential brotherhood of man is truly embodied and expressed
in a world organization with all the necessary practical safeguards to make it effective, these powers would naturally be
confided to that world organization.

THE EVIL OF TYRANNY

Now I come to the second danger of these two marauders which
threatens the cottage, the home, and the ordinary people—
namely, tyranny. We cannot be blind to the fact that the liberties
enjoyed by individual citizens throughout the British Empire are
not valid in a considerable number of countries, some of which
are very powerful. In these States control is enforced upon the
common people by various kinds of all-embracing police governments. The power of the State is exercised without restraint,
either by dictators or by compact oligarchies operating through
a privileged party and a political police. It is not our duty at this
time when difficulties are so numerous to interfere forcibly in the
internal affairs of countries which we have not conquered in war.
But we must never cease to proclaim in fearless tones the great
principles of freedom and the rights of man which are the joint
inheritance of the English-speaking world and which through
Magna Carta, the Bill of Rights, the Habeas Corpus, trial by jury,
and the English common law find their most famous expression
in the American Declaration of Independence.

All this means that the people of any country have the right, and
should have the power by constitutional action, by free unfettered
elections, with secret ballot, to choose or change the character or
form of government under which they dwell; that freedom of
speech and thought should reign; that courts of justice, independent of the executive, unbiased by any party, should administer
laws which have received the broad assent of large majorities or
are consecrated by time and custom. Here are the title deeds of
freedom which should lie in every cottage home. Here is the message of the British and American peoples to mankind. Let us
preach what we practise—let us practise what we preach. . . .

A shadow has fallen upon the scenes so lately lighted by the Allied victory. Nobody knows what Soviet Russia and its Communist international organization intends to do in the immediate fu-

ture, or what are the limits, if any, to their expansive and prose-lytizing tendencies. I have a strong admiration and regard for the valiant Russian people and for my wartime comrade, Marshal Stalin. There is deep sympathy and goodwill in Britain—and I doubt not here also—towards the peoples of all the Russias and a resolve to persevere through many differences and rebuffs in establishing lasting friendships. We understand the Russian need to be secure on her western frontiers by the removal of all possibility of German aggression. We welcome Russia to her rightful place among the leading nations of the world. We welcome her flag upon the seas. Above all, we welcome constant, frequent and growing contacts between the Russian people and our own people on both sides of the Atlantic. It is my duty, however, for I am sure you would wish me to state the facts as I see them to you, to place before you certain facts about the present position in Europe.

From Stettin in the Baltic to Trieste in the Adriatic, an iron curtain has descended across the Continent. Behind that line lie all the capitals of the ancient states of Central and Eastern Europe. Warsaw, Berlin, Prague, Vienna, Budapest, Belgrade, Bucharest and Sofia, all these famous cities and the populations around them lie in what I must call the Soviet sphere, and all are subject in one form or another, not only to Soviet influence but to a very high and, in many cases, increasing measure of control from Moscow. Athens alone—Greece with its immortal glories—is free to decide its future at an election under British, American and French observation. The Russian-dominated Polish Government has been encouraged to make enormous and wrongful inroads upon Germany, and mass expulsions of millions of Germans on a scale grievous and undreamed-of are now taking place. The Communist parties, which were very small in all these Eastern States of Europe, have been raised to pre-eminence and power far beyond their numbers and are seeking everywhere to obtain totalitarian control. Police governments are prevailing in nearly every case, and so far, except in Czechoslovakia, there is no true democracy.

Turkey and Persia [Iran] are both profoundly alarmed and disturbed at the claims which are being made upon them and at the pressure being exerted by the Moscow Government. An attempt is being made by the Russians in Berlin to build up a quasi-Communist party in their zone of Occupied Germany by showing special favours to groups of left-wing German leaders. At the end of the fighting last June, the American and British Armies withdrew westwards, in accordance with an earlier agreement, to a depth at some points of 150 miles upon a front of nearly four hundred miles, in order to allow our Russian allies to occupy this vast expanse of territory which the Western Democracies had conquered.

If now the Soviet Government tries, by separate action, to build up a pro-Communist Germany in their areas, this will cause new serious difficulties in the British and American zones, and will give the defeated Germans the power of putting themselves up to auction between the Soviets and the Western Democracies. Whatever conclusions may be drawn from these facts—and facts they are—this is certainly not the Liberated Europe we fought to build up. Nor is it one which contains the essentials of permanent peace.

NEEDED: A NEW EUROPEAN UNITY

The safety of the world requires a new unity in Europe, from which no nation should be permanently outcast. It is from the quarrels of the strong parent races in Europe that the world wars we have witnessed, or which occurred in former times, have sprung. Twice in our own lifetime we have seen the United States, against their wishes and their traditions, against arguments, the force of which it is impossible not to comprehend, drawn by irresistible forces, into these wars in time to secure the victory of the good cause, but only after frightful slaughter and devastation had occurred. Twice the United States has had to send several millions of its young men across the Atlantic to find the war; but now war can find any nation, wherever it may dwell between dusk and dawn. Surely we should work with conscious purpose for a grand pacification of Europe, within the structure of the United Nations and in accordance with its Charter. That I feel is an open cause of policy of very great importance. . . .

I have felt bound to portray the shadow which, alike in the west and in the east, falls upon the world. I was a high minister at the time of the Versailles Treaty and a close friend of Mr Lloyd George, who was the head of the British delegation at Versailles. I did not myself agree with many things that were done, but I have a very strong impression in my mind of that situation, and I find it painful to contrast it with that which prevails now. In those days there were high hopes and unbounded confidence that the wars were over, and that the League of Nations would become all-powerful. I do not see or feel that same confidence or even the same hopes in the haggard world at the present time.

On the other hand I repulse the idea that a new war is inevitable; still more that it is imminent. It is because I am sure that our fortunes are still in our own hands and that we hold the power to save the future, that I feel the duty to speak out now that I have the occasion and the opportunity to do so. I do not believe that Soviet Russia desires war. What they desire is the fruits of war and the indefinite expansion of their power and doctrines. But what we have to consider here today while time remains, is the permanent prevention of war and the establishment of conditions of freedom and democracy as rapidly as possible in all countries. Our difficulties and dangers will not be removed by closing our eyes to them. They will not be removed by mere waiting to see what happens; nor will they be removed by a policy of appeasement. What is needed is a settlement, and the longer this is delayed, the more difficult it will be and the greater our dangers will become.

STRENGTH IS SURVIVAL

From what I have seen of our Russian friends and Allies during the war, I am convinced that there is nothing they admire so much as strength, and there is nothing for which they have less respect than for weakness, especially military weakness. For that reason the old doctrine of a balance of power is unsound. We cannot afford, if we can help it, to work on narrow margins, offering temptations to a trial of strength. If the Western Democracies stand together in strict adherence to the principles of the United Nations Charter, their influence for furthering those principles will be immense and no one is likely to molest them. If, however, they become divided or falter in their duty and if these all-important years are allowed to slip away then indeed catastrophe may overwhelm us all.

THE TRUMAN DOCTRINE: THE UNITED STATES WILL SUPPORT NATIONS THREATENED BY AGGRESSORS

HARRY S. TRUMAN

Although the Soviet Union (USSR) entered World War II on the side of the Allies, it never really trusted, nor was trusted by, the Western Allies, whom it joined in mutual enmity against Germany. Shortly after the end of the war the USSR set out to strengthen itself through political and military expansion. It demanded—and gained—significant control in Eastern Europe through force and aggressive export of its idealistic but repressive Communist philosophy. Fearing that the USSR would become another Germany, overpowering weaker nations through totalitarianism, England and the other European Allies did what they could to support those nations threatened by the USSR, but when the USSR and local Communist insurgents began to threaten Greece and Turkey, England told the United States that it lacked the resources to defend the Mediterranean sphere.

President Harry S. Truman responded by asserting that the United States must aid these threatened countries. His address to Congress, which stated what came to be known as the Truman

From Harry S. Truman's address to Congress, February 21, 1947, Washington, D.C.

Doctrine, set the tone for U.S. foreign policy for the next several decades. Truman pledged that the United States would aid all countries threatened by "armed minorities or outside pressures," both of which were tacitly understood to refer to the Soviet Union.

The United States had a long history of shifts between isolationism and intervention in foreign affairs; now it declared that it would intervene when necessary. This policy became the basis of U.S. interventions in many countries—even supporting repressive or corrupt governments—where Communists threatened to take over. Truman's speech is presented below.

M r. President, Mr. Speaker, Members of the Congress of the United States:
The gravity of the situation which confronts the world today necessitates my appearance before a joint session of the Congress. The foreign policy and the national security of this country are involved.

One aspect of the present situation, which I wish to present to you at this time for your consideration and decision, concerns Greece and Turkey.

The United States has received from the Greek Government an urgent appeal for financial and economic assistance. Preliminary reports from the American Economic Mission now in Greece and reports from the American Ambassador in Greece corroborate the statement of the Greek Government that assistance is imperative if Greece is to survive as a free nation.

I do not believe that the American people and the Congress wish to turn a deaf ear to the appeal of the Greek Government.

Greece is not a rich country. Lack of sufficient natural resources has always forced the Greek people to work hard to make both ends meet. Since 1940, this industrious and peace loving country has suffered invasion, four years of cruel enemy occupation, and bitter internal strife.

When forces of liberation entered Greece they found that the retreating Germans had destroyed virtually all the railways, roads, port facilities, communications, and merchant marine. More than a thousand villages had been burned. Eighty-five per cent of the children were tubercular. Livestock, poultry, and draft animals had almost disappeared. Inflation had wiped out practically all savings.

As a result of these tragic conditions, a militant minority, exploiting human want and misery, was able to create political chaos which, until now, has made economic recovery impossible.

Greece is today without funds to finance the importation of

those goods which are essential to bare subsistence. Under these circumstances the people of Greece cannot make progress in solving their problems of reconstruction. Greece is in desperate need of financial and economic assistance to enable it to resume purchases of food, clothing, fuel and seeds. These are indispensable for the subsistence of its people and are obtainable only from abroad. Greece must have help to import the goods necessary to restore internal order and security, so essential for economic and political recovery.

The Greek Government has also asked for the assistance of experienced American administrators, economists and technicians to insure that the financial and other aid given to Greece shall be used effectively in creating a stable and self-sustaining economy and in improving its public administration.

The very existence of the Greek state is today threatened by the terrorist activities of several thousand armed men, led by Communists, who defy the government's authority at a number of points, particularly along the northern boundaries. A Commission appointed by the United Nations Security Council is at present investigating disturbed conditions in northern Greece and alleged border violations along the frontier between Greece on the one hand and Albania, Bulgaria, and Yugoslavia on the other.

Meanwhile, the Greek Government is unable to cope with the situation. The Greek army is small and poorly equipped. It needs supplies and equipment if it is to restore the authority of the government throughout Greek territory. Greece must have assistance if it is to become a self-supporting and self-respecting democracy.

ONLY THE UNITED STATES CAN HELP

The United States must supply that assistance. We have already extended to Greece certain types of relief and economic aid but these are inadequate.

There is no other country to which democratic Greece can turn.

No other nation is willing and able to provide the necessary support for a democratic Greek government.

The British Government, which has been helping Greece, can give no further financial or economic aid after March 31. Great Britain finds itself under the necessity of reducing or liquidating its commitments in several parts of the world, including Greece.

We have considered how the United Nations might assist in this crisis. But the situation is an urgent one requiring immediate action and the United Nations and its related organizations are not in a position to extend help of the kind that is required.

It is important to note that the Greek Government has asked for our aid in utilizing effectively the financial and other assistance we may give to Greece, and in improving its public administration. It is of the utmost importance that we supervise the use of any funds made available to Greece; in such a manner that each dollar spent will count toward making Greece self-supporting, and will help to build an economy in which a healthy democracy can flourish.

No government is perfect. One of the chief virtues of a democracy, however, is that its defects are always visible and under democratic processes can be pointed out and corrected. The Government of Greece is not perfect. Nevertheless it represents eighty-five per cent of the members of the Greek Parliament who were chosen in an election last year. Foreign observers, including 692 Americans, considered this election to be a fair expression of the views of the Greek people.

Harry S. Truman

The Greek Government has been operating in an atmosphere of chaos and extremism. It has made mistakes. The extension of aid by this country does not mean that the United States condones everything that the Greek Government has done or will do. We have condemned in the past, and we condemn now, extremist measures of the right or the left. We have in the past advised tolerance, and we advise tolerance now.

Greece's neighbor, Turkey, also deserves our attention.

TURKEY'S NEED

The future of Turkey as an independent and economically sound state is clearly no less important to the freedom-loving peoples of the world than the future of Greece. The circumstances in which Turkey finds itself today are considerably different from those of Greece. Turkey has been spared the disasters that have beset Greece. And during the war, the United States and Great Britain furnished Turkey with material aid.

Nevertheless, Turkey now needs our support.

Since the war Turkey has sought financial assistance from Great Britain and the United States for the purpose of effecting that modernization necessary for the maintenance of its national integrity.

That integrity is essential to the preservation of order in the Middle East.

The British government has informed us that, owing to its

own difficulties can no longer extend financial or economic aid to Turkey.

As in the case of Greece, if Turkey is to have the assistance it needs, the United States must supply it. We are the only country able to provide that help.

I am fully aware of the broad implications involved if the United States extends assistance to Greece and Turkey, and I shall discuss these implications with you at this time.

One of the primary objectives of the foreign policy of the United States is the creation of conditions in which we and other nations will be able to work out a way of life free from coercion. This was a fundamental issue in the war with Germany and Japan. Our victory was won over countries which sought to impose their will, and their way of life, upon other nations.

THE UNITED STATES MUST HELP ENSURE PEACE AND FREEDOM FROM COERCION

To ensure the peaceful development of nations, free from coercion, the United States has taken a leading part in establishing the United Nations. The United Nations is designed to make possible lasting freedom and independence for all its members. We shall not realize our objectives, however, unless we are willing to help free peoples to maintain their free institutions and their national integrity against aggressive movements that seek to impose upon them totalitarian regimes. This is no more than a frank recognition that totalitarian regimes imposed on free peoples, by direct or indirect aggression, undermine the foundations of international peace and hence the security of the United States.

The peoples of a number of countries of the world have recently had totalitarian regimes forced upon them against their will. The Government of the United States has made frequent protests against coercion and intimidation, in violation of the Yalta agreement, in Poland, Rumania, and Bulgaria. I must also state that in a number of other countries there have been similar developments.

TWO WAYS OF LIFE

At the present moment in world history nearly every nation must choose between alternative ways of life. The choice is too often not a free one.

One way of life is based upon the will of the majority, and is distinguished by free institutions, representative government, free elections, guarantees of individual liberty, freedom of speech and religion, and freedom from political oppression.

The second way of life is based upon the will of a minority

forcibly imposed upon the majority. It relies upon terror and oppression, a controlled press and radio; fixed elections, and the suppression of personal freedoms.

I believe that it must be the policy of the United States to support free peoples who are resisting attempted subjugation by armed minorities or by outside pressures.

I believe that we must assist free peoples to work out their own destinies in their own way.

I believe that our help should be primarily through economic and financial aid which is essential to economic stability and orderly political processes.

The world is not static, and the status quo is not sacred. But we cannot allow changes in the status quo in violation of the Charter of the United Nations by such methods as coercion, or by such subterfuges as political infiltration. In helping free and independent nations to maintain their freedom, the United States will be giving effect to the principles of the Charter of the United Nations.

A Free Nation's Collapse Would Affect Others

It is necessary only to glance at a map to realize that the survival and integrity of the Greek nation are of grave importance in a much wider situation. If Greece should fall under the control of an armed minority, the effect upon its neighbor, Turkey, would be immediate and serious. Confusion and disorder might well spread throughout the entire Middle East.

Moreover, the disappearance of Greece as an independent state would have a profound effect upon those countries in Europe whose peoples are struggling against great difficulties to maintain their freedoms and their independence while they repair the damages of war.

It would be an unspeakable tragedy if these countries, which have struggled so long against overwhelming odds, should lose that victory for which they sacrificed so much. Collapse of free institutions and loss of independence would be disastrous not only for them but for the world. Discouragement and possibly failure would quickly be the lot of neighboring peoples striving to maintain their freedom and independence.

Should we fail to aid Greece and Turkey in this fateful hour, the effect will be far reaching to the West as well as to the East.

We Must Take Action

We must take immediate and resolute action.

I therefore ask the Congress to provide authority for assistance to Greece and Turkey in the amount of $400,000,000 for the period ending June 30, 1948. In requesting these funds, I have taken into consideration the maximum amount of relief assistance which would be furnished to Greece out of the $350,000,000 which I recently requested that the Congress authorize for the prevention of starvation and suffering in countries devastated by the war.

In addition to funds, I ask the Congress to authorize the detail of American civilian and military personnel to Greece and Turkey, at the request of those countries, to assist in the tasks of reconstruction, and for the purpose of supervising the use of such financial and material assistance as may be furnished. I recommend that authority also be provided for the instruction and training of selected Greek and Turkish personnel.

Finally, I ask that the Congress provide authority which will permit the speediest and most effective use, in terms of needed commodities, supplies, and equipment, of such funds as may be authorized.

If further funds, or further authority, should be needed for purposes indicated in this message, I shall not hesitate to bring the situation before the Congress. On this subject the Executive and Legislative branches of the Government must work together.

This is a serious course upon which we embark.

I would not recommend it except that the alternative is much more serious. The United States contributed $341,000,000,000 toward winning World War II. This is an investment in world freedom and world peace.

The assistance that I am recommending for Greece and Turkey amounts to little more than 1 tenth of 1 per cent of this investment. It is only common sense that we should safeguard this investment and make sure that it was not in vain.

THE WORLD'S FREE PEOPLE LOOK TO US FOR SUPPORT

The seeds of totalitarian regimes are nurtured by misery and want. They spread and grow in the evil soil of poverty and strife. They reach their full growth when the hope of a people for a better life has died. We must keep that hope alive.

The free peoples of the world look to us for support in maintaining their freedoms.

If we falter in our leadership, we may endanger the peace of the world—and we shall surely endanger the welfare of our own nation.

Great responsibilities have been placed upon us by the swift movement of events.

I am confident that the Congress will face these responsibilities squarely.

INDIA'S
INDEPENDENCE DAY

TIME

British influence in Indian began with the arrival in about 1600 of the British East India Company, a trading organization that bought cotton goods to trade for spices in the East Indies (Indonesia). By the 1750s, India was a full-fledged British colony. Indians rebelled in the mid-1800s, but the British put down the rebellion. Not until Mahatma Gandhi assumed leadership of the Indian National Congress (an Indian nationalist organization) in 1920 did India's efforts to gain independence develop a focused campaign. After decades of protest, petitioning, and nonviolent resistance to British authority, Britain agreed in 1940 to negotiate Indian independence if India would fight with the Allies in World War II against the Japanese. In 1947 Britain released India from its colony status. Marring the event was the inability of India's Hindu and Muslim populations to coexist peacefully. Their conflict was so severe that United Nations–sponsored negotiations divided India into two countries—India (Hindu) and Pakistan (Muslim). In mid-August 1947 India was partitioned, and the two countries gained their independence. Almost immediately, the two new nations began battling over Kashmir, a northern province, and conflict continued in the following years.

India's independence marked the beginning of the end of the British Empire, which in 1914 covered almost one-fourth of the earth's surface and contained almost one-fourth of the world's population.

The author of the following account, published in *Time* magazine, was in New Delhi on the day India gained its independence. The account captures the atmosphere in the country on that day.

As the great day approached, Indians thanked their varied gods and rejoiced with special prayers, poems and songs. Poetess Sarojini Naidu set the theme in a radio message: "Oh lovely dawn of freedom that breaks in gold and purple over the ancient capital . . . !"

BLESSING WITH ASHES

Even such an agnostic as Jawaharlal Nehru, on the eve of becoming India's first Prime Minister, fell into the religious spirit. From Tanjore in south India came two emissaries of Sri Amblavana Desigar, head of a sannyasi order of Hindu ascetics. Sri Amblavana thought that Nehru, as first Indian head of a really Indian Government ought, like ancient Hindu kings, to receive the symbol of power and authority from Hindu holy men.

With the emissaries came south India's most famous player of the *nagasaram*, a special kind of Indian flute. Like other sannyasis, who abstain from hair-cutting and hair-combing, the two emissaries wore their long hair properly matted and wound round their heads. Their naked chests and foreheads were streaked with sacred ash, blessed by Sri Amblavana. In an ancient Ford, the evening of Aug. 14, they began their slow, solemn progress to Nehru's house. Ahead walked the flutist, stopping every 100 yards or so to sit on the road and play his flute for about 15 minutes. Another escort bore a large silver platter. On it was the *pithambaram* (cloth of God), a costly silk fabric with patterns of golden thread.

When at last they reached Nehru's house, the flutist played while the sannyasis awaited an invitation from Nehru. Then they entered the house in dignity, fanned by two boys with special fans of deer hair. One sannyasi carried a scepter of gold, five feet long, two inches thick. He sprinkled Nehru with holy water from Tanjore and drew a streak in sacred ash across Nehru's forehead. Then he wrapped Nehru in the *pithambaram* and handed him the golden scepter. He also gave Nehru some cooked rice which had been offered that very morning to the dancing god Nataraja in south India, then flown by plane to Delhi.

Later that evening Nehru, and other men who would be India's new rulers on the morrow, went to the home of Rajendra Prasad, president of the Constituent Assembly. On his back lawn four plantain trees served as pillars for a temporary miniature temple. A roof of fresh green leaves sheltered a holy fire attended by a Brahman priest. There, while several thousand women chanted hymns, the ministers-to-be and constitution-makers passed in front of the priest, who sprinkled holy water on them. The oldest woman placed dots of red powder (for luck) on each man's forehead.

Tryst with Destiny

Thus dedicated, India's rulers turned to the secular business of the evening. At 11 o'clock they gathered in the Constituent Assembly Hall, ablaze with the colors of India's new tricolor flag—orange, white and green. Nehru made an inspired speech: "Long years ago we made a tryst with destiny, and now the time comes when we shall redeem our pledge. . . . At the stroke of midnight hour, when the world sleeps, India will awake to life and freedom."

And as the twelfth chime of midnight died out, a conch shell, traditional herald of the dawn, sounded raucously through the chamber. Members of the Constituent Assembly rose. Together they pledged themselves "at this solemn moment . . . to the service of India and her people. . . ." Nehru and Prasad struggled through the thousands of rejoicing Indians who had gathered outside to the Viceroy's House (now called the Governor General's House) where Viscount Mountbatten, who that day learned he would become an earl, awaited them. There, 32 minutes after Mountbatten had ceased to be a Viceroy, Nehru and Prasad rather timidly, almost bashfully, told Mountbatten that India's Constituent Assembly had assumed power and would like him to be Governor General.

The People's Day

Delhi's thousands rejoiced. The town was gay, with orange, white and green. Bullocks' horns and horses' legs were painted in the new national colors, and silk merchants sold tri-colored saris. Triumphant light blazed everywhere. Even in the humble Bhangi (Untouchable) quarters, candles and oil lamps flickered brightly in houses that had never before seen artificial light. The government wanted no one to be unhappy on India's Independence Day. Political prisoners, including Communists, were freed. All death sentences were commuted to life imprisonment. The Government, closing all slaughterhouses, ordered that no animals be killed.

The people made it their day. After dawn half a million thronged the great expanse of the Grand Vista and parkway, near the Government buildings of New Delhi. Wherever Lord and Lady Mountbatten went that day, their open carriage, drawn by six bay horses, was beset by happy, cheering Indians who swept aside police lines. A Briton received a popular ovation rarely given even to an Indian leader. "*Mountbattenji ki jai* [Victory to Mountbatten]," they roared, adding the affectionate and respectful suffix "*ji*" usually reserved for popular Indian leaders.

Now and then Nehru (who sometimes shows the instincts of a traffic policeman) harangued the crowd to be more orderly. One he espied a European girl caught up in the swirl. She was Pamela Mountbatten, the Governor General's 18-year-old daughter. Nehru literally slugged his way through the crowd to rescue her, brought her to the platform.

In the Council House the Constituent Assembly heard Mountbatten take the oath as Governor General. "Regard me as one of yourselves," he told them, "devoted wholly to the furtherance of India's interests." Then he swore in the new Indian Government. Messages of congratulation from over the world were read. The most original was a greeting in verse from Chinese Ambassador Lo Chia-luen. It read:

> India be free!
> Won't that be
> A Himalayan dream?
> How fantastic,
> How absurd an idea,
> That never occurred to me!

FREEDOM'S ARCHITECT

Mountbattenji drew the biggest applause of the day when he said: "At this historic moment let us not forget all that India owes to Mahatma Gandhi—the architect of her freedom through nonviolence. We miss his presence here today and would have him know how he is in our thoughts."

The Mahatma, who more than any other one man had brought independence to India, was not in New Delhi on the day of days. He was in troubled Calcutta, mourning because India was still racked by communal hatred. (In the Punjab last week, even more than in Calcutta, communal warfare blazed. Nearly 300 were killed.)

Gandhiji had moved into a Moslem house in Calcutta's Moslem quarter, which had been assailed by his fellow Hindus. He appealed to Hindus to keep peace. Angry young Hindu fanatics broke up a prayer meeting at his house. For the first time, Indians stoned Gandhi's house. Gandhi spoke sadly to the crowd: "If you still prefer to use violence, remove me. It is not me but my corpse that will be taken away from here."

But on Independence Day even Calcutta's violence turned to rejoicing. Moslems and Hindus danced together in the streets, were admitted to each others' mosques and temples. Moslems crowded round Gandhi's car to shake his hand, and sprinkled him with rosewater. For the disillusioned father of Indian independence, there might be some consolation in the rare cry he heard from Moslem lips: *"Mahatma Gandhi Zindabad"* (Long Live Gandhi).

THE TRANSISTOR

SHARON BEGLEY

Teenagers in the 1950s coveted the newly compact portable radio. For the first time, teens could have music wherever they went. No longer was it necessary to sit beside a furniture-size console radio encumbered by electric cords. Today, it's hard to imagine life without miniature radios, color televisions, personal computers, and various other electronic devices that make our lives easier and more interesting. A single invention made the electronics revolution possible—the transistor. Developed at mid–twentieth century by Bell Lab scientists, the transistor changed people's lives. Journalist Sharon Begley describes the transistor's origin in the following article. Begley has been an editor and writer at *Newsweek* since 1977 and has been a senior science writer for the magazine since 1990.

"Nature abhors a vacuum tube," cracked Bell Labs physicist John Pierce. So did almost everyone else by the 1940s. Sure, vacuum tubes boosted the power of the phone network's electrical signals, which weaken as they travel. But vacuum tubes were too bulky, unreliable and inefficient to support what AT&T expected to be a boom in demand for telecommunications after the end of World War II. So as peace loomed, in the summer of 1945, Bell Labs established a group to forge the future out of semiconductors, materials whose properties lie midway between an electrical insulator's and a conductor's. In the fall of 1947, in a monthlong burst of inspiration, Bell scientists invented the device that came to embody, even create, the future. The tiny transistor changed the way we bank, drive, cook, communicate, listen to music, watch television and otherwise work, play and live.

The inventors were an unlikely trio. William Brattain was a farm boy and a born tinkerer. William Shockley, hard-driving, ambitious and impatient, was named manager of semiconductor research in 1945. His ego would eventually fracture the team. "Whispering John" Bardeen, the low-key, famously self-effacing theorist, would become the only person ever to win two Nobels in physics.

In 1925 a British scientist had theorized that if an electric field enveloped a semiconductor, then the semiconductor would conduct electricity differently. In some cases, it would amplify incoming current. That appealed to the Bell scientists charged with finding replacements for vacuum tubes. But the phenomenon remained maddeningly theoretical; try as they might, no one could make semiconductors jack up a signal. Finally, in March 1946, Bardeen hit on the reason. Electrical fields were not having the desired effect on, say, a bar of silicon because the surface of the silicon is riddled with cul-de-sacs, he suggested, making it possible for electrons to enter but not to leave. The surface seemed to be positively charged on the outside, attracting electrons in, but negative on the inside, repelling them when they start to move. The electrons were stuck. As a result the flow of electrons—which is all a current is—could not increase. Applying an electric field did nothing.

For the next 20 months Bell's team turned to the most basic of research—the quantum properties of solids—as it sought ways to liberate the electrons in the semiconductor. "Without understanding solids from a quantum mechanical point of view," says William F. Brinkman, vice president of R&D at Bell Labs, "the transistor could not have been invented." On Nov. 17, 1947, Brattain launched the experiments that would bring success. He began with a splash—literally: he bathed silicon in various electrolytes (liquids that contain electric charges), such as acetone and distilled water. The electrolytes changed the electrical properties of silicon's surface. When Brattain shined a light on the treated silicon, a larger current flowed than from untreated silicon (silicon was known to produce a current in response to light; today that is the basis for solar cells). Apparently, the electrolytes set up an electric field that bulldozed the cul-de-sacs, allowing the electrons to escape.

On Nov. 21 Bardeen went to Brattain with a new suggestion for making silicon amplify a signal. "Come on, John!" Brattain exclaimed. "Let's go out in the laboratory and make it!" They put a drop of distilled water on a slab of silicon. They pushed a tungsten wire through the drop and onto the silicon. They used a bat-

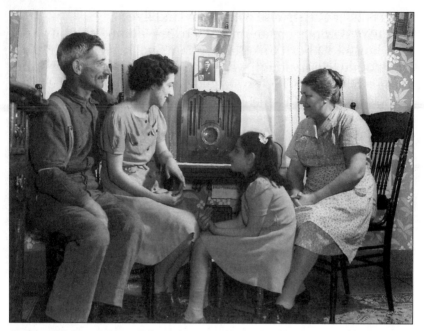

Before the invention of the transistor, which allowed people to carry small radios in their hands, families gathered around larger, more cumbersome radio consoles.

tery to apply one volt to the drop, hoping to stir up the positive and negative charges in the silicon just below the wire. Current through the contact point increased 10 percent: positive charges in the distilled water pulled the silicon's electrons to the surface, making more electrons flow and thus amplifying the current. Carpooling home that evening, Brattain said he'd "taken part in the most important experiment that I'd ever do in my life," according to an AT&T oral history quoted in "Crystal Fire," a book on the transistor by Michael Riordan and Lillian Hoddeson.

But hurdles remained. The silicon boosted current only 10 percent, not enough to outdo vacuum tubes. Brattain and Bardeen tried every variation they could think of to better their results. Germanium instead of silicon. Gold foil instead of tungsten. A viscous liquid called glycol borate—"gu"—instead of distilled water. On Dec. 16 they jury-rigged their final contraption. "It was marvelous!" Brattain recalled: their transistor boosted power 450 percent. The key realization was that "holes"—weird quantum-mechanical entities that are the *absence* of electrons—carried current in silicon. When Bardeen returned home that evening, he mumbled to his wife, Jane, as she peeled carrots, "We discovered something important today."

But Shockley was far from elated at Bardeen and Brattain's

success. He argued that work he had done in 1945 had sparked their invention, but AT&T's lawyers had filed a patent only on Brattain and Bardeen's device. Shockley worked obsessively on his own. On Jan. 23, 1948, he had his brainstorm: a sandwich. The bread would be semiconductor material with an excess of electrons; it was dubbed "n-type." The meat would be "p-type," with an excess of positively charged holes. When he attached wires and applied a voltage, holes streamed across the n-material into the p-area. His "junction transistor" amplified current just like Brattain and Bardeen's "point-contact" transistor. He tinkered with it in total secrecy. The rift in the team was now a canyon. Bardeen, fed up with Shockley, resigned in 1951.

In 1952 Bell Labs offered to license the point-contact transistor for $25,000 against future royalties. They had few takers apart from a small Japanese start-up called Sony. Its first transistor radio sold, in 1954, for $49.95 (more than $300 in 1995 dollars). Bell Labs produced the point-contact transistor for 10 years. But by 1954 production of the junction transistor had overtaken it. In 1956 Brattain, Bardeen and Shockley shared the Nobel in physics.

As the price of a transistor plunged—from $45 to $2 in the 1950s to .00001 cent today—the applications mushroomed. In 1959 sales of solid-state transistors overtook sales of vacuum tubes, and there has been no going back. Before the transistor "the whole phone network was analog and the switches were electromechanical; the transistor changed that to digital transmissions and electronic switches," says Ian Ross, Bell Labs president from 1979 to 1991. Today transistors packed by the millions onto microprocessors run car engines, cell phones, missiles, satellites, gas pumps, ATM machines, microwave ovens, computers, CD players and every other modern electronic toy and tool. In 1997 more than half a billion transistors will be manufactured. Every second.

ISRAEL BECOMES A NATION

RINNA SAMUEL

In 1897 Theodore Herzl founded the World Zionist Movement in Basel, Switzerland. The organization's goal was to establish a Jewish state in Palestine, the historic homeland of the Jews. During World War I, the British wrested control of Palestine from the Ottoman (Turkish) Empire and made commitments to both Jews and Arabs regarding territorial control. In support for Arab help against the Turks, the British promised Palestinian Arabs independence, but in the 1917 Balfour Declaration, the British also expressed support for a Jewish homeland within the state of Palestine and encouraged Jewish emigration there. At the time, there were fewer than one hundred thousand Jewish residents and a half-million Arabs in Palestine.

Jews continued to emigrate there in small numbers during the next twenty years, but when Hitler and the Nazis began their murderous campaign against the Jews in the 1930s, those Jews who could started to flee to Israel in greater numbers. This led to increased conflict between Jews and Arabs, traditional enemies who did not want to share their country with another sizable ethnic group. At the end of World War II, many Holocaust survivors in Europe had little desire to try to rebuild their lives in the countries where they had suffered so much pain and loss. As a result, many emigrated to other countries, including Israel.

The following article recounts the events following World War II and leading up to the establishment of Israel as an independent nation. The author, Rinna Samuel, lives in Israel and has written several books about the country and its history.

Excerpted from *A History of Israel*, by Rinna Samuel. Copyright © Rinna Samuel 1989. Reprinted by permission of George Weidenfeld & Nicolson Ltd.

Gradually, though not yet fully, the truth regarding the fate of European Jews [in World War II] began to seep out. A disbelieving world was forced to realize that Hitler's monstrous design had almost been completed, that six million Jews had been murdered by unspeakable means and that a remnant remained, leftovers of a catastrophe of such dimensions that, half a century later, survivors of the death camps, old men and women, would still be testifying—in courts, through books, on film—that, yes, however dreadful, it had all really taken place. In the summer of 1945, when horrified and sickened Allied troops liberated the camps, food, clothing and medicine were rushed from all over the civilized world to the dazed and disabled men and women who had experienced what no group of people had ever experienced before—and lived. Everything possible was done for them—with one exception: no government said it wanted them, would cherish them, would take all and any who wished to become its citizens.

In the summer of 1945, the battle lines were drawn, the struggle (*ma'avak* in Hebrew) between the mandatory power and the Jews of the Land, focusing on immigration, reached a stage of irreversibility; uneven sides faced each other stonily across an abyss. If confusion ever existed about the issues involved, it was now dispelled; everything was clear to everyone. As early as 1942, in an emergency conference held in New York, [Chaim] Weizmann, [David] Ben-Gurion and other Zionist leaders called for an opening of the gates of Palestine, with the Jewish Agency being given control of immigration and 'the necessary authority for upbuilding the country . . .', and urged '. . . that Palestine be established as a Jewish Commonwealth integrated in the structure of the new democratic world'. The Arabs took longer with their statement of intent; in 1945, Egypt, Saudi Arabia, Syria and Lebanon finally declared war against the Nazis and, with British aid, formed the Arab League, which at once declared Palestine to be an Arab state as promised by the [British] White Paper of 1939. . . .

THE UNITED STATES ENTERS THE FRAY

When, in a letter to British Prime Minister Clement Attlee, US President Harry Truman appealed for admission to Palestine of an additional 100,000 'displaced persons' (DPs) from the camps, the British refused to consider his request, suggesting instead that, since the Americans were so concerned with the plight of the Jews, an Anglo-American Committee of Inquiry study the problem.

In retrospect, it is possible that had Attlee agreed to Truman's proposal, the current Middle Eastern situation would have been very different. But he did not, and an Anglo-American Committee was duly established, the eighteenth fact-finding body to deal with Palestine. Diligently it went the European rounds, interviewed DPs, spoke to representatives of the British and US Armies of Occupation, to leaders of British and US Jewry, and in February 1946 arrived in the Land where it heard more testimony, not least the Jewish Agency report encapsulating Jewish history from the destruction of the Second Temple. While the Committee deliberated, the situation in Palestine worsened: the certificates permitted by the White Paper were used up and all official immigration stopped. The British announced a new policy: 1,500 certificates a month, if the Arabs agreed. When the Arabs said 'No', the British gave the Agency the certificates anyhow, but the ludicrous allocation solved little. Jewish resistance stiffened; the British, unable—despite a blockade and use of destroyers, aircraft and tanks—to break the will of the Yishuv [Jewish community], began to view the Jews *en masse* as political offenders, which helped explain the virtually unlimited powers handed to British soldiers, detectives and constables.

The Anglo-American Committee of Inquiry Report, published in May 1946, accepted neither the idea of immediate independence nor that of partition. 'Jew shall not dominate Arab and Arab shall not dominate Jew,' it proclaimed, and reminded everyone that the Christian churches too had a right in the country, thus sounding a new, if not particularly welcome, note. Its practical proposal was a trusteeship under the newly constituted United Nations. It further recommended admitting the 100,000 refugees and removing restrictions on land sales to Jews. The British government, faced by standard Arab threats, announced that it would only consider admitting the 100,000 when both sides disarmed. Nobody around was anxious to become a trustee or understood what this meant; the DPs still languished in their enclosures; the Yishuv exploded. The matter of self-restraint was no longer academic; splitting off from the Haganah [the Jewish military defense organization], with which it had been briefly united, the right-wing Irgun Zvai Leumi (its mentor the long-exiled Vladimir Jabotinsky, its commander Menachem Begin), and the much smaller, more extreme Stern Gang, openly revolted against the British, while official Jewish leadership expressing itself through the Haganah permitted the use of force in the cause of immigration, but prohibited the singling-out of British personnel.

When news came of the British rejection of the Anglo-American Committee's recommendations for the 100,000 certificates, the Haganah wrecked bridges and railways throughout the Land. The British then rounded up and jailed most of the Yishuv leadership, raiding and ransacking settlements in their frantic search for hidden arms. The extremist groups followed with flamboyant and deadly action, blowing up government offices in Jerusalem's King David Hotel, killing nearly 100 Britons, Jews and Arabs. The British decreed curfews for days on end, ordered detentions, passed death sentences and started shipping to Cyprus the illegal immigrants on whose pitiable behalf all this was happening.

BRITISH POSITION WAS UNTENABLE

By 1947, the British position was untenable; bullets and bayonets used against Palestinian Jews and DPs were not going to solve anything nor be tolerated much longer, either in Britain or by world opinion. In Palestine, British troops were now ghetto people: forbidden to associate with Jews, and terrified of the retaliation meted out for every action against the Yishuv by one of the three underground organizations; the Palestine administration was locked up in heavily guarded compounds; and habeas corpus was a thing of the past. Martial law was no fun for the ruled, but it made life impossible for the rulers. Nor was illegal immigration the sole area of Jewish defiance; the creation of Jewish settlements in prohibited areas also carried the message of the Yishuv's denial of the White Paper. In short, 'untenable' was an economical way of saying that, for the British, remaining in Palestine was exceedingly unpleasant, inordinately expensive and not worth the trouble. Let the United Nations see what it can do, said Mr Bevin in the House of Commons in February 1947.

So UNSCOP (the United Nations Special Committee on Palestine) entered the post–World War II lexicon. The Committee, like its immediate predecessor, came to Palestine, talked to everyone—except the Arabs who refused to acknowledge it—met with leaders of the Arab states, journeyed to Germany and Austria, after having been treated, unfathomably, by the British to a display of the harrowing consequences of the Government's decision to force the return to Germany (using combat troops) of the over 4,500 illegal immigrants (they included 2,000 children) who arrived in Palestine in July 1947 aboard an old American ship renamed the *SS Exodus*. On 31 August, from the former Palace of the League of Nations, UNSCOP issued its report recommending, as the Peel Commission had done, the termination of the mandate, the partition of Palestine into an Arab state and a Jewish state, a special arrangement for Jerusalem, and economic union for the whole country. By 29 November, the UNSCOP Majority Report (a minority report upheld by India, Yugoslavia and Iran suggested a federal Arab-Jewish state), slightly amended, was accepted by the UN General Assembly in New York. Thirty-three

countries voted 'Yes'; thirteen voted 'No'; ten, including Great
Britain abstained. The United Nations had created its first ward;
speaking through it, most of the world had authorized the realization of the dream of Jewish independence, liberty and refuge.

As for implementation of UN Resolution 181 (11), familiar
stances were again adopted: the Arab states announced that they
would oppose partition by force; the Jews, with mixed feelings,
accepted it; the British, upon whose co-operation its success depended, said that, since both sides had not agreed to the UN Resolution, the British Government would have no part of the proceedings, would not let UN representatives into the country
while the mandate was still operative, and fully intended to remain in exclusive control until 15 May 1948. Ernest Bevin's ran-
cour was most apparent in the British refusal to abide by the Resolution's requirement that the mandatory power evacuate a port
(and surrounding area) for the reception of immigrants.

The news of the passing of the Resolution reached Palestine at
1 A.M. on the night between the 29th and the 30th of November. In
the compound of the Jewish Agency building in Jerusalem, hundreds of people, British soldiers among them, joyously held
hands, embraced each other, sang and danced. Golda Meir, a rank-
ing member of the Jewish Agency Executive, recalled the scene:

> From the balcony of my office I spoke for a few min-
> utes . . . not really to the mass of people below me . . .
> it was . . . to the Arabs. 'You have fought your battle
> against us in the UN,' I said, 'the UN . . . have had their
> say. The partition plan is a compromise; not what you
> wanted, not what we wanted. . . . Let us now live in
> friendship and peace.'

A NATION NOT AT PEACE

That day, an Arab ambush killed seven Jews; next day, the Arabs
of Palestine declared a three-day strike. The celebration only
lasted a few hours and not everyone in the Yishuv danced or
sang. No one knew then that the war which had already broken
out would last nearly sixteen months, consist of close to forty
military operations, and involve mobilization of what amounted
to the entire Jewish population of the Land (in May 1948, about
650,000 people)—of whom a staggering 1 per cent were to be
killed—to meet the assault of five regular Arab enemies plus a
million Arabs of Palestine. No one knew this, but then no one
knew whether the state would ever come into being, or, having
been born, would survive its birth.

The British and the Arabs were as good as their word. Until

May 1948, the British, seemingly bent on the creation of chaos, engaged in highly selective attention and inattention. Insofar as immigration was concerned, the administration adhered strictly to White Paper legalities, as though nothing had changed; DPs without certificates, bound for the land, were hunted, seized and deported to camps in Cyprus. However, when it came to government stores, installations and essential records such as land registry deeds (Ben-Gurion went in vain to the High Commissioner to ask for these), it turned out that whatever was not handed to the Arabs or destroyed was simply 'lost'. The Arabs, for their part, switched from random raids and killings to increasingly focused attacks on Jewish settlements and vital roads, concentrating their efforts on isolating Jerusalem. Bolstered by British indifference to the weekly quota of murder and destruction (and even greater indifference to the vulnerability of the Jewish population), seduced by lurid descriptions of the joys awaiting them in conquered Tel Aviv, bands of Palestinian Arabs and irregulars from across the borders were on the offensive throughout the Land. As for the Haganah, driven further underground with each passing month, aware that full-scale warfare would break out as soon as the British departed Palestine's inhospitable shores, knowing precisely what hung in the balance and how meagre its military supplies—a few thousand rifles, a few hundred machine-guns, a mixed bag of other weapons, nine small planes—stepped up its arms procurement, mainly in Czechoslovakia, and hurriedly trained new immigrants with wooden rifles and dummy bullets. It vowed to hold on to all Jewish settlements, regardless of their size or the ferocity of the attack mounted against them—which was almost, though not quite, accomplished. Above all, the road from the coastal plain to Jerusalem had to be kept open or Jerusalem, the core of the Land, and its 100,000 Jews already under siege, might be cut off and captured, the only access to the rest of the country being a winding forty-mile mountain road, dominated by the Arabs who controlled most of the hilly regions of Palestine. The noose had to be loosened, and soon.

THE UNITED NATIONS GETS INVOLVED

A UN Implementation Committee came, looked around and returned to New York to wonder aloud whether the Jewish state had any chance of making it; were there no alternatives, considering the turmoil and toll? In April 1948, Ben-Gurion sent a convoy into battle for Jerusalem's life. On the first vehicle were scribbled the words: 'If I forget thee, O Jerusalem, let my right hand lose its cunning.' That convoy got through but was the last for a

long time, the longest time, in fact, that Jerusalem had been be-
sieged since the Crusades. There was no food, petrol or electricity, and one bucket of water per family; when the British finally
left, there was also a shortage of news, perhaps, under the circumstances, the greatest deprivation.

On 14 May, General Sir Alan Cunningham, last British High
Commissioner to Palestine, left Jerusalem's Government House
in full dress uniform, flew to Haifa, took a salute from a company
of the Palestine Police, shook hands with Haifa's Jewish mayor
and Arab deputy mayor, boarded a waiting British cruiser and,
from its deck, watched the Union Jack lowered. The evening before, he had broadcast a farewell message: 'It would be easy . . .
to say sometimes "here we did right", and no doubt at other
times, "there we did wrong". . . . the way ahead has not always
been clear . . . in this respect we are more than content to accept
the judgment of history.' And he prayed that peace might come
to Palestine, even at that late hour.

The British withdrawal left the Land devoid of air or sea mail,
tax collection, car registration, functioning health controls, even
much local currency. The thirty years of the mandate came to an
end, abruptly, humiliatingly and arbitrarily, doing little justice to
the high hopes that had accompanied the beginning of the great
venture, or to the many men of distinction and ability associated
with it. The long-term legacy of some of the best of British tradition would, in the future, be incorporated into that of the State of
Israel, but on the day of Sir Alan's embarkation, this could not be
taken for granted. In fact, the breach was to heal with unforesee-
able rapidity; although Great Britain abstained from voting, in
1949, for Israel's admission to the UN, early that year Ernest
Bevin announced *de facto* recognition and, shortly afterwards, the
appointment of Britain's first diplomatic representative to the
Jewish state.

NATIONHOOD IS DECLARED

At exactly 4 P.M. that Friday afternoon, in Tel Aviv's small art museum on the boulevard named for Baron Rothschild, against a
background of flags and a picture of Theodor Herzl, in the presence of some 200 deeply moved people who rose to their feet, in
a short ceremony (the time and place of which had been kept secret till then), David Ben-Gurion read out Israel's Proclamation
of Independence. The 979 Hebrew words, which took about
twenty minutes to read, stressed the unbroken link between the
Land and the Jewish people; referred to Herzl and the Balfour
Declaration; declared that the state would be called Israel; that it
would be 'open to Jewish immigration and the ingathering of ex-

iles'; that it would 'promote the development of the country for the benefit of all its inhabitants' and be based on liberty, justice and peace 'as envisaged by the Prophets of Israel'; and that it would loyally uphold the principles of the UN Charter. It called upon the United Nations to assist the Jewish people in the building of its state and appealed 'in the very midst of the onslaught launched against us . . . to the Arab inhabitants of the State of Israel . . . to play their part in the development of the state on the basis of full and equal citizenship and due representation in all its bodies and institutions'. To the Arab states and peoples, the Proclamation offered 'peace and good neighbourliness', and promised that the State of Israel would 'make its contribution to the progress of the Middle East as a whole'.

The traditional Jewish blessing was intoned ('Blessed be Thou, Oh Lord our God, King of the Universe, who has kept us alive and made us endure and brought us to this day'). Then, the Secretary of what was now the Provisional Government called upon those members of the Provisional State Council (evolved from the Jewish autonomous agencies under the mandate) to sign the Proclamation; the Zionist anthem, the *Hatikvah* ('The Hope') was sung; just after 4.30 P.M. Ben-Gurion said: 'The State of Israel has arisen. This meeting is ended.'

MAHATMA GANDHI AND NONVIOLENT RESISTANCE

ALOYSIUS FONSECA

Mohandas Karamchand Gandhi, better known by the title Mahatma, was one of the most influential figures of the twentieth century. Born in 1869 to a middle-class Hindu family, Gandhi was trained in the law, which he practiced in Africa from 1893 to 1914. While there he campaigned for equal rights for Indian settlers, and upon his return to India in 1919, he became active in the nationalist movement to gain India's independence from Britain. As head of the Indian National Congress, he led by example, promoting noncooperation with and nonviolent resistance to the British government. He urged boycotting of British products and encouraged use of native Indian products. He took part in hunger strikes protesting British policies. He encouraged friendship between the Hindu and Muslim communities and urged them to work together against their colonial masters.

Early in World War II, Great Britain pledged to give India its independence if India would fight with the Allies against the Japanese. Gandhi refused to fight and spent most of the war in prison. Following the war, he was involved in independence negotiations with Britain, and his leadership was instrumental in attaining India's independence in 1947.

Gandhi himself was not what people usually picture when they think of rebels. He did not lead guerrilla troops in gun battles against the authorities. As a Hindu, Gandhi deeply believed in the sacredness of life, and violence was anathema to him.

From "Gandhi and Nonviolence," by Aloysius Fonseca, *America*, October 4, 1969. Copyright © 1969. All rights reserved. Reprinted with permission from America Press, Inc., www.americapress.org.

Gandhi believed that social justice could be attained through peacefully refusing to obey unjust laws.

Gandhi's impact was far broader than on India alone. His methods and ideals influenced the struggle for human rights worldwide. A prime example is Martin Luther King Jr., who modeled his efforts in the American civil rights movement after Gandhi. The antiapartheid protestors in South Africa, too, tried to follow Gandhi's example in their fight to end that race-based system.

In the following article, written twenty years after Gandhi's assassination, Aloysius Fonseca discusses the principles Gandhi lived by and their effect. At the time he wrote this, Fonseca, a Catholic Jesuit priest and social worker in northern India, was the editor of *Social Action*, published by the Indian Social Institute, New Delhi, India.

It is almost impossible to compress within the span of a few pages such a complex personality as that of Mahatma Gandhi, or even to discuss adequately his philosophy and techniques of nonviolence. But I am making the attempt because, in an age of increasing violence, the Mahatma's repudiation of brute force and his message of *satyagraha* (truth force) exercises a peculiar fascination on the minds and hearts of many of the world's leading personalities, and of countless others in humbler positions. More than twenty years after his death, Gandhi and what he stood for produce an impact that is imperceptible and yet powerful enough to arouse admiration and create new hope among those who despair of our present civilization. Many of his concepts and practices, such as *ahimsa* (nonviolence), *satyagraha* (truth force), *sarvodaya* (welfare of all), have passed into international circulation and become part of the heritage of modern man and the inspiration of his struggle for human deliverance.

Because they were so strange and outlandish when he first expounded them, Gandhi's ideas have provoked intense controversy. Yet this naked fakir, as he was derisively hailed by the British press, secured independence for his people from one of the most powerful imperialist nations in history. It is this juxtaposition of seeming powerlessness and mighty influence, of traditionalism and modernism, of loving his enemies while fighting against them, of overcoming violence by nonviolence that has aroused the admiration of the world for this frail figure in his loincloth, trudging the dusty roads of India in order to free his countrymen and transform the lot of the outcastes of society.

An Enigmatic Figure

Even to his own people, however, Mahatma Gandhi was an enigmatic figure, often leaving them puzzled. To his most intimate followers he was occasionally a cause of irritated surprise and bewilderment. Writing about him after his death, Jawaharlal Nehru could say:

> What a problem and puzzle he has been not only to the British government but to his own people and his closest associates. Perhaps in every other country he would be out of place today, but India still seems to understand, or at least appreciate, the prophetic-religious type of man, talking of sin and salvation and nonviolence.

> Indian mythology is full of stories of great ascetics who, by the rigor of their sacrifices and self-imposed penance, built up a 'mountain of merit' that threatened the dominion of some of the lesser gods and upset the established order. These myths have come often to my mind when I have watched the amazing energy and inner power of Gandhiji coming out of some inexhaustible spiritual reservoir. He was obviously not of the world's ordinary coinage; he was minted of a different and rare variety, and often the unknown stared at us through his eyes.

Modern India owes more than it can ever realize to Gandhi. Had it not been for Gandhi, India might not have been a free nation today, the Constitution of India might not have breathed such a spirit of freedom, justice and equality in a society whose social structures had for centuries supported the caste system and the exploitation of the outcaste. Although Gandhi had been brought up in a strict orthodox Hindu caste, he became the great upholder of the millions of outcastes in India, living among them and striving to bring about a change in the attitudes of the caste people, who visited him in the unclean quarter of the village where he used to reside. For him, the great cleavage between "pure" and "impure" was not so much external and social as essentially internal.

Passion for Social Justice

There is no doubt that during his early years in England, as a young student, Gandhi came into contact with the culture and literature of Christianity. One of the books that made a deep impression on his mind was Ruskin's *Unto This Last*. Ruskin, the artist and poet, awakened in Gandhi a profound appreciation of the creative work of every craftsman and imbued his mind with a passion for social justice on behalf of the less privileged classes. Ruskin's inspiration served Gandhi in his struggle against social injustice in India, which was supported by the religious sanctions of the caste system.

During his stay in South Africa, Gandhi made a deep study of the Bible. He was above all impressed by the Sermon on the Mount. And he would often read and meditate on this passage from the gospel. But all the same, he remained a staunch Hindu to the end, being convinced that he was following the dictates of his conscience. No one could ever impugn the fact of his deep sincerity and honesty.

Gandhi's outlook on life was deeply influenced by certain traditional principles that formed part of the philosophy, the religious beliefs and practices of Hinduism, in particular by the Bhagavad Gita, which he liked to read and to meditate upon. To some extent, Gandhi was eclectic in his selection of what he thought to be the essence of religion. But his religious convictions and his spiritual interests provided him with a certain number of fundamental principles, which he outlined and gradually developed during the long political struggle for Indian independence.

LOVE OF TRUTH

One of the first was his complete submission to the truth and love for it. *Satyameva jayate* (Truth will always conquer). One must therefore assiduously seek for the truth. Gandhi entitled his autobiography *My Experiments With Truth.* All his life long, the Mahatma remained a great seeker of the truth because he firmly believed that truth was unassailable and impregnable. Its power over human behavior was unlimited. Once it was seen in all its clarity, nothing could prevent its triumphant progress toward realization. It is for this reason that Gandhi could sometimes be so obdurate in certain decisions that he took. It was at the moment when the truth in a situation burst upon his mind that he felt convinced he had to follow its beckoning, and nothing could stop him or make him change his decision.

Since Gandhi was deeply implicated in politics, as we understand the term (although he himself believed he was fighting for the moral right of Indians to be free and therefore was leading a moral battle), he developed a special philosophy of his own, which lay at the basis of much of his activity. His social system, which he named *sarvodaya* (welfare of all), was made up of several assumptions that he took for granted. In the first place, Gandhi was convinced that the good of the individual is assured in the good of all, that a barber's work has the same value as a lawyer's, and that the life of labor is the life worth living. Through *sarvodaya*, Gandhi aimed at forming a new social order that would be a peaceful nonviolent society in which "everyone would belong to everyone else and all would strive harmoniously toward the achievement of the greatest good of all."

Since *sarvodaya* aimed at the integral development of the individual, Gandhi—as he is quoted in the volume *Yeravda Mandir* (Navajivan Press, Ahmedabad)—wished to have a "civilization in the real sense of the term, consisting not in the multiplication but in the deliberate and voluntary reduction of wants." Gandhi, however, did not overemphasize the spiritual aspect at the cost of neglecting material requirements. For he asked, as quoted in the same volume: "How am I to talk of God to the millions who have to go without two meals a day? To them God can only appear as bread and butter." Finally, in this striving for *sarvodaya*, he attached the greatest importance to the means that must be used to achieve the end. Both means and end had to be good and pure.

In setting Indian independence as his goal, Gandhi was moved by what he believed was the "force of truth" (*satyagraha*). For him the simple, clear fact that a people like Indians had to be free was so evident that he found it intolerable to realize they were subject to foreign rule. Independence therefore for him became an objective demanded by truth itself. In order to achieve independence, Gandhi chose the means to reach it, namely, *ahimsa* (nonviolence). *Ahimsa* is not a peculiar Gandhian invention. It is as old as Indian philosophy and is deeply ingrained in the philosophy of some of the Hindu sects, such as the Jains. Jain *sadhus* and nuns often cover their mouths to prevent the destruction of life when they breathe. Gandhi certainly inherited this great respect for life and all living things from his cultural environment.

BELIEF IN NONVIOLENCE

The Mahatma elaborated his concept of nonviolence in several striking passages. For instance, as quoted by Jawaharlal Nehru in *Mahatma Gandhi*, he says: "Nonviolence is the law of our species, as violence is the law of the brute." In his own *Nonviolence in Peace and War* he describes *ahimsa* as "love in the Pauline sense, and yet something more than the love defined by St. Paul, although I know St. Paul's beautiful definition is good for all practical purposes. *Ahimsa* includes the whole of creation and not only humans."

While the initial concept of *ahimsa* conveyed little more than a vague gentleness, Gandhi enriched the notion with a very positive meaning and broadened its connotation to include passive resistance of a kind that could withstand great violence with remarkable fortitude, patience and equanimity—all for the sake of the truth. Thus he linked *ahimsa* with *satyagraha,* or "truth force," which in his estimation was so inherently powerful as to burst all social and political barriers once it was grasped in its fullness.

Further, Gandhi regarded *satyagraha* not merely as an expedient to use where force was impossible but as a weapon superior to force. It was on these two pillars of *satyagraha* and *ahimsa* that he built up his structure of nonviolent resistance, which finally brought the British Empire to its doom.

It must be emphasized that the starting point of a *satyagraha* campaign is the radical wrongness of a situation. To convert something that is evil, one must be fully conscious and aware of the evil; one must have a precise understanding of what is wrong, and what factor in the situation embodies the evil so starkly that a stand has to be made. To achieve this insight, one requires nonviolence of the mind, which enables one to get rid of hate, passion and prejudice. Truth must be sought in a spirit of love; otherwise it will never be found.

BANISH ANGER

Through the gaining of such an insight, one catches a glimpse of the Absolute Truth in the essential truth present in a specific situation. The *satyagrahi* (volunteer in *satyagraha*) draws great strength from the contemplation of such truth; it enables him to dedicate himself completely to its service by bringing about the realization of the truth in the troubled situation prevailing here and now. In Gandhi's words, quoted by Geoffrey Ashe in *Gandhi: A Study in Revolution* (Asia Pub. House, Bombay): "Truth is God and the way to find Him is nonviolence. Anger must be banished, and fear and falsehood. . . . Purified, you get power. It's not your own, it's God's."

Strengthened by this faith, the *satyagrahi* refuses to submit to the wrong or co-operate with it. He takes to the path of action, which often involves public acts of dissent and disobedience. His action may finally result in the setting up of new political or economic institutions to replace wrong by right. In the process, all violence must be precluded. Violence leads only to spiritual blindness, whereas the practice of nonviolence removes hatred and sets the two parties in a new light. They come to appreciate each other's worth.

Gandhi also expected his *satyagrahi* to submit silently and patiently to the blows and the truncheons of established authority while protesting against an injustice. He should not retaliate with violence. He must even be ready to face prison joyfully and courageously. Nor must he allow bitterness or rancor to invade his mind. *Satyagraha* implies self-reliance. It also calls for enormous self-control.

Victory Through Suffering

The secret of the *satyagrahi* is that he conquers through suffering. He makes his enemy ashamed of his violent attacks upon an unresisting victim. It is through his own martyrdom that the *satyagrahi* hopes to bring about a changed attitude, a conversion of not so much the defeat of the enemy heart. It is his endeavor to unnerve the arm that rains down the blows, and by his patient suffering to win over the mind that directs them. The ultimate result does not imply victory for one side or the other. It rather implies a reconciliation of both sides in a higher unity, after the wrong has been righted.

Gandhi's philosophy and technique of nonviolence have been strongly criticized because they seem to lend themselves to lawbreaking. Gandhi would submit that some laws may be broken in the interest of a higher law. Even the great Chancellor of Henry VIII's England, St. Thomas More, who died for resisting a royal tyrant, could maintain that he was "the king's good servant, but God's first." Gandhi's concept of nonviolence is very much in the same stream of thought and action as that of Thomas More's passive resistance. His study of the British legal system during his formative years in England, and his acceptance of the "rule of law" as the supreme arbiter in the relations between the citizen and the state, had deeply influenced his attitude toward the lawmaker and enabled him to see at what point the legislator had overstepped the bounds of his authority.

Gandhian Civil Disobedience

It must be noted that Gandhian civil disobedience, when used as a nonviolent technique, was very clearly and explicitly concentrated on a single issue. It was never a general attack on law and order. In other words, it was never anarchical. It did not aim to bring about anarchy. For instance, Gandhi fought for the right of Indians to live at peace in the Transvaal. He did this by organizing all his efforts and those of his collaborators on the infringement of a single law. He and his followers readily obeyed all the other laws of the state.

Obviously, every act of disobedience to this one law would raise a public outcry; it would also draw the attention of the public to the lawbreaker. At the same time, it would begin to shake the complacency of the lawgiver in the justice of the law and to rouse the citizen to inquire into its unjust aspects. But Gandhi would never allow his followers to violate a whole series of laws.

Gandhi was very careful not to sow confusion in their minds or among the general public. They had to see the issue very clearly, and its essential injustice. It was only then that the nonviolent struggle could really take shape and achieve its purposes despite violent determination on the part of the opponent.

Such sharp focusing on a single law was not easy for Gandhi when he launched the civil disobedience movement in India against the British government. In the first place, the Indian public had never been acquainted with the technique of nonviolence as Gandhi had developed it in South Africa. In the early days of the movement, civil disobedience easily erupted into violence, and in one instance the mob, infuriated by the blows of the police, turned violent, shut the policemen in the police station and burned it down. Immediately Gandhi called off the struggle and fasted to make amends for the crime. It was only several years after he had preached nonviolence and faced the blows of the police himself and gone to prison that his *satyagrahis,* or volunteers in *satyagraha,* began to realize the meaning of nonviolence and its heroic demands on human courage and patience.

SUCCESSFUL CAMPAIGN

A typical example of a successful nonviolent struggle was the march on Dandi by the seashore in order to scrape the salt off its surface. This action was aimed to disobey the salt law by which the British had imposed a tax on salt. The police were waiting for the marchers, and as soon as they reached the sands where the salt was exposed, the policemen used their staves on the heads of the unresisting *satyagrahis.* Many of them fell down unconscious and bleeding, but not a single one raised his hand against the persecutor. The story of this heroic struggle echoed throughout the land and was publicized throughout the world. It had an unnerving effect on the administration. The British government in India soon found itself isolated from the people and disparaged for its cruelty. Its prestige was swept away at one stroke.

As Nehru clearly maintains, it was to Indians with a living tradition of *ahimsa* that Gandhi appealed. This fact partly explains his success. On the other hand, as Dr. Rajendra Prasad conceded, Gandhi was also fortunate in having to wrestle with the British, who believed in the "rule of law" and therefore the exercise of self-restraint in the use of authority. Gandhi never believed in any kind of secret activity in his struggle for independence. Everything was done openly with the fullest cognizance of the government. His program was thrashed out in public meetings, and his calls for civil disobedience were known to the authorities long beforehand. What really took them unawares was the peculiar technique of nonviolence that he used. After some time, even his judges began to admire him and treated him with the greatest courtesy. And when the British at last withdrew from India, they left without misgivings or bitter feelings. On the contrary, their respect and affection for India were strengthened and increased. It was the same with the Indians in their friendly attitudes toward the British.

All the same, while many leading Indians doubted the impact of nonviolence on the British public, even Nehru was compelled to admit that "these movements (noncooperation and civil disobedience) exercised tremendous pressure on the British government and shook the government machinery." He continued: "But the real importance, to my mind, lay in the effect they had on our own people, and especially the village masses. Poverty and a long period of autocratic rule . . . had thoroughly demoralized and degraded them. . . .

"Noncooperation dragged them out of the mire and gave them self-respect and self-reliance . . . they acted courageously and did not submit so easily to unjust oppression; their outlook widened and they began to think a little in terms of India as a whole; they discussed political and economic questions (crudely no doubt) in their bazaars and meeting places. . . . It was a remarkable transformation, and the Congress, under Gandhi's leadership, must have the credit for it. It was something far more important than constitutions and the structure of government. It was the foundation on which a stable structure or constitution could be built.

"All this, of course, involves a cataclysmic upheaval of Indian life. Usually in other countries this has involved a vast amount of hatred and violence. And yet in India, thanks to Mahatma Gandhi, there was, relatively speaking, exceedingly little of this. We developed many of the virtues of war without its terrible evils."

REVOLUTION WITHOUT VIOLENCE

These brief comments of Nehru on the impact of Gandhi's efforts for over 14 years illuminate with precision Gandhi's real contribution to the movement for independence. Nonviolence was forged by the Mahatma into a technique for bringing about a revolution without violence, bitterness or hatred. In this art, Gandhi is the supreme master, and the manner in which he organized masses of illiterate and demoralized people into a disciplined force has won him the admiration and respect of the entire world. His critics, even in his own country, have been innumerable and vociferous. But the point remains that despite their sophisticated disbelief and against their advice, Gandhi followed his own inner promptings and achieved results where they would have completely failed.

In an editorial in *Civiltà Cattolica* of May 18, 1968, violent revolution was strongly repudiated as a means of bringing about a more just and equitable social order. It was stated: "Christianity is profoundly revolutionary. . . . The Christian must fight against social injustice, against social discrimination, must oppose political and economic regimes that tend to reduce man to a condition of slavery, to oppress him politically and to maintain him in a condition of economic misery and moral abjection. The Christian must oppose the international imperialism of money, which contributes toward keeping peoples and continents in conditions of alarming misery and tragic underdevelopment." It was left to Mahatma Gandhi to show us the method of nonviolence to achieve such ends. His method helps to channel social protest to predetermined ends through which change is effected. His method is fully in consonance with the spirit of the cross, and the objectives it seeks can never include triumph over one's enemies, but rather their conversion and salvation.

But this victory is not an easy one. It requires first of all self-conquest and self-purification before an attempt can be made to convince others of the justice of one's cause. It is strange that while Christian nations take to violence to achieve their goals and seek to justify the use of violence, a convinced and staunch Hindu should have discovered the link between truth and non-violence to bring about social change. In spite of his success, Gandhi's nonviolent methods have captured neither the Indian mind nor that of the rest of the world, except in a few rare cases, like Martin Luther King, Danilo Dolci and Gandhi's closest follower, Vinoba Bhave. Such lessons are hard to learn, but all of us must learn them, because the only alternative is war with its Pyrrhic victories, its bitterness and the seeking for revenge it arouses in the vanquished enemy.

Gandhi's way of nonviolence is the hard and narrow path through which men learn the value of self-sacrifice in the interest of universal truth and the hard lesson of vanquishing others by vanquishing themselves. This paradox is not strange to Christian theology though often far removed from Christian practice. It needs to be absorbed in slow stages, or step by step, as Gandhi's favorite Christian hymn, "Lead Kindly Light," has it:

> Keep thou my feet: I do not ask to see
> The distant scene: one step is enough for me.

WORLD HISTORY BY ERA

1950–1959

CHAPTER 2

THE RED MENACE

BY JOSEPH R. MCCARTHY

On February 9, 1950, a Wisconsin senator raised himself out of obscurity and began the four-year campaign that would bind his name with a notorious period of American political history. Joseph R. McCarthy was nearing the end of his first senatorial term and needed a hook to draw his constituency to reelect him. Invited to speak at a Republican Women's Club Lincoln Day dinner in Wheeling, West Virginia, McCarthy tapped into a deep-seated fear afflicting Americans of the time—communism.

During the Great Depression of the 1930s, communism had appealed to many people as a promising humanitarian philosophy. It promoted political and economic equality and promised to raise the poor out of their struggle. In fact, its precepts were instrumental in the founding of one of America's most powerful organizations, the CIO (Congress of Industrial Organizations), and the Communist Soviet Union (USSR) and the United States were Allies during World War II. But a key tenet of communism was the importance of the state: The good of the whole—or, it often seemed in practice, the good of government officials—was more important than the good of any individual. This philosophy diametrically opposed the Western—particularly American—view that individual rights were of utmost importance.

Shortly after the end of the war, the USSR began aggressively seeking control of Eastern European nations near its borders, and the United States and other Western nations feared that the Soviet Union would pursue aggressive policies in Europe and other democratic nations, trying to convert them by force or propaganda to communism. Fear of Communist subversion ran high. In 1947 U.S. president Harry Truman signed an executive order establishing a loyalty program for all federal officials; government employees were required to sign oaths that they were not

From Joseph R. McCarthy's speech to the Ohio County Republican Women's Club, February 9, 1950, Wheeling, WV, read into the *Congressional Record*, February 20, 1950.

Communists. In that same year, he established the Truman Doctrine, which committed the United States to supporting nations threatened by aggressors. Implicitly, it was understood that the aggressors Truman was pledging to defend against were Russian Communists.

Joseph McCarthy tapped into the fear of communism when he gave his notorious Wheeling, West Virginia, speech. He asserted that America had far more to fear from subversive enemies within than from a Communist invasion from without. He also asserted that he had undeniable evidence that Communists were employed by the State Department and were helping form U.S. policy.

McCarthy's speech was quoted in the next day's newspapers, and his charges caught fire. Within a short time, McCarthy was involved in a highly publicized campaign to root out Communists from the government. While some thought McCarthy was a fraud and a demagogue, many others believed his charges. The careers and reputations of many individuals, both in the public and private sectors, were ruined, sometimes on little or no evidence, when McCarthy leveled charges of un-Americanism and traitorous activities against them in what became known as the Red Scare.

Intimidated by the disastrous consequences of being accused by McCarthy and the fear of being accused, many people were fearful of challenging him. By 1954 he had spread his accusations of Communist infiltration to include the U.S. Army. The Army-McCarthy hearings were televised to the nation, and this exposure was the beginning of McCarthy's downfall.

Throughout his anticommunism campaign, he had used brutal tactics, virulently attacking hundreds of alleged Communists and Communist sympathizers. Many of these people were blacklisted from their profession, whether any truth was found in McCarthy's charges or not. On television, the American public could see McCarthy's methods more clearly for what they were. By the end of 1954, the Senate had censured McCarthy, and the public saw him as, at best, a bullying buffoon. A backlash against McCarthyism and the so-called red menace began. Many people now believed that McCarthy had made up all his charges and so there must be no Communist threat—from within—at all. Today, evidence suggests that McCarthy was not completely wrong in his assertions that Soviet spies were working in the American government, but his wrong-headed methods cost him—and the accusations he made—credibility. Today, the term *McCarthyism* is synonymous with witch-hunting tactics—unwarranted political smears.

McCarthy's Wheeling, West Virginia, speech is reprinted here.

L adies and gentlemen, tonight as we celebrate the one hundred and forty-first birthday of one of the greatest men in American history, I would like to be able to talk about what a glorious day today is in the history of the world. As we celebrate the birth of this man who with his whole heart and soul hated war, I would like to be able to speak of peace in our time, of war being outlawed, and of world-wide disarmament. These would be truly appropriate things to be able to mention as we celebrate the birthday of Abraham Lincoln. . . .

Five years after a world war has been won, men's hearts should anticipate a long peace and men's minds should be free from the heavy weight that comes with war. But this is not such a period—for this is not a period of peace. This is a time of the "cold war." This is a time when all the world is split into two vast, increasingly hostile armed camps—a time of a great armaments race.

Today we can almost physically hear the mutterings and rumblings of an invigorated god of war. You can see it, feel it, and hear it all the way from the hills of Indochina, from the shores of Formosa, right over into the very heart of Europe itself.

The one encouraging thing is that the "mad moment" has not yet arrived for the firing of the gun or the exploding of the bomb which will set civilization about the final task of destroying itself. There is still a hope for peace if we finally decide that no longer can we safely blind our eyes and close our ears to those facts which are shaping up more and more clearly. And that is that we are now engaged in a show-down fight—not the usual war between nations for land areas or other material gains, but a war between two diametrically opposed ideologies.

SOVIET MORAL DIFFERENCES DIVIDE THE WORLD

The great difference between our western Christian world and the atheistic Communist world is not political, ladies and gentlemen, it is moral. There are other differences, of course, but those could be reconciled. For instance, the Marxian idea of confiscating the land and factories and running the entire economy as a single enterprise is momentous. Likewise, Lenin's invention of the one-party police state as a way to make Marx's idea work is hardly less momentous.

Stalin's resolute putting across of these two ideas, of course, did much to divide the world. With only those differences, however, the East and the West could most certainly still live in peace.

The real, basic difference, however, lies in the religion of immoralism—invented by Marx, preached feverishly by Lenin, and carried to unimaginable extremes by Stalin. This religion of immoralism, if the Red half of the world wins—and well it may—

this religion of immoralism will more deeply wound and damage mankind than any conceivable economic or political system.

Karl Marx dismissed God as a hoax, and Lenin and Stalin have added in clear-cut, unmistakable language their resolve that no nation, no people who believe in a God, can exist side by side with their communistic state.

Karl Marx, for example, expelled people from his Communist Party for mentioning such things as justice, humanity, or morality. He called this soulful ravings and sloppy sentimentality.

While Lincoln was a relatively young man in his late thirties, Karl Marx boasted that the Communist specter was haunting Europe. Since that time, hundreds of millions of people, and vast areas of the world, have fallen under Communist domination. Today, less than 100 years after Lincoln's death, Stalin brags that this Communist specter is not only haunting the world, but is about to completely subjugate it.

FINAL, ALL-OUT BATTLE

Today we are engaged in a final, all-out battle between communistic atheism and Christianity. The modern champions of communism have selected this as the time. And, ladies and gentlemen, the chips are down—they are truly down. . . .

Lest there be any doubt that the time has been chosen, let us go directly to the leader of communism today—Joseph Stalin. Here is what he said—not back in 1928, not before the war, not during the war—but 2 years after the last war was ended: "To think that the Communist revolution can be carried out peacefully, within the framework of a Christian democracy, means one has either gone out of one's mind and lost all normal understanding, or has grossly and openly repudiated the Communist revolution."

And this is that was said by Lenin in 1919,which was also quoted with approval by Stalin in 1947:

"We are living," said Lenin, "not merely in a state, but in a system of states, and the existence of the Soviet Republic side by side with Christian states for a long time is unthinkable. One or the other must triumph in the end. And before that end supervenes, a series of frightful collisions between the Soviet Republic and the Bourgeois states will be inevitable."

Ladies and gentlemen, can there be anyone here tonight who is so blind as to say that the war is not on? Can there be anyone who fails to realize that the Communist world has said, "The time is now"—that this is the time for the show-down between the democratic Christian world and the Communist atheistic world?

Unless we face this fact, we shall pay the price that must be paid by those who wait too long.

Six years ago, at the time of the first conference to map out the [World War II] peace—Dumbarton Oaks—there was within the Soviet orbit 180,000,000 people. Lined up on the antitotalitarian side there were in the world at that time roughly 1,625,000,000 people. Today, only 6 years later, there are 800,000,000 people under the absolute domination of Soviet Russia—an increase of over 400 percent. On our side, the figure has shrunk to around 500,000,000. In other words, in less than 6 years the odds have changed from 9 to 1 in our favor to 8 to 5 against us. This indicates the swiftness of the tempo of Communist victories and American defeats in the cold war. As one of our outstanding historical figures once said, "When a great democracy is destroyed, it will not be because of enemies from without, but rather because of enemies from within."

ENEMIES WITHIN

The truth of this statement is becoming terrifyingly clear as we see this country each day losing on every front.

At war's end we were physically the strongest nation on earth and, at least potentially, the most powerful intellectually and morally. Ours could have been the honor of being a beacon in the desert of destruction, a shining living proof that civilization was not yet ready to destroy itself. Unfortunately, we have failed miserably and tragically to arise to the opportunity.

The reason why we find ourselves in a position of impotency is not because our only powerful potential enemy has sent men to invade our shores, but rather because of the traitorous actions of those who have been treated so well by this Nation. It has not been the less fortunate or members of minority groups who have been selling this Nation out, but rather those who have had all the benefits that the wealthiest nation on earth has had to offer—the finest homes, the finest college education, and the finest jobs in Government we can give.

This is glaringly true in the State Department. There the bright young men who are born with silver spoons in their mouths are the ones who have been worst. . . .

Now I know it is very easy for anyone to condemn a particular bureau or department in general terms. Therefore, I would like to cite one rather unusual case—the case of a man who has done much to shape our foreign policy.

When Chiang Kai-shek was fighting our war, the State Department had in China a young man named John S. Service. His task, obviously, was not to work for the communization of China. Strangely, however, he sent official reports back to the State Department urging that we torpedo our ally Chiang Kai-shek and stating, in effect, that communism was the best hope of China.

Later, this man—John Service—was picked up by the Federal Bureau of Investigation for turning over to the Communists secret State Department information. Strangely, however, he was never prosecuted. However, Joseph Grew, the Under Secretary of State, who insisted on his prosecution, was forced to resign. Two days after Grew's successor, Dean Acheson, took over as Under Secretary of State, this man—John Service—who had been picked up by the FBI and who had previously urged that communism was the best hope of China, was not only reinstated in the State Department but promoted. And finally, under Acheson, placed in charge of all placements and promotions.

Today, ladies and gentlemen, this man Service is on his way to represent the State Department and Acheson in Calcutta—by far and away the most important listening post in the Far East.

COMMUNISTS IN THE STATE DEPARTMENT

Now, let's see what happens when individuals with Communist connections are forced out of the State Department. Gustave Duran, who was labeled as (I quote) "a notorious international Communist," was made assistant to the Assistant Secretary of State in charge of Latin American affairs. He was taken into the State Department from his job as lieutenant colonel in the Communist International Brigade. Finally, after intense congressional pressure and criticism, he resigned in 1946 from the State Department—and, ladies and gentlemen, where do you think he is now? He took over a high-salaried job as Chief of Cultural Activities Section in the office of the Assistant Secretary General of the United Nations. . . .

Then there was a Mrs. Mary Jane Kenny, from the Board of Economic Warfare in the State Department, who was named in an FBI report and in a House committee report as a courier for the Communist Party while working for the Government. And where do you think Mrs. Kenny is—she is now an editor in the United Nations Document Bureau.

Another interesting case was that of Julian H. Wadleigh, economist in the Trade Agreements Section of the State Department for 11 years and was sent to Turkey and Italy and other countries as United States representative. After the statute of limitations had run so he could not be prosecuted for treason, he openly and brazenly not only admitted but proclaimed that he had been a member of the Communist Party—that while working for the State Department he stole a vast number of secret documents—and furnished these documents to the Russian spy ring of which he was a part.

You will recall last spring there was held in New York what was known as the World Peace Conference—a conference which was labeled by the State Department and Mr. Truman as the sounding board for Communist propaganda and a front for Russia. Dr. Harlow Shapley was the chairman of that conference. Interestingly enough, according to the new release put out by the Department in July, the Secretary of State appointed Shapley on a commission which acts as liaison between UNESCO and the State Department. . . .

This, ladies and gentlemen, gives you somewhat of a picture of the type of individuals who have been helping to shape our foreign policy. In my opinion the State Department, which is one of the most important government departments, is thoroughly infested with Communists.

Enemies Guiding Our Policy

I have in my hand 57* cases of individuals who would appear to be either card carrying members or certainly loyal to the Communist Party, but who nevertheless are still helping to shape our foreign policy.

One thing to remember in discussing the Communists in our Government is that we are not dealing with spies who get 30 pieces of silver to steal the blueprints of a new weapon. We are dealing with a far more sinister type of activity because it permits the enemy to guide and shape our policy.

In that connection, I would like to read to you very briefly from the testimony of Larry E. Kerley, a man who was with the counter espionage section of the FBI for 8 years. And keep in mind as I read this to you that at the time he is speaking, there was in the State Department Alger Hiss, the convicted Alger Hiss; John Service, the man whom the FBI picked up for espionage—Julian Wadleigh, who brazenly admitted he was a spy and wrote newspaper articles in regard thereto, plus hundreds of other bad security risks.

The FBI, I may add, has done an outstanding job, as all persons in Washington, Democrats and Republicans alike, agree. If J. Edgar Hoover had a free hand, we would not be plagued by Hisses and Wadleighs in high positions of power in the State Department. The FBI has only power to investigate.

Here is what the FBI man said. . . .

In accordance with instructions of the State Department to the FBI, the FBI was not even permitted to open an espionage case

---

*McCarthy originally used the number 208, but he changed it when he read the speech into the *Congressional Record*.

against any Russian suspect without State Department approval. . . .

Mr. ARENS. Did the State Department ever withhold from the Justice Department the right to intern suspects?. . .

Mr. KERLEY. They withheld the right to get out process for them which, in effect, kept them from being arrested, as in the case of Schevchenko and others.

Mr. ARENS. In how many instances did the State Department decline to permit process to be served on Soviet agents?

Mr. KERLEY. Do you mean how many Soviet agents were affected?

Mr. ARENS. Yes.

Mr. KERLEY. That would be difficult to say because there were so many people connected in one espionage ring, whether or not they were directly conspiring with the ring.

Mr. ARENS. Was that order applicable to all persons?

Mr. KERLEY. Yes; all persons in the Soviet-espionage organization.

Mr. ARENS. What did you say the order was as you understood it or as it came to you?

Mr. KERLEY. That no arrests of any suspects in the Russian-espionage activities in the United States were to be made without the prior approval of the State Department. . . .

Now the reason for the State Department's opposition to arresting any of this spy ring is made rather clear in the next question and answer.

"Senator O'CONOR. Did you understand that that was to include also American participants?

"Mr. KERLEY. Yes; because if they were arrested that would disclose the whole apparatus, you see.". . .

INFLUENCE OF A RED SPY

This brings us down to the case of one Alger Hiss who is important not as an individual any more, but rather because he is so representative of a group in the State Department. It is unnecessary to go over the sordid events showing how he sold out the Nation which had given him so much. Those are rather fresh in all of our minds.

However, it should be remembered that the facts in regard to his connection with this international Communist spy ring were made known to the then Under Secretary of State Berle 3 days after Hitler and Stalin signed the Russo-German alliance pact. At that time one Whittaker Chambers—who was also part of the spy ring—apparently decided that with Russia on Hitler's side, he could no longer betray our Nation to Russia. He gave Under

Secretary Berle—and this is all a matter of record—practically all, if not more, of the facts upon which Hiss' conviction was based.

Under Secretary Berle promptly contacted Dean Acheson and received word in return that Acheson (and I quote) "could vouch for Hiss absolutely"—at which time the matter was dropped. And this, you understand, was at a time when Russia was an ally of Germany. This condition existed while Russia and Germany were invading and dismembering Poland, and while the Communist groups here were screaming "war-monger" at the United States for their support of the allied nations.

Again in 1943, the FBI had occasion to investigate the facts surrounding Hiss' contacts with the Russian spy ring. But even after that FBI report was submitted, nothing was done.

Then late in 1948—on August 5—when the Un-American Activities Committee called Alger Hiss to give an accounting, President Truman at once issued a Presidential directive ordering all Government agencies to refuse to turn over any information whatsoever in regard to the Communist activities of any Government employee to a congressional committee.

Incidentally, even after Hiss was convicted—. . .

It is interesting to note that the President still labeled the exposé of Hiss as a "red herring."

If time permitted, it might be well to go into detail about the fact that Hiss was Roosevelt's chief adviser at Yalta when Roosevelt was admittedly in ill health and tired physically and mentally—and when, according to the Secretary of State, Hiss and Gromyko drafted the report on the conference. . . .

According to the then Secretary of State Stettinius, here are some of the things that Hiss helped to decide at Yalta. (1) The establishment of a European High Commission; (2) the treatment of Germany—this you will recall was the conference at which it was decided that we would occupy Berlin with Russia occupying an area completely circling the city, which, as you know, resulted in the Berlin airlift which cost 31 American lives; (3) the Polish question; (4) the relationship between UNRRA and the Soviets; (5) the rights of Americans on control commissions of Rumania, Bulgaria, and Hungary; (6) Iran; (7) China—here's where we gave away Manchuria; (8) Turkish Straits question; (9) international trusteeships; (10) Korea.

Of the results of this conference, Arthur Bliss Lane of the State Department had this to say: "As I glanced over the document, I could not believe my eyes. To me, almost every line spoke of a surrender to Stalin."

As you hear this story of high treason, I know that you are saying to yourself, "Well, why doesn't the Congress do something about it?" Actually, ladies and gentlemen, one of the important reasons for the graft, the corruption, the dishonesty, the disloyalty, the treason in high Government positions——one of the most important reasons why this continues is a lack of moral uprising on the part of the 140,000,000 American people. In the light of history, however, this is not hard to explain.

APATHY TO EVIL

It is the result of an emotional hang-over and a temporary moral lapse which follows every war. It is the apathy to evil which people who have been subjected to the tremendous evils of war feel. As the people of the world see mass murder, the destruction of defenseless and innocent people, and all of the crime and lack of morals which go with war, they become numb and apathetic. It has always been thus after war.

However, the morals of our people have not been destroyed. They still exist. This cloak of numbness and apathy has only needed a spark to rekindle them. Happily, this spark has finally been supplied.

As you know, very recently the Secretary of State proclaimed his loyalty to a man guilty of what has always been considered as the most abominable of all crimes—of being a traitor to the people who gave him a position of great trust. The Secretary of State in attempting to justify his continued devotion to the man who sold out the Christian world to the atheistic world, referred to Christ's Sermon on the Mount as a justification and reason therefore, and the reaction of the American people to this would have made the heart of Abraham Lincoln happy.

When this pompous diplomat in striped pants, with a phony British accent, proclaimed to the American people that Christ on the Mount endorsed communism, high treason, and betrayal of a sacred trust, the blasphemy was so great that it awakened the dormant indignation of the American people.

He has lighted the spark which is resulting in a moral uprising and will end only when the whole sorry mess of twisted, warped thinkers are swept from the national scene so that we may have a new birth of national honesty and decency in Government.

THE NUCLEAR BOMB RULED THE WORLD

GAR ALPEROVITZ AND KAI BIRD

Shortly after World War II the era of East-West military, political, and ideological tension called the Cold War began. For four decades Eastern powers—primarily the Soviet Union—and Western powers—primarily the United States—taunted, spied on, and subverted one another. What allowed these world powers to continue their antagonistic relationship without ever breaking into out-and-out war? The authors of the following article, Gar Alperovitz and Kai Bird, argue that the nuclear bomb made it possible.

First used by the United States to end World War II's war in the Pacific, the atomic bomb and its successors became a sword of Damocles hanging over the world. The ever-present threat of nuclear annihilation deterred the two major powers from escalating any conflict beyond the use of conventional weapons, and brought the art of brinkmanship to new levels.

Gar Alperovitz is a historian and political economist. He is Lionel R. Bauman professor of political economy at the University of Maryland, College Park, and a fellow of the Institute for Policy Studies in Washington, D.C. He is the author of *The Decision to Use the Atomic Bomb*, as well as many other books and articles. Kai Bird is a biographer and contributing editor for the *Nation*. He has written essays and book reviews for *The New York Times*, the *Los Angeles Times*, *Foreign Policy*, the *Journal of Diplomatic History*, and other publications.

From "The Centrality of the Bomb," by Gar Alperovitz and Kai Bird, *Foreign Policy*, Spring 1994. Reprinted with permission.

Russia and the United States [have] always gotten along for a hundred and fifty years history with Russia friendly and helpful. Our respective orbits do not clash geographically and I think on the whole we can probably keep out of clashes in the future.

—Secretary of War Henry Stimson
April 1945

Before the atom bomb was used, I would have said, yes, I was sure we could keep the peace with Russia. Now I don't know. . . . People are frightened and disturbed all over. Everyone feels insecure again.

—General Dwight Eisenhower
Visiting Moscow, August 1945

Even though the Cold War's abrupt, peaceful demise [with the dissolution of the Soviet Union in 1991] rendered useless most of the assumptions and theories advanced to explain that strange conflict, orthodox historians have kept on writing about it as if what actually happened had been inevitable. Moreover, they largely avoid the specific role the atomic bomb played in fueling the Cold War. In fact, the bomb was a primary catalyst of the Cold War, and, apart from the nuclear arms race, the most important specific role of nuclear weapons was to revolutionize American policy toward Germany. The bomb permitted U.S. leaders to do something no American president could otherwise have contemplated: rebuild and rearm the former Nazi state. That in turn had extraordinary, ongoing consequences.

The bomb also made the Korean and Vietnam wars possible: Had the weapon not been available to protect the U.S. global flank in Europe, such episodes would always have been "the wrong war in the wrong place at the wrong time," to use General Omar Bradley's words. Finally, those who believed early on that America and Russia could reach a great power accommodation were probably right—and such an accommodation may well have been delayed for four decades because the atomic bomb appeared precisely when America and the Soviet Union were beginning to feel their way to a new post–World War II relationship.

Not only does that explanation of the Cold War offer a good measure of common sense, but a vast body of new archival research lends powerful support to the hypothesis. This is not to say that frictions, rivalries, and areas of conflict would not have existed between the major powers had there been no atomic bomb. What needs to be explained is the extreme militarization of great power relations that came to be called "the Cold War."

Historians like to see patterns, trends, and continuity in long periods of development, but they rarely pause to reflect upon the extreme chanciness of the timing of historically important events. Consider the prehistory of nuclear weapons. Physicist Hans Bethe once observed that it was only very "slowly and painfully, through a comedy of errors, [that] the fission of uranium was discovered."

It was by mere chance, for instance, that Enrico Fermi made his critical 1934 discoveries about the capacity of the atom's nucleus to capture slow neutrons. Fermi's seemingly accidental findings built on a line of development that began with Albert Einstein's famous 1905 papers and continued with subsequent reports and inventions by scientists such as Leo Szilard (in connection with the cyclotron) and James Chadwick (in connection with the existence of the neutron).

Most accounts do not acknowledge that had twentieth-century physics not been moving at the particular rate it did, America would never have gotten to the 1939 Szilard-Einstein letter to President Franklin Roosevelt, the 1941 MAUD Committee report, and then the Manhattan Project—to a sufficiently advanced point, that is, where large sums of money and engineering expertise could have produced an atomic bomb by August 1945. As Bethe's remark suggests and others have noted, events might just as well have moved a decade or two slower or perhaps faster.

With that in mind, it is instructive to reflect on what might have happened (or, more precisely, what probably would not have happened) if the "independent track" of scientific historical development had not reached fruition in 1945. What might the postwar world have looked like in the absence of an early U.S. atomic monopoly?

GERMANY AND THE BOMB

At Yalta, Roosevelt had been quite clear about two fundamentals: First, given the domestic political concerns of a country taught to fear and hate Germany in the course of two world wars, he believed that the former Nazi state simply had to be eliminated as a serious security threat in the postwar period. It was both a strategic and an absolute political requirement. Second, as is well-known, Roosevelt felt that the American people would not permit him to keep American troops in Europe for long after the war. Given strong "isolationist" sentiments that appeared in Congress and the popular press, he was almost certainly correct in his judgment.

Those constraints produced the main requirements of Roosevelt's postwar security policy: He needed a rough agreement with the other dominant military power—the Soviet Union—to control Germany directly, and he needed a concrete way (beyond rhetoric) to weaken Germany's underlying military potential. Exaggerated discussions of "pastoralization" apart, Roosevelt's strategy centered on the notion of "industrial disarmament" to weaken Germany's military-industrial complex—and simultaneously to cement American-Soviet cooperation. Reductions in German industry could also provide the short-term reparations Joseph Stalin desperately sought to help rebuild the war-torn Soviet Union.

Related to that strategy, of course, were implications for Roosevelt's de facto acceptance of a Soviet sphere of influence in Eastern Europe. To the extent Stalin was certain that Germany would not rise again, at least in theory Soviet policy could be more relaxed in Eastern Europe. The Yalta agreement embodied big-power control of Germany, large-scale reparations, and an extremely vague declaration on the status of Eastern Europe.

Often overlooked is that from the American point of view, the advent of nuclear weapons gave Washington an alternative to constructing a European peace in cooperation with the Soviet Union. At Yalta, Washington had essentially agreed to a neutralized Germany, but with the bomb U.S. policymakers realized they could afford the risks of acting unilaterally. The western por-

At the Yalta Conference, Winston Churchill, Franklin Delano Roosevelt, and Joseph Stalin (pictured) discussed ways to keep Germany from rising to power again.

tion of Germany could safely be reconstructed economically and, later, integrated into a West European military alliance. Only the atomic monopoly permitted that with little fear of German resurgence and without regard to Soviet security interests.

BOMB LESSENED SOVIET THREAT

At Potsdam, American leaders explicitly understood that the atomic test the United States had conducted at Alamogordo, New Mexico, had upended the assumptions of policy. Compare, for instance, the views of President Harry Truman's closest adviser, James Byrnes, before and after Alamogordo. On June 6, 1945, six weeks before the blast, the diary of Ambassador Joseph Davies records that Byrnes, about to become secretary of state, "discussed the entire Russian situation at great length":

> It was clear that without Russian cooperation, without a primary objective for Peace, another disastrous war would be inevitable. . . . Nor did he think that our people on sober second thought would undertake fighting the Red Army and Russia for a hopeless cause of attempting to control the ideology or way of life which these various rival groups wished to establish in the various countries.

Although Russian cooperation was needed before the bomb, many scholars now recognize that the successful atomic test gave Truman "an entirely new feeling of confidence," as he put it. It provided Secretary of State Byrnes in particular with what he called "a gun behind the door" that he believed could make Russia "more manageable." One of many similar conversations from the period was recorded by Secretary of War Stimson in his diary shortly after Hiroshima: "Byrnes was very much against any attempt to cooperate with Russia. His mind is full of his problems with the coming meeting of foreign ministers and he looks to having the presence of the bomb in his pocket, so to speak, as a great weapon to get through the thing."

In connection with the U.S. approach to Germany, the atomic bomb altered policy in two quite specific ways that went to the heart of Rooseveltian strategy. Shortly after the atomic test Byrnes simply abandoned the Yalta understanding that had set German reparations at roughly $20 billion (half of which would go to the Soviet Union). Another Davies diary entry on July 28, 1945, shows that he did so explicitly relying on the atomic bomb: "[Byrnes] was having a hard time with reparations . . . , [but the] details as to the success of the atomic bomb, which he had just received, gave him confidence that the Soviets would agree as to these difficulties."

Moreover, according to Davies, the secretary of state was also quite clear about the shift in fundamental power relations in Europe: "Because of the New Mexico development [Byrnes] felt secure anyway." Byrnes suggested that "the New Mexico situation had given us great power, and that in the last analysis it would control." Several American policymakers (notably Benjamin Cohen, an assistant to Byrnes) had believed that international control of the Ruhr industrial heartland might be the key to a compromise approach. In principle, it could achieve security without necessarily weakening the German economic reconstruction effort. But—again, shortly after the report of the successful nuclear test—Byrnes rejected that proposal as well.

Many scholars now understand that the atomic bomb altered the Truman administration's general postwar approach to the USSR. What needs to be grasped is the specific implications the weapon had for the continuing U.S. approach to Germany. That there was a close link between the bomb and the German problem in the minds of U.S. policymakers was made quite explicit again, for instance, in two August 22, 1945, meetings with General Charles de Gaulle. Here Truman and Byrnes together urged that "the German danger should not be exaggerated." De Gaulle, however, continued to emphasize French fears—and, like Roosevelt's advisers and the Russians, urged direct security measures to manage the longer-term German threat (including international control of the Ruhr and severing the west bank of the Rhine from Germany). Finally, Truman and Byrnes—responding explicitly to de Gaulle's concern about Germany—became blunt: "The atomic bomb will give pause to countries which might [be] tempted to commit aggressions."

Although U.S. policymakers still worried about the potential power of a united German state, very early in the postwar period they clearly understood that Germany no longer presented a fundamental military threat. The new nuclear monopoly substantially relieved the Truman administration of the central foreign-policy and military concern of Roosevelt and his advisers. "In the last analysis it would control" as Byrnes said—even if the American people forced the withdrawal of U.S. troops from the Continent, even if American-Soviet cooperation failed, and even if Germany were not disarmed industrially. Put another way, the bomb made it possible to pursue a policy described by scholars in recent years as "double containment"—that is, the division of Germany could be used to contain both the Germans and the Soviets.

SCARING STALIN

The problem was obviously not quite the same from the Soviet point of view. In the first place, the new weapon itself now posed a threat. Generalized fear provoked by the new weapon was only one aspect of the problem: In the fall of 1945 and spring of 1946, American policy moved slowly but steadily away from Roosevelt's approach to Germany. Partly as a result of French obstruction on the Allied Control Council, partly out of understandable fear of economic chaos and political disorder, and partly—but not at the outset—out of frustration with Soviet policy, U.S. policy shifted from industrial disarmament to rebuilding German economic power. A major turning point was probably the decision to stop reparation shipments in May 1946—dramatically followed by the tough speech Byrnes gave that September in Stuttgart.

That shift occurred at the same time that policymakers began to play up the bomb as a strategic factor. The U.S. stockpile of assembled weapons was actually quite small, but the potential of the nuclear monopoly was also obviously extraordinary—as was advertised by the atomic tests in June 1946 at Bikini Atoll in the Pacific. Code-named "Operation Crossroads," the blasts took place at the same time Byrnes and Soviet foreign minister Vyacheslav Molotov were again trying to reach agreement over Germany. *Pravda* took note of the mushroom cloud over Bikini and accused Washington of plotting an atomic war. And as the arsenal grew (50 weapons were available by 1948), the Truman administration steadily found the courage to act more forcefully and unilaterally in Germany.

Reams have been written about the extreme Russian security fears of the German threat. Stalin, in Nikita Khrushchev's judgment, "lived in terror of an enemy attack." The Soviet premier observed in April 1945 that Germany "will recover, and very quickly"—but apparently he initially believed that "quickly" meant as many as 10 or 15 years. Sometime at the end of 1947, as Michael McGwire observes in a recent study, "Stalin shifted focus . . . to the more immediate threat of war within 5–6 years against a capitalist coalition led by the Anglo-Saxon powers."

Recently released Soviet documents offer additional insight. Soviet ambassador to the United States Nikolai Novikov, for instance, painted a deeply disturbing picture of American intentions toward the Soviet Union in 1946. Citing the U.S. "establishment of a system of naval and air bases stretching far beyond the boundaries of the United States" and the "creation of ever newer types of weapons," Novikov believed that Washington was preparing for war. In the heart of Europe, he

emphasized, America was "considering the possibility of terminating the Allied occupation of German territory before the main tasks of the occupation—the demilitarization and democratization of Germany—have been implemented. This would create the prerequisites for the revival of an imperialist Germany, which the United States plans to use in a future war on its side."

U.S. leaders fully understood Russian fears of Germany. Ambassador Averell Harriman, for instance, later recalled that "Stalin was afraid of Germany, Khrushchev was afraid of Germany, the present people [Brezhnev] are afraid of Germany—and I am afraid of Germany . . . [the Soviets] have a feeling that the Germans can arouse a situation which will involve us and that will lead to a disaster."

SOVIET DEFENSIVE POLICY

Obviously, the critical turning point came with the decision to partition Germany and rearm West Germany. American leaders recognized that the Soviets would view even the restoration of significant German economic power as a threat—and that this would have painful repercussions in Eastern Europe. At a cabinet meeting in late 1947, Secretary of State George Marshall predicted that because of U.S. actions in Germany the Soviets would have to "clamp down completely" on Czechoslovakia, and that when they did, it would be a "purely defensive move."

Was Marshall's basic insight into a critical dynamic feature of the early Cold War correct? Was Soviet policy in Central and Eastern Europe primarily defensive and a reaction to American policy toward Germany? It is difficult to know, of course, but others also recognized the point early on. In his opinion columns at the time, Walter Lippmann, for instance, regularly pointed out the obvious connection between what happened in Germany and what happened in Eastern Europe. Unless the German problem were settled first, he urged, the Russians were unlikely ever to relax their hold on Eastern Europe. Lippmann believed that Byrnes's strategy of pressing forward on Eastern Europe without simultaneously promoting a reasonable settlement of the German issue was demanding too much. "We must not set up a German government in the two or three Western zones," Lippmann urged the Wall Street lawyer and future secretary of state John Foster Dulles in 1947. "We must not make a separate peace with it."

A steadily expanding body of research and documentary evidence suggests that Marshall's fundamental insight and Lippmann's early judgment offer the most plausible explanation for one of the most dramatic and painful features of the Cold War—

Stalin's clampdown on Eastern Europe. The Soviet archives have yet to divulge anything definitive about Stalin's intentions at the end of World War II. However, even Harriman, who is usually portrayed as a hardliner in early postwar dealings with Moscow, thought the Soviet dictator had no firm plan at the outset: "I had a feeling," Harriman observed, "that they were considering and weighing the pros and cons of cooperating with us in the post-war world and getting the benefit of our cooperation in reconstruction."

SOVIET AMBIVALENCE

Recent scholarship has uncovered far more indications of ambivalence—and, indeed, a great deal more caution and cooperation—in Soviet policy during 1945 and 1946 than is commonly recognized. A number of developments helped produce judgments about the Soviet Union like Harriman's:

- General elections in Hungary in the fall of 1945 held under Soviet supervision resulted in the defeat of communist-supported groups.
- In September 1945, Moscow unilaterally withdrew troops from Norway, despite its long-standing claims on Bear Island and Spitzbergen.
- In the wake of the December 1945 Moscow agreements, the government in Romania was enlarged to include noncommunists, after which both the United States and Great Britain recognized it.
- The Soviet military also withdrew from Czechoslovakia at that time, and free elections produced a coalition government of communists and non-communists committed to keeping the country's doors open to both the East and the West.
- In the spring of 1946, Soviet troops left the Danish island of Bornholm.
- In accord with his "percentage agreement" with Winston Churchill, Stalin abandoned the Greek communists at a critical juncture in their civil war, leaving Greece within the Western sphere of influence.
- In Austria, the Soviet army supervised free elections in their occupation zone and, of course, withdrew after the signing of the Austrian Peace Treaty in 1955.
- The Soviets warned the French communist leader, Maurice Thorez, against attempting "to seize power by force since to do so would probably precipitate an international conflict from which the Soviet Union could hardly emerge victorious." (American intelligence obtained a report on that conversation in November 1946.)

- Despite a short delay, Soviet troops in 1946 did pull out of Iran—a country bordering the Soviet Union—after a brief and, in retrospect, rather modest international dispute.
- Perhaps most revealing, former Soviet officials who had defected to the West documented that important railway lines running from the Soviet Union through Eastern Europe were yanked up in the very early postwar period. The working assumption appeared to be that since there would be only a short occupation, Soviet forces should hurry to remove as much useful material as possible.
- Nor did Stalin pursue an aggressive policy in the Far East during the early years. Indeed, for a good period of time Stalin supported Nationalist Chinese leader Chiang Kai Shek—much to the lasting chagrin of Chinese communist leaders. And Red Army troops departed Manchuria in May 1946.

Many historians now accept that substantial evidence exists that Stalin neither planned nor desired the Cold War. Finland and Austria—neutral but free states—serve as alternative models for border-area countries that the Soviet Union might have accepted had a different dynamic been established after World War II.

Of course, Soviet policy in Eastern Europe was to shift dramatically, especially after 1947 and 1948. Along with the announcement of the Truman Doctrine, the Marshall Plan also appears to have been far more threatening to Stalin than was previously understood: It suggested the creation of a powerful "economic magnet" to draw Eastern Europe into the Western orbit. Once it was clear that Germany was to be rebuilt and later rearmed, the crackdown in Eastern Europe became irrevocable.

ATOMIC DIPLOMACY

That interpretation returns us to a central point, namely that the U.S. decision to rearm West Germany was made possible only by the atomic bomb. Modern writers often forget the degree of concern in the U.S. foreign policy establishment and elsewhere about the former Nazi state in the early postwar years. Even after the outbreak of the Korean War—and even with the atomic bomb— Truman's high commissioner in Germany, John McCloy, initially opposed the creation of a German national army. So too did his successor, James Conant. And when they changed their minds, both men had to deal with the unrelenting opposition of the French. As late as August 1950, the State Department declared it "opposed, and still strongly opposes, the creation of German national forces."

Further, Truman himself was deeply worried about the Germans—again, even with the bomb. Among many indications of Truman's worry was a memo to Secretary of State Dean Acheson in June 1950:

> We certainly don't want to make the same mistake that was made after World War I when Germany was authorized to train one hundred thousand soldiers, principally for maintaining order locally in Germany. As you know, that hundred thousand was used for the basis of training the greatest war machine that ever came forth in European history.

Truman also recognized that he faced very powerful domestic political opposition to rearming a nation that had so recently caused the deaths of so many American boys. "From today's perspective, the rearmament of Germany seems natural and almost inevitable," writes historian Frank Ninkovich in a recent study.

> To achieve it, however, American policy makers had to clear a long series of hurdles, including self-doubts, widespread European reluctance, and Soviet obstructionism. . . . The amazing thing, then, is not that rearmament took place with such enormous difficulty, but that it happened at all.

Amazing, indeed! All but unimaginable in the absence of nuclear weapons or popular support for maintaining major conventional forces. As Roosevelt had forecast, the American people overwhelmingly demanded rapid demobilization after the war. In June 1945, the United States had more than 12 million men and women under arms, but one year later the figure was only 3 million, and by June 1947 demobilization had left the armed services with no more than 1.5 million personnel. Congress defeated universal military training in 1947 and in 1948; defense spending in general declined rapidly during the first postwar years. Such domestic political realities left U.S. policymakers empty-handed: They did not have sufficient conventional forces to hold down the Germans.

Given such realities—and considering the extraordinary difficulty of achieving German rearmament even with U.S. possession of the atomic bomb—it is all but impossible to imagine the early rearmament of the former Nazi enemy had there been no atomic bomb. Put another way, had the scientific-technical track of development that yielded the knowledge required to make an atomic weapon not chanced to reach the point it had by 1939, the central weapon in America's postwar diplomatic arsenal would not have existed.

There is a further reason why we believe this hypothesis explains the early Cold War dynamic: German rearmament and the

U.S. Cold War conventional buildup, many scholars recognize, probably could not have happened without the dramatic U.S. decision to enter the Korean War. That decision, in turn, was made possible only by the atomic bomb—and, hence, the train of subsequent events is difficult to imagine in the absence of the bomb.

THE BOMB ENABLED THE UNITED STATES TO INTERVENE IN KOREA

Even with the atomic bomb virtually every important American military leader was extremely skeptical about a land war in Asia. The Korean peninsula, of course, had been arbitrarily divided in 1945 by Moscow and Washington, and both powers were well aware that their client regimes in Pyongyang and Seoul were committed to unifying the country under their own flags. Each regime had guerrilla units operating in the other's territory in what amounted to a simmering civil war. (Washington was actually restricting the supply of offensive weapons to the Syngman Rhee regime in South Korea for fear that they would be used in an invasion of the North.)

By late 1949, as is well known, Truman's National Security Council (NSC) advisers had concluded that Korea was of little strategic value to the United States and that a commitment to use military force in Korea would be ill-advised. Early in 1950, both Acheson and the chairman of the Senate Foreign Relations Committee, Tom Connally, had publicly stated that South Korea lay outside the perimeter of U.S. national security interests.

Most important, to pledge troops to a land war in Asia would expose the American "European flank," since moving troops to Asia would weaken the American presence on the Continent. As General Bradley recounted in his memoirs, "We still believed our greatest potential for danger lay in Soviet aggression in Europe." And, "to risk widening the Korean War into a war with China would probably delight the Kremlin more than anything else we could do." The famous Bradley comment quoted earlier summarized the general view within the Joint Chiefs of Staff: Fighting in Korea would involve the United States "in the wrong war, at the wrong place, at the wrong time, and with the wrong enemy." When an invasion of the South did occur in June 1950, the Truman administration's decision to intervene amounted to an astonishing policy reversal.

If, even with the atomic bomb, U.S. military leaders hesitated to pledge land forces to the defense of Korea, then without the atomic bomb—which to the generals would have meant a totally exposed European "flank"—a decision to protect South Korea would have been practically impossible.

And again, very few would disagree with the proposition that the Korean War, in turn, provided a crucial fulcrum upon which the Cold War pivoted. Most scholars accept that NSC-68, the document outlining a massive rebuilding of the U.S. military, was going nowhere in early 1950; the defense budget was being cut, not raised. The political drama surrounding the Korean War permitted an extraordinary escalation both in Cold War hysteria and in military spending. Before Korea such spending was around 4 per cent of gross national product (GNP); during the war it peaked at nearly 14 per cent. After Korea it stabilized to average roughly 10 per cent of GNP during the 1950s—an unimaginable extravagance before that time. (The buildup, in turn, established a structure of forces and political attitudes without which the subsequent intervention in Vietnam is difficult to imagine.)

Most important, Germany almost certainly could only have been rearmed in the domestic political atmosphere that accompanied the chaotic Korean conflict, along with the qualitative political shift in Cold War tensions that the war brought. The entire scenario depended ultimately upon the odd historical timing that put nuclear weapons in American hands at a particular moment in the twentieth century.

U.S. Overreaction?

What of "the Cold War" per se—the larger, overarching dynamic? Recall that the issue is not whether the usual tensions between great powers would or would not have existed. The issue is whether the relationship would have had to explode into the extremely militarized form it took.

Recently declassified archival materials from both sides should destroy the traditional assumption that the Soviet army at the end of World War II offensively threatened Western Europe. In 1945, roughly half the Soviet army's transport was horse-drawn, and it would remain so until 1950. Moreover, Soviet troops demobilized massively and dramatically in the early postwar period. Soviet documents suggest that Stalin's army shrank from 11,365,000 in May 1945 to 2,874,000 in June 1947.

While there is debate about how widely such information was known or heeded by top U.S. officials, a number of scholars have recently cited evidence suggesting that U.S. policymakers fully understood that the Soviet Union had neither the intention nor the capability to launch a ground invasion of Western Europe. In December 1945, for instance, the State Department circulated an intelligence estimate concluding that for at least five years "the United States need not be acutely concerned about the current intentions of the Soviet Union [and has] considerable latitude in determining policy toward the USSR." A Joint Chiefs of Staff report at the end of 1948 estimated the Soviets might be able to marshal only some 800,000 troops for an attack force. Two years later, the CIA used the same figure in its intelligence estimate. Similarly, documents recapped in Frank Kofsky's recent *Harry S. Truman and the War Scare of 1948* provide devastating proof that American military intelligence estimates consistently concluded that the Soviets could not and did not want to wage war. One illustration is a high-level briefing given directly to Truman in late 1948:

> The Russians have dismantled hundreds of miles of railroads in Germany and sent the rails and ties back to Russia. There remains, at the present time . . . only a single track railroad running Eastward out of the Berlin area and upon which the Russians must largely depend for their logistical support. This same railroad line changes from a standard gage going Eastward, to a Russian wide gage in Poland, which further complicates the problem of moving supplies and equipment forward.

George Kennan, for one, "never believed that they [the Soviets] have seen it as in their interests to overrun Western Europe militarily, or that they would have launched an attack on that region generally even if the so-called nuclear deterrent had not existed."

Credible documentation has also emerged from the Russian archives that Stalin repeatedly rejected North Korean leader Kim Il-Sung's requests for support of an invasion of South Korea. As one scholar, Kathryn Weathersby, has explained in a recent working paper, Stalin reluctantly "approved the plan only after having been assured that the United Sates would not intervene." Even then he apparently did so because Kim Il-Sung would otherwise have pursued the war anyway with support from the communist Chinese. As Weathersby concludes, "it was Soviet weakness that drove Stalin to support the attack on South Korea, not the unrestrained expansionism imagined by the authors of NSC-68."

Moreover, Bruce Cumings's sweeping two-volume history, *The Origins of the Korean War,* demonstrates that the U.S. command in South Korea knew at the time that South Korean irregular army units had been provoking the North Koreans for months. A once clear-cut case of communist aggression is now seen by most knowledgeable historians as a complicated civil war that dated back at least to 1945.

MYTH OF SOVIET POWER

The Russian archives also show that often neither Stalin nor his successors could control the regimes in Eastern Europe, Cuba,

China, North Korea, or North Vietnam. "It's a big myth that Moscow directed a unified monolith of socialist states," argues Deborah Kaple of Columbia University's Harriman Institute. Newly uncovered documents, for instance, make it clear that the Sino-Soviet split existed almost from the day Mao Tse-tung seized power. And other recent archival discoveries suggest that East Germany's Walter Ulbricht largely initiated the Berlin crisis of 1958–1961, forcing a reluctant Khrushchev to engage in brinkmanship diplomacy.

All of these events suggest a broadly defensive post–World War II Soviet foreign policy that on occasion accommodated American security interests. The monolithic enemy of Cold War fame, many now agree, existed mainly in the imaginations of America's ardent anticommunist cold warriors. At the very least, these events suggest Stalin appeared willing to cut a deal with Washington in the critical early postwar years.

This analysis does not suggest that the American-Soviet relationships could have been a tranquil sea of cooperation. But the unusual and dangerous over-militarization of foreign policy during the Cold War demands an explanation on its own terms—and the atomic bomb is the first item in that lexicon.

This essay has not attempted to untangle the many factors that led to the end of the Cold War. One related issue, however, may be noted: The advent of nuclear weapons (and the U.S. nuclear monopoly in particular) upset the balance of power in general and especially in Europe, where from the Soviet point of view the critical issue was Germany. However, once the Soviet Union had its own nuclear weapons and a credible way to deliver them—and Germany had no such weapons—then the implicit balance of power in general and in Europe, too, was essentially restored, albeit at a higher level.

Before that time the Soviets kept Germany relatively weak by occupation, reparations, and tight control of the invasion routes. After the Soviet Union had secured nuclear weapons (and once the implications were digested and fought out by policy elites), Soviet policy could relax all three prongs of its earlier strategy. Old military and foreign policy *apparatchiks* [blindly devoted officials] did not easily abandon traditional assumptions, as the crackdown in Czechoslovakia in 1968 suggests. The preconditions for ending the Cold War, however, were established only after the basic power relationship between the Soviet Union and the United Sates was rebalanced.

Might history have taken a different course? Many high-level Western policymakers believed an accommodation with the Soviet Union was a reasonable possibility in the early postwar

years. The United States was also in a position to encourage Soviet cooperation with the lure of desperately needed long-term
economic aid. Indeed, had the United States lacked a nuclear
weapons monopoly—and given the rapid pace of U.S. demobilization and Congress's rejection of universal military training—
such an approach might well have been the only acceptable option from the U.S. point of view.

All of this, of course, is "counter-factual" history. As the late
philosopher Morris Cohen observed in 1942, however, "we cannot grasp the full significance of what happened unless we have
some idea of what the situation would have been otherwise." But
in a sense all history is implicitly counter-factual—including,
above all, the counter-factual orthodox theory that had the
United States not taken a tough stand after World War II, there
would have been no "long peace" and disaster would inevitably
have befallen the Continent, the world, and the United States.

U.S. RESPONSIBILITY FOR THE COLD WAR

In *A Preponderance of Power,* Melvyn Leffler concludes that because of its enormous strength the United States must also bear
a preponderance of responsibility for the Cold War. That important judgment, like Stimson's rejected 1945 plea for an immediate, direct, and private effort to cut short what became the nuclear era, brings into focus the question of just how wise were the
"wise men" who crafted America's Cold War policies at the moment when the two great tracks of twentieth-century scientific
and global political development converged. At the very least,
they failed to find a way to avoid one of history's most costly and
dangerous—indeed, literally world-threatening—struggles.

THE BEAT GENERATION

BRUCE COOK

"Woe unto those who spit on the Beat Generation, the wind'll blow it back," writes Jack Kerouac, author of the classic "Beat" novel *On the Road.* To many people, Kerouac personified the Beat movement—the iconoclastic literary movement that set conventional culture back on its heels. As Bruce Cook writes in the following article, the Beats changed society. The popular stereotype depicted the Beats, also called beatniks or hipsters, as living a loose lifestyle, men in goatees and berets, women in tight black clothing, spouting poetry in dark, smoky coffeehouses with bongo drums and jazz music playing in the background. The Beats reacted against the conservative, materialistic society of the 1950s, and their reaction brought a new sense of rebellion and wildness to the literary scene.

Best known for their poetry, the Beats also wrote novels, painted canvases, performed music, and smoked marijuana. They were influenced by Eastern religions, especially Buddhism, and jazz rhythms. Kerouac, poets Allen Ginsberg and Lawrence Ferlinghetti, and novelist William Burroughs were among the best-known Beats. Their experiments in literary form as well as subject matter scandalized, titillated, and inspired their own generation as well as succeeding ones.

In the following viewpoint, Bruce Cook describes the Beats' influence and the conflict between them and the other leading literary group of the day, the intellectual academics. Cook is director of piano studies at Diablo Valley College in California. He has extensive experience in musical performance, ethnomusicology, and transpersonal psychology. He views the Beats as archetypi-

cally American, following the most American of traditions: protest and dissent.

I soon came to regard the Beats as my generation. I felt the
same keen sense of identification with them that thousands of
others my age did, and I had the same feeling that I was lucky
to be in on the beginning of something big, if only as a spectator.
For yes, even in January 1958, it was possible to detect the vague
shape of change on the horizon. And if the Beats meant anything
to complacent, conformist Eisenhower America, it was change.

But if the Beats were "my" generation, it should be emphasized, probably, that this did not make me a member of the Beat
Generation. I got to know them just as did the rest of those who
were my age—by reading their books, attending their poetry
readings, and following the hectic accounts of their misadven-
tures in magazines and newspapers. Eventually I came to know
personally a couple of the writers associated with the Beat movement—but only a couple; this was a few years after that initial
exciting moment when the Beats seemed to be everything—and
the only thing—that was happening.

And yet I retained the sense of identification with them that I
first began to feel on that trip back to the States. This was because
I was in fundamental agreement with what I perceived, in broad
outline, to be their program. Which meant that I was against the
same things they were against—elitism on the one hand, mass
movements on the other, and that if I had been pressed to characterize my personal aesthetic in a single word, that word would
have been "populist." (A sculptor named Jack Burnham says,
"The goal of a democratic society should be to make every man
an artist." I like that.) This by way of declaring my bias.

THE BEATS HERALDED CHANGE

Because of the affinity I felt for the Beats, I kept an eye on them
long after the public had forgotten them and what they stood for.
And it was because I never forgot that, really, that I was never
quite as surprised as I might otherwise have been at how the
1960s turned out. For the almost schizophrenic change that has
been worked in the temper of our times was predicted a decade
before, implicit in every poem, novel, and prose piece produced
by the Beat Generation.

Indeed there has been a change. The single most conspicuous
fact of the present time is the great alteration that has come about
in the character and attitudes of the under-thirty generation.
They *are* different. Who could deny it? No longer docile, as we

were, they present their demands where we submitted our requests in triplicate. Or more impressive still, they drop out in disgust from a culture we slavered to serve.

I must say that I am impressed by this new lot. Yet not so impressed that I am convinced, as many seem to be, that those under thirty are a new breed entirely, a generation without forebears, precursors, or precedents. No, even though many of the young themselves seem unaware of it, the present generation is caught in the usual umbilical relationship to the past. And it may give us some idea of the future in store for us if we give their cord a tug and see where it leads. When we do, we will find that it goes back directly to that legion of artists and frustrated artists, novelists and would-be novelists, poets and poets manqué, those mothers (maintaining the metaphor) known then and ever after as the Beat Generation.

During their moment in the spotlight they received the full treatment from the media—coverage in the news magazines, special attention in *Life*, lots of time on the talk shows, and even a television documentary or two devoted to them. And now, although nearly all the writers who emerged from the movement are still being published, the Beat Generation, if remembered at all today, is recalled as some distant phenomenon, an isolated cultural event of the 1950s. And those of the present generation who have inherited so much from them have only the haziest notion of the Beat Generation, why, what, or even who it was.

WHO WERE THE BEATS?

All right, *who* were the Beats? Were they truly, as they called themselves, a generation? A movement? Or were they merely—as was said so often of them by members of the literary establishment of that day—a fad, a phenomenon of publicity, a creation of the Luce publications?

If you had gone out and asked who the Beats were on any college campus in, say, 1958, you would have heard the same three names mentioned over and over again in response. The first of them would surely have been that of Jack Kerouac. Now dead, Kerouac was the victim of his own restless urgings and of the deep-seated alienation he felt from the culture that created him and from the counterculture he helped create. His death, which came in the fall of 1969 wrote a sort of full stop to the Beat episode. Once the obituaries and memoirs of Kerouac had come in, many who were a part of it all felt that the Beat Generation was finally a thing of the past. For hadn't he been the star of the show? Wasn't it his ruggedly handsome Canuck face that had appeared in the magazines and been seen so often on television?

Hadn't he even been the first to dub his generation Beat?

Yes, according to John Clellon Holmes, it was Kerouac who christened them all, though no one would ever claim that he originated the term. Beat, in the sense of beaten, frustrated, played out, has been around for many, many years. Its fustian, ungrammatical quality suggests it may have originated in the nineteenth-century West or rural South. In the 1940s it had a vogue among jazz musicians who used to embellish it with little variations, such as "I'm beat right down to my socks." A friend of Kerouac's, Herbert Huncke, who was then living an underground life as a Times Square hustler, petty thief, and drug addict, had picked it up from the jazzmen and used it often with frequent variations. So there was nothing really remarkable in Jack Kerouac using the word in that way when he attempted to characterize the new attitude he saw in his contemporaries. "It's a sort of furtiveness," Clellon Holmes quotes him as saying, "like we were a generation of furtives. You know, with an inner knowledge there's no use flaunting on that level, the level of the 'public,' a kind of beatness—I mean being right down to it, to ourselves, because we all *really* know where we are—and a weariness with all the forms, all the conventions of the world. . . . It's something like that. So I guess you might say we're a *beat* generation.". . .

THE BEATS LIBERATED US

It is difficult, separated as we are by time and temper from that period, to convey the liberating effect that *On the Road* had on young people all over America. There was a sort of instantaneous flash of recognition that seemed to send thousands of them out into the streets, proclaiming that Kerouac had written their story, that *On the Road* was their book. There was such community of feeling in this response that critics began to speak with some certainty, though without much respect, of Kerouac's as the new literary generation. . . .

THE BEATS AND THE LITERARY ESTABLISHMENT

The Beats themselves had precious little rapport with the official culture of their own day. Once they were established, neither Jack Kerouac nor Allen Ginsberg ever received favorable reviews. They were ridiculed, reviled, and scoffed at. Harold Rosenberg, in one of his more memorable phrases, called the Beats a "herd of independent minds." And Norman Podhoretz, who was then even younger than most of the Beats and just beginning to make his reputation as a critic, labeled them "know-nothing Bohemians," and set forth his judgment in what was soon to become his characteristic stentorian tone of disapproval: "The plain truth is that the primitivism of the Beat Generation serves first of all as a cover for an anti-intellectualism so bitter that it makes the ordinary American's hatred of eggheads seem positively benign."

Anti-intellectualism was, as we shall see, a charge often tossed in their direction. And though we shall deal with it again in passing, let us note with particular reference to Podhoretz's severe judgment that an intellectual, if he is anything, is a man who is in touch with his own time, one who knows what's happening and why. And by that modest standard, any one of the Beat writers was as much an intellectual as he. Why? Because the Beats had perceived and managed to touch something essential that was only then beginning to take shape in the America of the 1950s. It was a very important and widespread something, compounded of a deep hunger for individual recognition, a desire to speak frankly and honestly about things that mattered, and, finally, a need for passionate personal involvement in major undertakings.

Perhaps these are not unusual qualities at all. Perhaps they can be found in Americans of any decade. They may be merely the common needs and characteristic qualities of the young at any time or in any place. But they were of special importance to the Beats and their followers because these, after all, were the 1950s—the era of Joe McCarthy, the HUAC hearings, and a series of spy trials that together spread a brooding pall of suspicion over all of American society. It was a time during which most of the adult population was trapped in an intricate edifice of social conformity built of fear, suppressed hostility, and the simple desire to get along. And finally, it was also a time when many adult Americans experienced personal prosperity and some degree of affluence for the first time in their lives; the middle class was expanded in that decade by many millions who could well remember extreme poverty from the depression years. Most of them had worked hard and waited a long time to get where they were. And once comfortably established, they embraced the values and symbols of middle-class life with all the fervor of religious converts.

A THREAT TO THE STATUS QUO

In this context the Beats were of considerable social importance to the 1950s, for they soon came to be regarded as a threat to all this because they questioned the conservative, corporate, and suburban values that were then so widely and publicly extolled. The Beats not only questioned, they challenged them, and were soon widely publicized as rebels against the system. And if, as a revolt, theirs may have had serious inadequacies in shape, definition, and direction, still it attracted thousands—tens of thousands—of young people in a very short time.

In the literary culture, as well, this was a period of stasis and conformity. Two groups—the New Critics of the colleges and universities and that group of New York intellectuals known variously as the Family and the *Partisan Review* crowd—dominated the arena without themselves ever really falling into serious contention. They shared. A sort of polite trust prevailed between the two that was based on overlapping interests and mutual advantage. Outsiders—and there were many of them—spoke wryly of this coalition as the *"Kenyon Review–Partisan Review* axis."

THE NEW CRITICS

But make no mistake: the two groups were quite distinct. For their part, the New Critics were academic in about every way it was possible for them to be. They were schoolmen who devoted their time and intellectual energies to the close reading of texts, from which they drew conclusions on points so fine as to often seem irrelevant. Their poetry—to generalize recklessly—was crabbed, pinched, and reticent, and their fiction introspective and oblique. Politically, they were either indifferent or conservative. Socially, there was a definite disposition to the Ciceronian ideals of the ante-bellum South and a tendency to share a fantasy of the agrarian past at the expense of the urban present. They were elitists at heart, and they drew their strength from the sudden rise of the universities in America following World War II and from the growing popular faith that through education a new elite would be created that might be expected to solve all the problems and guide the way into that brave new world of the future.

THE NEW YORK INTELLECTUALS

The New York crowd, on the other hand, was intensely political. No matter what the text at hand, they could be counted on to examine it fundamentally as a political document. Their style had survived from the 1930s. Nearly all had at that time gone through a period of keen enthusiasm for Marxism. One by one, however, they all became disenchanted and dissociated themselves from orthodox Marxism. This was the case, certainly, with the *Partisan Review* itself, which was well known in the 1930s as an independent Marxist political journal, though it was then categorized as "Trotskyite." Gradually, however, as the personal political commitment of its editors and contributors began to cool—for most this happened during the war—their attention became focused more and more on literary subjects. Yet while the content of their articles had gradually changed, their manner and fundamental concern had not. These have remained essentially political. Criticism for this group consisted largely in gathering a certain number of recent novels within a generalization and denouncing it as evidence of some especially pernicious social tendency. Their rhetoric is the sort that invariably seems to draw them into intellectual demolition of their opponents. They specialized in feats of literary overkill, and their favorite targets have always been sitting ducks. Yet if nothing more, the New York group was, is, and always will be *serious*—concerned with the great issues, refusing steadfastly to be amused.

Thus the scene is set. Here are the two groups—New Critics and New Yorkers—occupying center stage. They perform their familiar routines to the scattered applause of an indifferent audience. All right, the show may *not* be very interesting but respect and good feeling prevail: a sense of order and authority is present in the world of letters. Suddenly, from the wings there appears onstage a wild, shabbily dressed, and unshaven bunch who mill in disorder about the stage, shouting obscenities, jeering, and making light of all the heavy weight of intellect assembled there. Where order was, there is now anarchy.

That wasn't how it really happened, but that is how members of the literary establishment *thought* it was happening. For these who held so tenaciously to their position in center stage, the keenest irritation of all was not that the Beats, who were now crowding them out, were so ill-mannered and unserious. No, what bothered them most was that the audience they had been boring had suddenly become intensely interested.

A BEAT EVENT

This was quite literally apparent whenever the Beats gave a reading or made any sort of public appearance. I remember being present at such an event held at a Loop hotel in Chicago early in 1959. It was a reading given as a benefit to launch a new magazine with Beat leanings, *Big Table*, edited by the poet Paul Carroll. Attendance at the event in every way exceeded the expectations of the academic crowd that usually made up the audience at local poetry evenings such as this. The audience of over 700 completely filled the ballroom they had engaged, and in no time at all the aisles were packed and people were being turned away from the door. But the character of the audience must have surprised the regulars, too, for it was not the modest crowd of college students and young teachers who usually showed up. They were both younger and older than that, ranging from about mid-teens to grizzled middle age. And while there were certainly many there from the area's many colleges, the outsiders seemed to dominate, giving the audience a distinctly nonacademic, almost proletarian appearance.

The most eminent representative of the literary establishment present was the late Henry Rago, an academic in all but point of fact, who was then editor of *Poetry* magazine. He was there seated in the midst of a group of young university teachers. As it happened, I was introduced to him by one of the university teachers I knew and took a seat quite nearby. I couldn't help noticing Mr. Rago's reactions during the reading, and although they were never put into words, they were so expressive in their own way that I think they are worth noting here. When, for example, Gregory Corso began reading his poem, "Hair,"

> My beautiful hair is dead
> Now I am the rawhead
> O when I look in the mirror
> he bald I see is balder still
> When I sleep the sleep I sleep
> is not at will
> And when I dream I dream children waving
>   goodbye—
> It was lovely hair once
> it was
> Hours before shop windows gum-machine mirrors
>   with great combs
> pockets filled with jars of lanolin. . . .

I watched Mr. Rago sink deeper and deeper into his seat. He was clearly disturbed by what he heard, perhaps unhappy that he had even come, but he made no move to leave. As I recall, he endured the entire program, perhaps too much of a gentleman to leave (for he was always that), or more likely frozen in consternation at this awful new thing that was happening. In any case he did stay, but by the time Allen Ginsberg was reading his even then famous poem "Howl" ("I saw the best minds of my generation destroyed by madness, starving hysterical naked,/ dragging themselves through the negro streets at dawn looking for an angry fix . . ."), Henry Rago's face wore an expression of almost physical pain.

TOUCHING SOMETHING REAL

Yet this was clearly not how the rest of the audience heard it. They not only applauded at the appropriate places, they applauded at *in*appropriate places and did a bit of cheering and stamping, too. The response to the poems read and to the remarks made by the poets was so open and spontaneous that the feeling that night was quite like that of a jazz concert. This, of course, was precisely the open and swinging effect that the Beat poets strove for in all their readings, with or without musical accompaniment. The response was there. No doubt about it: Corso and Ginsberg had touched something real that night. . . .

The New York intellectual community . . . saw Ginsberg, Corso, Kerouac, and company not so much as a threat, but as writers of little intrinsic worth whose importance to them lay in their relation as inferiors to the senior group. (And they saw themselves—Mrs. Trilling makes this painfully clear—as defenders of the True Faith.) . . .

And yet the Beats survived. They not only survived, they prevailed. Why? And how, when neither Kerouac nor Ginsberg nor any of the rest received much more than muttered encouragement from critics, did they manage to pull off the sort of cultural revolution they boasted they would? If that seems excessive, then just think how different things are today from what they were when the Beats came along. Socially, culturally, even politically, the drift was set long before in their direction. The Beats simply managed to accelerate the pace so wildly that less than a decade after they had begun to amuse the readers of *Time, Life,* and *Newsweek,* America was so radically changed that those who had done the laughing could hardly believe it was the same country. ("Something's happening, but you don't know what it is, do you, Mr. Jones?")

It was not only that they touched something essential and responsive in their younger readers and listeners. The Beats also had behind them the force of a long, rich, and deeply American tradition.

ROCK AND ROLL IS HERE TO STAY

ED WARD

The 1950s saw the birth of arguably the most significant popular music movement of the twentieth century—rock and roll. The movement grew out of American black rhythm and blues music. Like many other aspects of American culture, popular music was racially segregated prior to this time. Mainstream white popular music included crooners like Frank Sinatra, the music from such popular musical theater productions as *Oklahoma!*, and Big Band swing or bebop, which were outgrowths of jazz.

In the early 1950s, however, a subversive musical revolution began in which the nation's youth were widely exposed to black music.

A few white disc jockeys began playing rhythm and blues music on mainstream radio stations, usually in late-night time slots. The music began to catch on with teens, and soon a few black artists became crossover hits. Still reluctant to risk trying to promote black artists to a mainstream white audience, record producers used white artists who did covers of black artists' music. When Elvis Presley made the scene with his rhythm-and-blues-derived music in 1953, teens raved—and so did their parents, but for different reasons. Teens were swept away by the primal attractions of Presley's and other rock-and-rollers' rhythms, emotional appeal, and sensuality. Parents, on the other hand, feared that such music would corrupt their children and lead them away from solid American family values. But the teens' voices prevailed. America was prosperous in the decade following World War II, and teens had money to spend—and they often spent it on rock and roll records.

By 1957 a Philadelphia television program dedicated to teens and their music went national. *American Bandstand*'s national debut set the show's tone with an appearance by southern rocker Jerry Lee Louis playing his wild hit "A Whole Lotta' Shakin' Goin' On."

Rock's popularity also brought mainstream acceptance to many black musicians, and in 1959 Berry Gordy established Motown Records, the first all-black record company that produced top-ten hits with such artists as Diana Ross and the Supremes, Smokey Robinson and the Miracles, and the Temptations.

In the following decades, rock and roll took many directions and spread around the world. Protest, folk, psychedelic, bubblegum, heavy metal, and punk were some of the offshoots of this music that was born in the 1950s and continues to dominate music sales around the world today.

In the article below, music writer Ed Ward describes some of the events of 1955, what he describes as a pivotal year in music history—"the year rock and roll was born." Ward has written for music publications *Crawdaddy, Rolling Stone, Creem,* and others.

As 1955 dawned, a solitary figure stood looking out the second-floor window of his home in Oak Park, Illinois. Dr. Charles A. Lauhead had been dismissed from his teaching position at the University of Michigan by colleagues who refused to believe that he had heard voices from outer space, telling him that a giant tidal wave would sweep over the Midwest, engulfing it and ending life there, and that the world would be destroyed shortly thereafter. What he didn't know was that there would be a wave, but it would not be of water, and that far from destroying life on Earth, it would enhance it for many. But as the year progressed, parents across the country would come to regard some of their children as if they were space aliens, so strange would their behavior become. . . .

CHUCK BERRY INVENTS "MAYBELLENE"

One day in 1955, [blues artist] Muddy Waters walked in [to Chess Records] with an artist from far left field: Chuck Berry, a country-and-western-singing black cosmetician from St. Louis who played blues guitar. Sure, he'd done three years for armed robbery in the 1940s, but when Muddy heard him in Chicago, he knew Berry had a future in music. Fortunately, too, he was no threat to Muddy's superiority as a bluesman; indeed, Chuck Berry was as unlike Muddy Waters as he could be. Like Muddy, he was rather dark-skinned, but his features showed that he had

Indian in his background. And when he was asked to play, he whipped out an old fiddle tune, "Ida Red," which had been recorded by everybody from Bob Wills to country music star, Lloyd "Cowboy" Copes.

It was Copes's version, in fact, that Berry's "Ida Red" most closely resembled, the version recorded when Copes was playing swing and hot licks, the period that produced his hit "Jamboree." But Berry had revised the song, putting Ida Red into a car and adding lyrics to the verse so that he could spit them out rapid-fire to sim- ulate the car chase that was the song's central action. It was a freakish mix- ture—no wonder Capitol and Mer- cury [record company] had already rejected Berry but there was some- thing about the song that [owners Phil and Leonard] Chess liked. The main problem was that "Ida Red" was p.d.—public domain—it couldn't be copyrighted, and that meant no royalties. So they asked Berry to think of another title, another name for the girl in the car, and his mind went back to the beauty shop in St. Louis and came up with "Maybellene."

Chuck Berry

Then the brothers dubbed a copy of "Maybellene" and gave it to Alan Freed [a white disk jockey who played black blues music], who liked it enough to attach his name to the credits, along with the name of one Russel D. Fratto and—oh, yes, Charles Edward Berry. Chess released "Maybellene" in July, and in exactly four weeks, it had hit the top of the rhythm-and-blues charts—at a time when people in the industry were complaining that the glut of records had made the rhythm-and-blues market sluggish.

But that was just the beginning: Soon the record broke into the pop charts at thirteen and it hovered in the Top Ten for weeks! Cover versions—if you can imagine a cover version of "Maybel- lene"—by the [easy-listening] Johnny Long Orchestra and the Ralph Marterie Orchestra, among others, sat choking on Chuck Berry's dust. . . .

LITTLE RICHARD MAKES THE SCENE

There was already a pile of tapes from various hopefuls at Spe- cialty [Records], and [Robert 'Bumps'] Blackwell [a gospel mu- sic producer] set about going through them. "One day," he remembered nearly thirty years later, "a reel of tape, wrapped in a piece of paper looking as though someone had eaten off it, came across my desk. . . . The voice was unmistakably star material. I can't tell you how I knew, but I knew. The songs were not out-and-out gospel, but I could tell by the tone of his voice and all those churchy turns that he was a gospel singer who could sing the blues."

At first, [Art] Rupe [a Specialty Records executive] waffled when Blackwell came raving into his office, urging him to sign "Little" Richard Penniman, but finally Bumps wore him down. Richard was still under contract to Peacock [Records]—where he'd cut some truly somnolent records with both his own band, the Tempo Toppers, and with Johnny Otis's orchestra—and going head to head with Don Robey was hardly what a struggling entrepreneur like Art Rupe wanted to do. But the singer himself approached Robey, who never knew there was another interested party, and got his contract price down to $600. Rupe wired him the money.

It was not until the first recording session, at Cosimo Matassa's J&M Studios in New Orleans, that Rupe or Blackwell ever laid eyes on their new artist. As Bumps recalled, it was a shock. "There's this cat in this loud shirt, with hair waved up six inches above his head. He was talking wild, thinking up stuff just to be different, you know? I could tell he was a mega-personality." Richard liked Fats Domino, which was encouraging, since Fats was hot, so Bumps set him up with Domino's band: Lee Allen on tenor sax, Alvin "Red" Tyler on baritone sax. Earl Palmer on drums, Edgar Blanchard and Justin Adams on guitars, Frank Fields on bass, and Huey "Piano" Smith and James Booker taking turns on the piano.

And then Richard froze. Well, not completely; after all, he was a seasoned performer at twenty-two, and he'd been making records since he was eighteen. But now it was like pulling teeth. Bumps was paying serious money for studio time and only got one keeper, "I'm Just A Lonely Guy," by Dorothy La Bostrie, a writer who had been hounding him forever. "The problem was that what he looked like and what he sounded like didn't come together," Blackwell recalled. "If you look like Tarzan and sound like Mickey Mouse it just doesn't work out . . . I didn't know what to do. I couldn't go back to Rupe with the material I had because there was nothing there that I could put out, nothing to merchandise."

Lunch break! Maybe they could get him drunk or something—anything to loosen him up. So they walked down the street to the Dew Drop Inn, a musicians' hangout, and Richard was transfigured the moment he entered the door. "We walk into the place, and the girls are there and the boys are there and he's got an audience. There's a piano, and that's his crutch. He's on stage reckoning to show Lee Allen his piano style. So *wow!* He gets to sing. He hits that piano, *didididididididi* . . . and starts to sing, Awop-bopa-loo-mop a good goddam—Tutti-Frutti, good booty. . . ."

It was just what Blackwell had been waiting for—something that matched the image—a hit song, although filthy, that the singer had picked up somewhere along the road people travel when they're very young, homosexual, and black in the Deep South. Blackwell knew that Dorothy La Bostrie was probably still hanging around the studio, waiting to pitch yet another set of lyrics, and so they rushed back to find her. There was hardly any time to rewrite the song and then get the whole band to rehearse it and cut it—and then Richard got embarrassed to play it in front of her. Bumps explained that La Bostrie was over twenty-one, a consenting adult, she needed money to raise her kids, and finally Richard turned to the wall and pounded out the song. "Fifteen minutes before the session was to end," Blackwell recalled, "the chick comes in and puts these little trite lyrics in front of me. I put them in front of Richard. Richard says he ain't got no voice left. I said. 'Richard, you've got to sing it.'" So they reset the mikes so that Richard could sing and play simultaneously, and fifteen minutes later they were listening to the playback:

"Awop bop a loo mop a lop bam boom! Tutti frutti! Aw rootie!" It sounded like Dr. Lauhead's space people had landed, and it was outrageous enough that it spent twenty weeks on the rhythm-and-blues charts, getting as high as number two, and had enough momentum to blast onto the pop charts, landing at number seventeen. Something about this weird singer's voice was affecting teenagers, that was certain.

Amazingly there were still those who thought that rock and roll was nothing but a momentary craze, something the teens would grow out of. . . .

ROCK AND ROLL: HARMFUL OR HARMLESS?

But there were others who continued to see rock and roll as an ominous symptom of decay. In Chicago in April 1955, fifteen thousand teenagers bombarded djs (at stations that were playing mostly pop records, if the truth be known) with letters patterned on a suggested model printed in a Catholic high school newspaper, accusing them of playing dirty records. In Boston, six djs formed a censorship board to screen new records, with the help of newspaper writers and religious leaders. In Bridgeport and New Haven, the police announced a ban on rock-and-roll dances.

Bridgeport Superintendent of Police John A. Lyddy claimed his department was merely responding to the pleas of hundreds of concerned parents and noted, "Teenagers virtually work themselves into a frenzy to the beat of fast swing music" at the dances. Disc jockey Marc Jennings, at WCMI in Huntington, West Virginia, announced that "tunes like . . . 'Hearts of Stone,' 'Ko Ko Mo,' and 'Tweedle Dee' are products of the mass hysteria prevalent in our world today." That the hysteria should have reached Huntington was certainly food for thought. No doubt about it, the rock-and-roll mania was becoming an epidemic.

Even *Life* magazine devoted a few pages—albeit not as many as for the Davy Crockett fad—to the latest bit of teenage craziness. Readers were treated to pictures of a dance that spontaneously erupted (in front of a *Life* photographer, conveniently enough) in the parking lot of a suburban Los Angeles supermarket: Alan Freed with some fans; San Francisco teenagers dancing on television; Herbert Hardesty of Fats Domino's band writhing on the floor, tenor sax afly; an integrated audience in the balcony of the Brooklyn Paramount at Alan Freed's first spectacular show, which broke all house records for attendance; New Haven's Police Chief Francis McManus warily eyeing a program for a rock-and-roll dance he'd just banned; and, as a last shot to show people it wasn't anything serious, two pictures of [famous ballroom dance instructor] Arthur Murray learning how to do the dance and then teaching it to one of his classes. "Rock and roll," the text said, "is both music and dance. The music has a rhythm often heavily accented on the second and fourth beat. The dance combines the Lindy and Charleston, and almost anything else. In performing it, hollering helps and a boot banging the floor makes it even better. The overall result frequently is frenzy.". . .

And in May 1955, it was discovered that class distinctions had nothing to do with rock and roll's ability to incite the baser passions: at Princeton University, it was reported, a student fired up "Rock Around the Clock" in his dorm room, and was answered right afterward by another student doing the same thing. Soon a mob had formed in the courtyard, chanting and stamping their feet, setting fire to trash cans as they moved beyond the halls of Old Nassau into the streets at midnight, until finally a dean was found to quell the boiling blue blood, reminding them of the dire consequences of being thrown out of Princeton. . . .

AMERICANS SUPPORT ENTERTAINMENT WITH THEIR POCKETBOOKS

By 1955, it was becoming clearer that Americans were enjoying entertainment as never before; that they were spending more money on it than ever; and that for the first time, the home was becoming a major entertainment venue. Television, a novelty three short years before, had become an appliance as common as the refrigerator with variety shows like Jackie Gleason's and Ed Sullivan's presenting the talent that network radio used to provide—only now you could see the performers. And nearly every home had a phonograph, whether it was a little fold-up child's model, a record changer that attached with a jack to the television set, or a large console. Some people—people with money—were indulging in the new "high-fidelity" craze, which required an investment of thousands of dollars in amplifiers, preamplifiers, FM tuners, and speakers with funny names like woofers and tweeters, as well as tape recorders. There was no denying that sound had made a quantum leap in five years, especially considering the advances being made with microgroove recording and long-playing records. By 1955, although most manufacturers were still making 78s for customers who hadn't changed over or wouldn't change over, they were becoming more expensive specialty items, and by June 1955, the ten-inch LP [long-playing record] was on its way out, too, as Columbia shifted completely to albums, along with 45s [small records containing only a few songs], and the other majors soon followed suit. . . .

Maybe the rock and roll phenomenon *wasn't* going to disappear as fast as some people thought. Ed Sullivan, respected columnist for the New York *Daily News*, with his own television program "The Toast of the Town" (the same name as his column) drawing a huge viewing audience on Sunday nights, had begun inviting these acts onto his show. Not only that, he hired Tommy "Dr. Jive" Smalls to give the audience a fifteen-minute taste of the shows he'd been doing in Harlem. Dr. Jive was up to the challenge and got some hard-core entertainment into his segment, too: La Vern Baker, Bo Diddley, the Five Keys, and tenor honker Willis Jackson's Orchestra.

The show came off well, but there was one hitch: Sullivan's producer had spotted Bo Diddley and thought, aha! A guy with a guitar! The fastest rising song in the country—in fact, the fastest-rising song in the history of the American record business—was "Sixteen Tons," which had been written in the mid-1940s by the fingerpicking guitar whiz Merle Travis and had just been recorded by Tennessee Ernie Ford. Sullivan hadn't been able to corral Tennessee Ernie for an appearance on the show, but the producer figured Diddley would do—like the rest of the entertainment establishment, he still thought it was the *song*, not the performer, that mattered. At first, Mr. Diddley insisted that he didn't know "Sixteen Tons." So the producers sat down with some members of the studio orchestra and the production crew and went over it with him. Just to make sure he got it right, they wrote the words down on big cue cards in big letters, in deference to his bad eyes. Everything was set for the live broadcast, and Dr. Jive introduced the guitar slinger, who blithely strolled onstage and performed—"Bo Diddley." As he strutted offstage, he was met by the production staff en masse, who demanded an explanation. "Man, maybe that was 'Sixteen Tons' on those cards" he drawled, "but all I saw was 'Bo Diddley!'" Coke-bottle lenses, you know. . . .

Those unpredictable rock and rollers! Why would anybody want to work with them? The answer came along the first week of December 1955.

THE KING CLINCHES CROSSOVER

DOUBLE DEALS HURL PRESLEY INTO STARDOM, screamed the front page of *Billboard.* THE BIG TIME AT 19. . . .

The very fact that RCA thought they could sell Elvis to everybody meant that they were thinking along the same lines as Sam Phillips: that the day had finally arrived when an artist who combined elements from each field would appeal to everyone—urban and rural, black and white—embodying a fusion that had been building since the days of Jimmie Rodgers (himself an RCA artist), Bob Wills, and Nat "King" Cole. But to the industry at that time, it seemed clear that this bumbling giant, this major label that had been ignoring the rhythm-and-blues and rock-and-roll explosion, had lost its corporate mind.

But then again, maybe everybody had. Alan Freed announced that he was going to star in a movie called *Rock Around the Clock* and lead an eighteen-piece band in the sanctum sanctorum of New York jazzdom, Birdland. He would be featured on trombone. His uptown counterpart, Dr. Jive, bought Small's Paradise, the legendary Harlem nightclub, from owner Edwin Smalls (no relation) and announced an all-R&B booking policy, even though he must have realized that teenagers couldn't drink and rarely frequented nightclubs. Decca [Records] went ahead and ignored cooler heads by releasing Bill Haley and His Comets' album *Rock Around the Clock,* which seemed as foolish as Atlantic's R&B album release. Sun Records, in its second coup of the year, won a lawsuit against Don Robey for inducing Junior Parker away from them despite a legally binding contract, and the judge made Robey pay not only the amount of the unexpired contract but damages as well. And at the year-end BMI awards, the publishing organization noted that sixteen of the twenty-eight songs cited for generating the most income over the year were R&B

tunes, and two of them, "Sincerely" and "Maybellene," were co-written by Alan Freed.

The statisticians were out in force, analyzing the year's developments. An outfit called Teen-Age Surveys, Inc., reported that teenagers still liked rock and roll, and that the slight decline in popularity of R&B detected in their poll was "insufficient to justify any claims that it is waning in popularity." They also advised America's churches to act hip and put some rock and roll into their programs for teenagers, since the teens were beginning to perceive church as, well, a little square. Kay Starr released something called "Rock and Roll Waltz," and any radio that wasn't exhorting you to buy early for Christmas was screaming *A wop bop a loo mop a lop bam boom!* Maybe Dr. Lauhead's space people had landed after all.

Peaceful Coexistence

NIKITA S. KHRUSHCHEV

Nikita S. Khrushchev became a Bolshevik at the time of the Russian Revolution and fought in both world wars. He became a member of the Politburo (the Russian Communist Party's major decision-making organization) following World War II. When dictator Joseph Stalin died in 1953, Khrushchev became first secretary of the Party and the head of the Soviet government until 1964. Within three years of his rise to power, he denounced the iron-fisted Stalin and his methods and set about creating a somewhat less harsh projection of communism. Unlike Stalin, he made gestures of friendship toward the West, although his country continued its campaign to strengthen communism in Eastern Europe and the Third World countries of Asia, Africa, and Central and South America through propaganda, aid, and force.

One of Khrushchev's major thrusts was to promote the idea of peaceful coexistence: He preached that communist and noncommunist nations ought to be able to live side-by-side without fear. His conviction was that communism would triumph not through military might but through economic and scientific superiority. When the Soviet Union began to fall on hard economic times, Khrushchev was forced to resign.

The following article is excerpted from one of Khrushchev's speeches in which he promoted peaceful coexistence.

Comrades, I should like to dwell on some fundamental questions concerning present-day international development, which determine not only the present course of

From Nikita S. Krushchev's speech to the Central Committee of the Communist Party of the Soviet Union, 20th Party Congress, February 14, 1956, Moscow.

events, but also the prospects for the future.

These questions are the peaceful coexistence of the two systems, the possibility of preventing wars in the present era, and the forms of transition to socialism in different countries.

Let us examine these questions in brief.

The peaceful coexistence of the two systems. The Leninist principle of peaceful coexistence of states with different social systems has always been and remains the general line of our country's foreign policy.

It has been alleged that the Soviet Union advances the principle of peaceful coexistence merely out of tactical considerations, considerations of expediency. Yet it is common knowledge that we have always, from the very first years of Soviet power, stood with equal firmness for peaceful coexistence. Hence, it is not a tactical move, but a fundamental principle of Soviet foreign policy.

MYTH OF SOVIET AGGRESSION

This means that if there is indeed a threat to the peaceful coexistence of countries with differing social and political systems, it by no means comes from the Soviet Union or the rest of the socialist camp. Is there a single reason why a socialist state should want to unleash aggressive war? Do we have classes and groups that are interested in war as a means of enrichment? We do not. We abolished them long ago. Or, perhaps, we do not have enough territory or natural wealth, perhaps we lack sources of raw materials or markets for our goods? No, we have sufficient of all those and to spare. Why then should we want war? We do not want it; as a matter of principle we renounce any policy that might lead to millions of people being plunged into war for the sake of the selfish interests of a handful of multi-millionaires. Do those who shout about the "aggressive intentions" of the U.S.S.R. know all this? Of course they do. Why then do they keep up the old monotonous refrain about some imaginary "communist aggression"? Only to stir up mud, to conceal their plans for world domination, a "crusade" against peace, democracy and socialism.

To this day the enemies of peace allege that the Soviet Union is out to overthrow capitalism in other countries by "exporting" revolution. It goes without saying that among us Communists there are no supporters of capitalism. But this does not mean that we have interfered or plan to interfere in the internal affairs of countries where capitalism exists. [French novelist and pacifist] Romain Rolland was right when he said that "freedom is not brought in from abroad in baggage trains like Bourbons." It is ridiculous to think that revolutions are made to order. We often hear representatives of bourgeois countries reasoning thus: "The

Soviet leaders claim that they are for peaceful coexistence between the two systems. At the same time they declare that they are fighting for communism, and say that communism is bound to win in all countries. Now if the Soviet Union is fighting for communism, how can there be any peaceful coexistence with it?" This view is the result of bourgeois propaganda. The ideologists of the bourgeoisie distort the facts and deliberately confuse questions of ideological struggle with questions of relations between states in order to make the Communists of the Soviet Union look like aggressors.

When we say that the socialist system will win in the competition between the two systems—the capitalist and the socialist—this by no means signifies that its victory will be achieved through armed interference by the socialist countries in the internal affairs of the capitalist countries. Our certainty of the victory of communism is based on the fact that the socialist mode of production possesses decisive advantages over the capitalist mode of production. Precisely because of this, the ideas of Marxism-Leninism are more and more capturing the minds of the broad masses of the working people in the capitalist countries, just as they have captured the minds of millions of men and women in our country and the People's Democracies. We believe that all working men in the world, once they have become convinced of the advantages communism brings, will sooner or later take

Nikita S. Khrushchev

the road of struggle for the construction of socialist society. Building communism in our country, we are resolutely against war. We have always held and continue to hold that the establishment of a new social system in one or another country is the internal affair of the peoples of the countries concerned. This is our attitude, based on the great Marxist-Leninist teaching.

The principle of peaceful coexistence is gaining ever wider international recognition. This principle is one of the corner-stones of the foreign policy of the Chinese People's Republic and the other People's Democracies. It is being actively implemented by the Republic of India, the Union of Burma, and a number of other countries. And this is natural, for there is no other way in present-day conditions. Indeed, there are only two ways: either peaceful coexistence or the most destructive war in history. There is no third way.

We believe that countries with differing social systems can do more than exist side by side. It is necessary to proceed further, to improve relations, strengthen confidence between countries, and co-operate. The historic significance of the famous Five Principles [mutual respect, mutual nonaggression, noninterference, equality and mutual benefit, and peaceful coexistence], advanced by the People's Republic of China and the Republic of India and supported by the Bandung Conference [1955 meeting of twenty-nine Asian and African nations that opposed colonialism and promoted economic and cultural cooperation] and the world public in general, lies in that they provide the best form for relations between countries with differing social systems in present-day conditions. Why not make these principles the foundation of peaceful relations among all countries in all parts of the world? It would meet the vital interests and demands of the peoples if all countries subscribed to these Five Principles.

PREVENTING WAR

The possibility of preventing war in the present era. Millions of people all over the world are asking whether another war is really inevitable, whether mankind which has already experienced two devastating world wars must still go through a third one? Marxists must answer this question taking into consideration the epoch-making changes of the last decades.

There is, of course, a Marxist-Leninist thesis that wars are inevitable as long as imperialism exists. This precept was evolved at a time when 1) imperialism was an all-embracing world system, and 2) the social and political forces which did not want war were weak, poorly organised, and hence unable to compel the imperialists to renounce war.

People usually take only one aspect of the question and examine only the economic basis of wars under imperialism. This is not enough. War is not only an economic phenomenon. Whether there is to be a war or not depends in large measure on the correlation of class, political forces, the degree of organisation and the awareness and resolve of people. Moreover, in certain conditions the struggle waged by progressive social and political forces may play a decisive role. Hitherto the state of affairs was such that the forces that did not want war and opposed it were poorly organised and lacked the means to check the schemes of the war-makers. Thus it was before the First World War, when the main force opposed to the threat of war—the world proletariat—was disorganised by the treachery of the leaders of the Second International. Thus it was on the eve of the Second World War, when the Soviet Union was the only country that pursued an active peace policy, when the other Great Powers to all intents and purposes encouraged the aggressors, and the Right-wing Social-Democratic leaders had split the labour movement in the capitalist countries.

In that period this thesis was absolutely correct. At the present time, however, the situation has changed radically. Now there is a world camp of socialism, which has become a mighty force. In this camp the peace forces find not only the moral, but also the material means to prevent aggression. Moreover, there is a large group of other countries with a population running into many hundreds of millions which are actively working to avert war. The labour movement in the capitalist countries has today become a tremendous force. The movement of peace supporters has sprung up and developed into a powerful factor.

PREVENTING IMPERIALIST WARMONGERING

In these circumstances certainly the Leninist precept that so long as imperialism exists, the economic basis giving rise to wars will also be preserved remains in force. That is why we must display the greatest vigilance. As long as capitalism survives in the world, the reactionary forces representing the interests of the capitalist monopolies will continue their drive towards military gambles and aggression, and may try to unleash war. But war is not fatalistically inevitable. Today there are mighty social and political forces possessing formidable means to prevent the imperialists from unleashing war, and if they do try to start it, to give a smashing rebuff to the aggressors and frustrate their adventurist plans. To be able to do this all anti-war forces must be vigilant and prepared, they must act as a united front and never relax their efforts in the battle for peace. The more actively the peoples defend peace, the greater the guarantees that there will be no new war.

Forms of transition to socialism in different countries. In connection with the radical changes in the world arena new prospects are also opening up in respect to the transition of countries and nations to socialism.

As far back as the eve of the Great October Socialist Revolution Lenin wrote: "All nations will arrive at socialism—this is inevitable, but not all will do so in exactly the same way, each will contribute something of its own in one or another form of democracy, one or another variety of the dictatorship of the proletariat, one or another rate at which socialist transformations will be effected in the various aspects of social life. There is nothing more primitive from the viewpoint of theory or more ridiculous from that of practice than to paint, 'in the name of historical materialism,' *this* aspect of the future in a monotonous grey. The result will be nothing more than Suzdal daubing."

Historical experience has fully confirmed Lenin's brilliant precept. Alongside the Soviet form of reconstructing society on socialist lines, we now have the form of People's Democracy.

In Poland, Bulgaria, Czechoslovakia, Albania, and the other European People's Democracies, this form sprang up and is being utilised in conformity with the concrete historical, social and economic conditions, and peculiarities of each of these countries. It has been thoroughly tried and tested in the course of ten years and has fully proved its worth.

Much that is unique in socialist construction is being contributed by the Chinese People's Republic, whose economy prior to the victory of the revolution was exceedingly backward, semi-feudal and semi-colonial in character. Having taken over decisive commanding positions, the people's democratic state is using them in the social revolution to implement a policy of peaceful reorganisation of private industry and trade and their gradual transformation into a component of socialist economy.

CREATIVE MARXISM IN ACTION

The leadership of the great cause of socialist reconstruction by the Communist Party of China and the Communist and Workers' Parties of the other People's Democracies, exercised in keeping with the peculiarities and specific features of each country, is creative Marxism in action.

In the Federative People's Republic of Yugoslavia, where state power belongs to the working people, and society is based on public ownership of the means of production, specific concrete forms of economic management and organisation of the state apparatus are arising in the process of socialist construction.

It is probable that more forms of transition to socialism will appear. Moreover, the implementation of these forms need not be associated with civil war under all circumstances. Our enemies like to depict us Leninists as advocates of violence always and everywhere. True, we recognise the need for the revolutionary transformation of capitalist society into socialist society. It is this that distinguishes the revolutionary Marxists from the reformists, the opportunists. There is no doubt that in a number of capitalist countries the violent overthrow of the dictatorship of the bourgeoisie and the sharp aggravation of class struggle connected with this are inevitable. But the forms of social revolution vary. It is not true that we regard violence and civil war as the only way to remake society.

It will be recalled that in the conditions that arose in April 1917 Lenin granted the possibility that the Russian Revolution might develop peacefully, and that in the spring of 1918, after the victory of the October Revolution, Lenin drew up his famous plan for peaceful socialist construction. It is not our fault that the Russian and international bourgeoisie organised counter-revolution, intervention, and civil war against the young Soviet state and forced the workers and peasants to take up arms. It did not come to civil war in the European People's Democracies, where the historical situation was different.

Degree of Violence Depends on Ruling-Class Resistance

Leninism teaches us that the ruling classes will not surrender their power voluntarily. And the greater or lesser degree of intensity which the struggle may assume, the use or the non-use of violence in the transition to socialism depends on the resistance of the exploiters, on whether the exploiting class itself resorts to violence, rather than on the proletariat.

In this connection the question arises of whether it is possible to go over to socialism by using parliamentary means. No such course was open to the Russian Bolsheviks, who were the first to effect this transition. Lenin showed us another road, that of the establishment of a republic of Soviets, the only correct road in those historical conditions. Following that course we achieved a victory of history-making significance.

Since then, however, the historical situation has undergone radical changes which make possible a new approach to the question. The forces of socialism and democracy have grown immeasurably throughout the world, and capitalism has become much weaker. The mighty camp of socialism with its population of over 900 million is growing and gaining in strength. Its gigantic internal forces, its decisive advantages over capitalism, are being increasingly revealed from day to day. Socialism has a great power of attraction for the workers, peasants, and intellectuals of all countries. The ideas of socialism are indeed coming to dominate the minds of all toiling humanity.

At the same time the present situation offers the working class in a number of capitalist countries a real opportunity to unite the overwhelming majority of the people under its leadership and to secure the transfer of the basic means of production into the hands of the people. The Right-wing bourgeois parties and their governments are suffering bankruptcy with increasing frequency. In these circumstances the working class, by rallying around itself the toiling peasantry, the intelligentsia, all patriotic forces, and resolutely repulsing the opportunist elements who are incapable of giving up the policy of compromise with the capitalists and landlords, is in a position to defeat the reactionary forces opposed to the popular interest, to capture a stable majority in parliament, and transform the latter from an organ of bourgeois democracy into a genuine instrument of the people's will. In such an event this institution, traditional in many highly developed capitalist countries, may become an organ of genuine democracy, democracy for the working people.

The winning of a stable parliamentary majority backed by a mass revolutionary movement of the proletariat and of all the working people could create for the working class of a number of capitalist and former colonial countries the conditions needed to secure fundamental social changes.

In the countries where capitalism is still strong and has a huge military and police apparatus at its disposal, the reactionary forces will of course inevitably offer serious resistance. There the transition to socialism will be attended by a sharp class revolutionary struggle.

KEY FACTOR: LEADERSHIP OF THE WORKING CLASS

Whatever the form of transition to socialism, the decisive and indispensable factor is the political leadership of the working class headed by its vanguard. Without this there can be no transition to socialism.

It must be strongly emphasised that the more favourable conditions for the victory of socialism created in other countries are due to the fact that socialism has won in the Soviet Union and is winning in the People's Democracies. Its victory in our country would have been impossible had Lenin and the Bolshevik Party not upheld revolutionary Marxism in battle against the reformists, who broke with Marxism and took the path of opportunism.

Such are the considerations which the Central Committee of the Party finds necessary to set out in regard to the forms of transition to socialism in present-day conditions.

A Challenge to Communism: The Hungarian Revolution

Timothy Foote

In World War II, Hungary sided with Nazi Germany, facilitating the extermination of many Hungarian Jews. In 1944 the Soviets expelled German troops from Hungary, and by 1946 Hungary had become a republic, headed by Imre Nagy. In 1948 the Communist Party gained control of the government, and Hungary became a socialist state.

Russian dictator Joseph Stalin imposed an iron fist throughout the USSR and the countries in its sphere of influence. When Stalin died in 1953, the new Soviet leader, Nikita Khrushchev, denounced Stalin and loosened the Soviet reins very slightly. The people of Hungary, however, were tired of Soviet repression enforced by puppet political leaders. Spontaneously, on October 23, 1956, an uprising began. What started as a peaceful student demonstration grew into a brief but significant revolution.

Although the Soviets quickly quelled the Hungarian uprising, the brief rebellion showed the Communists that they could not expect to complacently maintain control of their satellite nations. At the same time, it showed the Western nations that the Soviets would do what was necessary to keep their hold on the countries they claimed as Communist partners. This incident intensified Cold War animosity between East and West.

Excerpted from "'But If Enough of Us Get Killed Something May Happen . . . ,'" by Timothy Foote, *Smithsonian*, November 1986. Slightly revised by and reprinted with the permission of the author.

In the following article, journalist Timothy Foote recalls the revolution, which he observed firsthand as a reporter in Budapest at the time. Foote is a senior editor and writer at *Smithsonian* magazine.

T he 13 days that shook the Communist world began rather like an uplifting scene from a Cecil B. DeMille [epic film] extravaganza. Streams of students, and some workers, swelling into a crowd of thousands marching ten abreast, poured across the city's great bridges and through Budapest's wide streets toward the Parliament building.

They carried posters and waved Hungarian flags from which the Communist star had been snipped out with scissors. They sang patriotic songs and shouted slogans: "Russki go home!" "Disband the AVO!" (the old acronym for the security police whose initials had already become AVH). "We want Nagy!", a reference to Imre Nagy, a studious man with a walrus mustache who, though he had lived for 15 years in Moscow as a Russian citizen, was known as the most liberal of Hungary's notably savage Communist Party leaders. More than 10,000 crowded into Kossuth Square beside the Parliament building. They were genial. They simply had a petition, with a list of demands they wanted the government to listen to. These included the return of Nagy to power; the eventual withdrawal of the Red Army, which at the time had two divisions outside Budapest; an end to the power of some 35,000 security police whose use of kidnapping, torture and terrorism had turned the lives of thousands of Hungarians into a nightmare. (Hungary's population was, and is, 11 million. On an American scale an equivalent secret-police force would be more than 750,000 men.)

Such demands were not extreme. The demonstrators were not exactly asking for Eisenhower Republicanism. They just hoped to ease the worst of the Stalinist abuses. The tide seemed to be shifting in Eastern Europe. The American Secretary of State, John Foster Dulles, had grandly talked about "rolling back the Iron Curtain." Most important, the new Soviet Party Secretary, Nikita Khrushchev, had been struggling to get his country to give up many of Stalin's policies.

STALIN WAS DEAD, BUT REPRESSION WAS NOT

Stalin had thrown Marshal Tito of Yugoslavia out of the Comintern and tried to have him murdered because Tito said he wanted to run his own Yugoslav Communist Party in his own Yugoslav way. But in May of 1955, Khrushchev journeyed to Belgrade and reinstated Tito. "My father's socialist house," he declared, "has many mansions." Khrushchev began letting people out of the gulags to which Stalin had permanently consigned millions of Russians. He had quickly moved to spring Hungary's neighbor Austria from the limbo of four-power occupation, making her a free but essentially neutral state.

Yet on October 23, the day the crowd massed in front of Hungary's Parliament, Party Secretary Erno Gero, a hard-lining Stalinist, refused to treat the list of demands seriously. Instead, Gero threatened the petitioners and called them "enemies of the people." When they left Kossuth Square it was late in the day. They were angry now and full of energy.

Thousands headed for the Budapest radio station to demand that a petition be read over the air. The frightened station director at first agreed, then trickily had the reading put on a loudspeaker so the crowd could hear, but without actually broadcasting it. Someone in the crowd had a radio and discovered the ruse. Bricks began to fly. In the building the beleaguered AVH initially used blanks and tear gas, but finally fired bursts of gunfire into the crowd. Now a few Hungarian soldiers joined the rebels. Others handed their weapons over to the crowd, which eventually blasted the AVH from the radio building.

Enraged groups dashed to Stalin Square and began fruitlessly smashing at a 24-foot bronze statue of the Soviet dictator with bricks and sledgehammers. A worker with an acetylene torch, slicing the statue off at the ankles, finally brought it crashing down to be spat upon, dismembered, the parts paraded through the streets.

Raids on state arsenals began; weapons were handed out to anyone who wanted them, and the rebellion started in bitter earnest. By the next day two mechanized Russian divisions stationed nearby had been called into Budapest by the Hungarian Communist government. Fifty of the arriving Russian tanks rolled into Kossuth Square to encircle Parliament. Harassed by snipers, others took positions at crossroads or roamed the city trying to drive freedom fighters from the streets and impromptu strongholds. The Hungarian rebels, who had seen Soviet films about heroic guerrilla forces, began using homemade Molotov cocktails and now and then a captured antitank gun. Some Hungarian Army tanks joined the rebels too. During the next few days, just in the area around the Kilian Barracks on Ulloi Ut and the Corvin Theater, the streets were strewn with the innards of Russian tanks and armored cars.

On October 24 the Soviet Union agreed to have Nagy put back in power. He declared martial law, but could not make it stick.

He offered amnesty to any rebels who swiftly laid down their arms. There were no takers. Now the hope was that by yielding to a certain number of demands and promising to consider others, the Communist government might hang on to power and stabilize the country. On October 25 it was announced that the hated Gero was out as Party Secretary, to be replaced by Janos Kadar who, though he had once served as Interior Minister in charge of the security police, was counted as sympathetic because, in what has been aptly described as the "Shoots and Ladders" of Communist politics, he had also been imprisoned and tortured by the Stalinist wing of his party.

POWER OF THE REVOLUTION

By October 25, too, communications with Western Europe were all but cut off. But the power of the revolution was now clear. Stones had been torn up to make street barricades. Contemptuously tossed on top were portraits of Stalin and Party Secretary Matyas Rakosi, the Hungarian Communist most hated by his countrymen. Thousands of Hungarian workers joined the fight, not only in Budapest but around the country. In Magyarovar in western Hungary, the AVH had used automatic weapons on a crowd that wanted to tear a Soviet star off the front of a local barracks. When the shooting stopped, 85 people, including women and children, were dead. In industrial Gyor and other large regional cities like Miskolc, the leading Communist officials simply went into hiding and citizen committees took control, electing their own leaders. Rebel newspapers, mostly just a few pages long, written and run off at night in temporarily commandeered print shops, began to appear—as did local rebel radio broadcasts—to counteract the official radio which did not tell what was going on.

Nagy was still the rebels' main hope. After the Russian Army was called in, however, their demands included the withdrawal of all Russian soldiers from Hungary, amnesty for everyone who took part in the revolution, the dismissal from the government of all the worst Communist Party leaders, and the creation of a cabinet that included non-Communists. . . .

The first priority of Marxism-Leninism is that at all costs the Party must stay in power. The second is that the Party is always right. During the revolution, top Russian leaders Mikhail Suslov and Anastas Mikoyan shuttled in and out of Budapest. Once, for safety, they had to be brought from the airport in a Soviet tank. Yuri Andropov, the Russian Ambassador (later head of the KGB and still later General Secretary of the USSR), was always on hand. Before giving in to rebel demands, Nagy, still a good Party man, prudently checked things out with them. They lied to him, and both he and the world were fooled.

RUSSIAN STAKES WERE HIGH

The stakes were high. The Russians stood to lose not only their grip on the country, but perhaps much of their restive East European empire as well. Among hard-liners, Nikita Khrushchev's soft reforms were blamed. It was clear that he would now have to be very hard indeed to cover himself. He was also afraid of losing face outside Russia. The capitalists "will say we are either stupid or soft," he confided to Tito.

A Russian plan to clamp the lid down on Hungary by quietly sealing the borders and overrunning the countryside with ten divisions had already been set in motion. But that would take time and at first was only a worst-case scenario. Meanwhile, they could slowly give in to the revolution's demands, playing for time, while the Hungarians and the world outside thought there was hope of accommodation. Nagy might quiet things down with limited concessions. If not, they could be sure he would eventually go too far, giving them an excuse to step in. They had still another problem. "No matter what government they form," the first rebel fighter I met in Hungary told me, "there is no strong leader the people can really trust. Except Kossuth, and he's been dead for 60 years.". . .

The Kremlin was fearful of Western interference or United Nations inquiry, both of which the freedom fighters, as they lost confidence in Nagy's authority, increasingly hoped for and openly courted. They were desperate. Soon the United States and the United Nations were to be preoccupied with the Suez crisis and a threatened war in the Middle East. But from October 24 on, the Hungarian-language version of Radio Free Europe, paid for by the American CIA, had worked around the clock, relaying news and dispensing encouragement and occasional advice to the rebels. "A political victory must follow an armed victory," one broadcast said, discussing possible plans for a new government. "Don't hang your rifles on the wall."

Day to day, with most communications cut, it was not clear in the West, or even inside Hungary, exactly what was going on. To understand it, as one journalist put it, was like "trying to interpret the groans and thumps of a fight in a locked closet." Officially the border was closed. But medical supplies and food began to come in from neutral Austria, and a trickle of journalists followed. With a friend, photographer John Sadovy, I walked into Hungary near Hegyeshalom at midnight in a late October rain.

Russian Withdrawal

Hungarians tended to greet Western journalists then by asking "When will you send guns?" Like me, however, the bulk of the press did not get in until near the moment when it seemed that soon Budapest might not have to face Russian tanks again. An incredible thing had happened: the Russians had previously agreed to the disbanding of the security police and even the possibility of government by more than one party. Now, we learned, they had allowed Nagy to announce the one concession that gave the others meaning: withdrawal of Russian forces from Budapest, their eventual retirement from the whole country.

Late in the night, Soviet forces officially began to leave Budapest. This was the beginning of three intoxicating days when it seemed to the exhausted revolutionaries, and to the astonished world, that they had won. During this period a number of suppressed political parties were heard from for the first time since 1948 and nearly a dozen newspapers sprang up. In all, more than 17,000 political prisoners would be let out of jail.

There had been such heavy fighting that certain parts of the city looked as if they had been ravaged by full-scale war. Sidewalks were clogged with rubble. Gaping holes the size of trailer trucks had been punched in apartments by Soviet tank fire. Along Ulloi Ut and Jozsef Boulevard, Russian soldiers and Hungarians lay in broken postures, dead alongside their burned-out tanks, armored cars and self-propelled guns. Rebel work teams and curious citizens poked at the wreckage, inspecting, sometimes repairing and salvaging what they could. Men in white coats sprinkled snowy quicklime on the Hungarian and Russian dead. Small boys collected bullets. . . .

The young street fighters were eager to explain how tanks had been destroyed by drawing their attention toward the upper windows of buildings so that youngsters could dash in at street level close enough to throw Molotov cocktails. When they spoke of Russians their anger was clear and hard, but when they gritted out the word "AVO," fear and rage were almost palpable.

Meanwhile, church bells were ringing in Budapest. High on Gellert Hill, across the river, tiny figures could be seen swarming around the big bronze figure of a Soviet soldier, put up in 1947 at the feet of Budapest's 130-foot-tall female statue of Freedom. Heavy lines, in the distance looking only the thickness of black thread, were tied to it. Hauling like slaves, the Hungarian crowds rocked the figure of the soldier back and forth until it fell.

Next day there were grim rumors, but still no Russian tanks or troops in Budapest. Groups of freedom fighters began to hunt out pockets of security police. Some were taken prisoner but some were killed, especially after a half-day siege of Communist Party headquarters on Republic Square.

For several days, the noise of Russian tanks and troops ranging the countryside was all but drowned out by the noise of public and private Russian assertions that the Red Army would soon be gone for good. Imre Nagy twice questioned Moscow about it and got the same answer. He repeatedly asked Andropov and was told the troops coming in were "just protection" for the troops going out. Uneasy, Nagy nevertheless appealed to the revolutionary groups to lay down their arms, insisting the Russians had acceded to all Hungarian demands. He even sent Gen. Pal Maleter, thought to be a hero of the fighting around Kilian Barracks, to a meeting with Russian generals to arrange the final details of Russian withdrawal from the country. The Red Army brass had been claiming they wanted to delay departure until Communist statues had been set up again. They also wanted to arrange a good-bye military parade in Budapest.

On November 1 in Budapest, during an angry discussion with the Russians, Janos Kadar shook his fist and said, "I am a Hungarian. If you come in I will fight your tanks with my bare hands." Later, Kadar mysteriously disappeared. On the afternoon of November 4, Kadar's voice came over the radio broadcasting from a Russian command post outside the city. Calling for the creation of a new Hungarian communist party, he declared himself Hungary's new Premier. At almost exactly the same time fresh Russian divisions made their move on Budapest.

But by that time Nagy had already faced the fact of Soviet deception and betrayal, and taken the only course left to him. He declared Hungary's neutrality and took the country out of the Warsaw Pact.

RUSSIAN TANKS RETURN

This time there was nothing sporadic about the Russian attack. Soviet tanks rolled into town, blazing away at people and buildings as they came. The revolution was virtually crushed after three days. But the November calendar was to be full of last-ditch street fights, fires, imprisonments, mass deportation of students and workers to Russia. Kadar and the Red Army were kept busy, as Kadar put it, saving "the Hungarian proletarian dictatorship." Radio Moscow kept on claiming that the revolt was a counter-revolution, the work of America, West Germany, capitalism, fascism, "bishops, landowners and aristocrats." The free newspapers and political parties disappeared. The first wave of what would eventually be 200,000 refugees slipped into Austria.

General Maleter was seized while he sat negotiating with a

Russian general. Imre Nagy took refuge in the Yugoslavian embassy. But on November 22, promised amnesty by Kadar, he emerged and was instantly picked up. Though now deposed in favor of Kadar, he was still popular, still a threat. Like Maleter, Nagy was eventually hanged.

Kadar, who was a metalworker by trade, wooed the armed workers. But all over Hungary they held out against him, defending their plants and going on strike. During the revolution they had for the first time freely elected their own leaders rather than put up with Party puppets. As the Red Army threatened to move against them they seemed entirely abandoned, except for Hungarian humor. At "Red" Csepel, a huge factory complex built as part of Matyas Rakosi's ill-fated instant industrialization of Hungary, the following sign went up: "The 40,000 aristocrats and fascists of Csepel are on strike."

Hungarians, those who fled to the West and those who stayed behind, felt, still feel, a deep bitterness, especially toward America. With some reason they believed that the United States encouraged their sacrifice, then failed to help. Chatter about rolling back the Iron Curtain was political eyewash of the sort understood (and largely forgiven) as campaign rhetoric in America, but taken seriously in beleaguered Hungary.

When, on October 27, President Eisenhower conveyed to the Russian leaders that the United States was not looking for new allies in Eastern Europe, he mainly intended to make the Russians understand that they had nothing to fear from the West should they somewhat relax their stranglehold on Hungary. What the President's message really did was tell Khrushchev he could do what he had to do anyway—with impunity.

Courage never failed the Hungarians. Nor did a slightly self-deprecating, gallows laughter in adversity. Contemplating their thousands of dead, the scores of smashed schools and hospitals, the 20,000 houses ruined or damaged, they said: "Know where we went wrong in October? We interfered in our own affairs."

WHAT KIND OF COMMUNIST COUNTRY?

No one could then imagine that history would provide their tragedy with a hopeful epilogue, or cast up the betrayer Kadar as the resourceful architect of Hungary's current measure of freedom and prosperity. Once the Red Army came back, Hungary was clearly going to continue as a communist country. The question was, what kind of a communist country would it be? For the first two years Kadar earned a nickname, "The Butcher," as he busied himself with repression, reviving a new incarnation of the Communist Party and (under a new name) the secret police. But he soon proved adept both at getting the Kremlin to let him change the inflexible doctrines of communism that so often have led to despair and bankruptcy and he put his country in hock, borrowing millions of dollars to improve the standard of living. He also struck an unspoken deal with the Hungarian people: if they did not make trouble again, there was some chance of improving their lot.

There was, and is, no doubt about whether Hungary is communist. The land has been collectivized—individual ownership is strictly limited—and the state owns the major means of production. The government has—and sometimes uses—the machinery of repression. But, especially over the past 15 years, Kadar and a handful of brilliant Hungarian financiers have used the state's great power mainly to encourage, not stifle, individual initiative. The present economic system has been variously labeled as the New Mechanism and Goulash (or Paprika) Socialism. Hungarian experts sometimes describe it as "socialist, but with a tendency toward capitalism."

A NEW HUNGARY

Visitors can see spectacular if superficial results in Budapest. Among people over 40, one senses a certain somberness. But in public the atmosphere is free and the streets are bustling, full of well-dressed, mostly cheerful people. Store windows are full of consumer goods, fancy dresses, modern gadgetry. Coffee- and pastry-minded clients of Gerbaud, Budapest's fin de siècle rival to Demels in Vienna, spill out onto beautiful Vorosmarty Square, their tables shaded by bright red, yellow, blue and white umbrellas, each one advertising a different product. Bookstores are jammed, though books critical of the Soviet presence in Eastern Europe are almost impossible to obtain. . . .

The Soviet Union originally acquired its Eastern European empire as a defensive buffer. In its early days as an imperialist power, it rifled occupied territories for railroad tracks and raw materials, often forcing captive peoples to sell to Moscow at a loss, regardless of the hardship caused or the damage to local industries. Today Soviet methods and dealings are more complex. The empire, in fact, must often seem more trouble than it is worth. Experts in Sovietology point out, though, that Russian attachment to Eastern Europe is based on more than defense or economics. "The empire," Seweryn Bialer has written, "is perceived . . . as the basis for the future expansion of Soviet rule and . . . as confirmation of the historical trend toward the 'inevitable' victory of socialism over capitalism."

It cannot be lost on the Soviet leaders that the face and the future of international socialism would look a lot brighter if the Soviet Union and more of the Warsaw Pact nations could match the personal liberty and prosperity lately reached in Kadar's Hungary.

Kadar himself has been farsighted and skillful. But the great bargaining power that he had vis-à-vis the Soviet Union, and the power that still enables him to experiment with flexible, free-enterprising reforms, derives mainly from the willingness of Hungarians long ago to fight Soviet tanks practically with their bare hands. The revolution left behind the threat of future unrest if reforms were not made. It called the world's attention to the failure of Soviet policies. It demonstrated that even in a police state fully equipped with ideology, propaganda and lack of squeamishness, there is a point beyond which you cannot drive a strong and unified people without a certain peril.

In 1989, Hungary became free of communism.

SPUTNIK AND THE SPACE RACE

EDWIN DIAMOND AND STEPHEN BATES

Spurred by wartime military research, the science of rocketry rapidly advanced following World War II. At first, the United States and the Soviet Union built rockets to use as long-range weapons. But by the mid-1950s, both major world powers were working frantically and secretly to be the first to launch a rocket into space. Such an accomplishment would not only establish the winner's primacy—and by extension, the superiority of the political system it espoused—but would provide new ways to keep an eye on, contain, and, if necessary, strike down the enemy.

On October 4, 1957, the Soviet Union launched the first satellite. *Sputnik I* orbited the Earth for several months, all the while dealing a strong blow to America's confidence and its citizens' sense of security. Within a month of *Sputnik*'s launch, the Soviet Union launched a second satellite, this one carrying Laika, a live dog. By 1961 the Soviet Union had put the first man into space. Although U.S. president Dwight Eisenhower's response had been muted, the next president, John F. Kennedy, elected in 1960, placed great emphasis on America's space efforts. At his urging, the United States fought mightily to conquer the "new frontier" of space and achieved the ultimate victory when it landed men on the moon in 1969.

The following article describes the events surrounding the launch of *Sputnik I*. Author Edwin Diamond was a media critic and journalism professor at New York University. Stephen Bates is an editor, writer, and First Amendment scholar.

From "Sputnik," by Edwin Diamond and Stephen Bates, *American Heritage*, October 1997. Reprinted by permission of the authors.

I t wasn't the best of times, but it wasn't the worst of times either. Although a mild recession had cooled down the post–Korean War economy, many families were living comfortable lives in the autumn of 1957. There were 170 million Americans now, and more of them had taken a vacation that summer than ever before, just like the swells out in Southampton.

To be sure, there was turbulence in the air. Three years after *Brown v. Board of Education* had struck down school segregation, the governor of Arkansas, Orval Faubus, defied a federal judge's integration order. Reluctantly, President Dwight D. Eisenhower dispatched the 101st Airborne to enforce the Constitution at Little Rock's Central High School. Slowly, though, the walls of segregation were falling. In July of that long-ago summer, Althea Gibson of Harlem, U.S.A., scored a first. A decade after Jackie Robinson had broken the baseball color line, Gibson won the Wimbledon tennis singles championship and curtsied to the Queen of England.

No Americans were fighting abroad in 1957, though tens of thousands of GIs were deployed in Cold War hot spots from divided Berlin to the Korean demilitarized zone. The Americans and the Russians were methodically testing bigger and "dirtier" (more radioactive fallout) nuclear bombs while perfecting intercontinental missile systems to deliver them. But Nikita Khrushchev, the new Number One Red (as the newspapers referred to him), was talking peaceful competition between socialism and the Free World (as the same papers referred to our side), and summitry, not shooting, seemed to be the prospect between the United States and the U.S.S.R.

Everything in fact appeared to be converging on a broad consensual middle, a prospect that evoked varying responses. What enthusiasts touted as serene abundance (the Republicans had just produced a film called *These Peaceful and Prosperous Years*), critics scorned as soulless conformity and complacency—from Holden Caulfield's contempt for "phonies" to *The Man in the Gray Flannel Suit*'s self-doubt.

THE FIRST SATELLITE

Then, early in the evening of October 4, the sky seemed to fall, literally, on the American edifice. At 6:30 P.M. EST the Associated Press moved a bulletin: Moscow Radio had announced that "the Soviet Union has launched an earth satellite." Later in the evening NBC interrupted regular programming to give more details of the "man-made moon" and to play its high-pitched radio signal "as recorded by RCA engineers." The next morning's *New York Times* and *Washington Post* both gave three-line eight-column banners to the feat, the kind of headline reserved for a Pearl Harbor or a

D-day. The editors of *Newsweek* scrapped their planned feature on Detroit's new line of cars (trashing 1,309,990 cover copies—twenty tons of paper). The new cover showed an artist's conception of the Soviet satellite *Sputnik* (Russian for "fellow traveler"). Inside, the weekly explained "The Red Conquest," "The Meaning to the World," and, ominously, "Why We Are Lagging."

Overnight the self-assured center began coming apart. Inventive, free-enterprise America, home of Edison and the Wright brothers, Levittown and "modern laborsaving kitchen appliances," was being overtaken—surpassed?—by a backward, totalitarian, *Communist* nation. And the shock to can-do pride was the least of it. A missile gap apparently yawned, with the Soviets pulling decisively ahead in the ultimate nuclear weapons, ICBMs. Democrats in Congress charged that amiable Ike's midregister budgetary caution had jeopardized U.S. military prowess. It seemed that the energetic five-star architect of victory in the Big War had turned into a Burning Tree Country Club slacker (one cartoonist showed *Sputnik* whizzing past a golf ball), a myopic Pangloss, a President Magoo.

Sen. Stuart Symington of Missouri, a potential Democratic presidential candidate in 1960, demanded that the President call a special session of Congress to address the *Sputnik* crisis. Ike refused; he even declined to deliver a televised speech addressing the nation's apprehensions, so as not to appear "alarmist." Instead he chose to hold a news conference on October 9, five days after the Soviet announcement. It was, in the view of Eisenhower's biographer Stephen Ambrose, one of the most hostile Q&A sessions of Ike's presidency. Eisenhower repeatedly maintained that *Sputnik* was in essence meaningless. "As far as the satellite itself is concerned," he said, "that does not raise my apprehensions, not one iota."

AMERICANS PANIC

The reporters were, to put it mildly, skeptical. If the Soviets could orbit a satellite, they could fire a nuclear warhead across the ocean at Washington; if the Americans couldn't orbit a satellite, they couldn't shoot a warhead inside Soviet boundaries. Or so experts were telling journalists, and journalists were telling the public. War planners had been confident that the United States could fight off a nuclear strike launched by Soviet long-range bombers, but if Soviet *missiles* could reach the United States, as *Sputnik* hinted, then perhaps our way of life *was* doomed. *Life* magazine presented "The Case for Being Panicky."

Readers were persuaded. Soon Gallup found that half of all Americans believed the Soviets held the lead "in the development of missiles and long-distance rockets." By early 1958 more than a third of Americans thought that the Soviets "could wipe out most cities in the United States in a matter of a few hours with their new rockets and missiles." One out of three Americans also expected the outbreak of World War III by the early 1960s.

The news grew gloomier. In early November, just in time for the celebration of the fortieth anniversary of the Russian Revolution, the Soviets announced the launch of a second *Sputnik*, this one carrying Laika, the orbiting dog. No matter that Laika had a one-way ticket; the capsule accommodated enough oxygen to keep her alive for ten days (because a thermal-control system failed, she didn't last even that long). The Soviets began hinting at plans for manned spaceflights. "What will Americans find on the other side of the moon?" went the joke. "Russians."

In reality the United States was winning both the arms race and the nascent space race. There was indeed a "missile gap," but the lead belonged to the Americans. Ike, it turned out, knew something the rest of us didn't.

SPACE RACE BACKGROUND

Sputnik, like so many 1950s developments in military technology, had its roots in World War II. Hours after the satellite was launched, a U.S. military official complained, "We've got the wrong Germans!" He was mistaken. Most of "their" German rocket scientists—the Peenemunde group captured by the Soviets at the end of the war—had been repatriated. The four-hundred-thousand-pound three-stage rocket that launched *Sputnik* may have been an elaboration of the successful German V-2 design, but it was homegrown.

The best known of "our" Germans, those who had fled west to avoid capture by the Russians, was a civilian scientist for the U.S. Army Redstone missile command in Huntsville, Alabama, named Wernher von Braun. Smooth, handsome in a Hollywood-heavy sort of way, von Braun had been trying for years to get the government to make satellites a priority. His 1954 report "A Minimum Satellite Vehicle" outlined a plan for orbiting an American satellite by 1956. "It is only logical to assume that other countries could do the same," von Braun wrote, adding (emphasis in original): *"It would be a blow to U.S. prestige if we did not do it first."* He sought one hundred thousand dollars to start an Army satellite program. The request was turned down.

Instead the administration divvied up the tasks—and the pork—of missile development. In that 1950s spirit of compromise, every service got a piece of the action (as did the contractors allied with each service—Martin, Northrop, Convair, Aero-

Jet General). Even though von Braun and the Army were far ahead in testing rocket designs, the Defense Department gave the Navy the satellite assignment. A new Navy Vanguard rocket would be developed to lift a four-pound satellite and its modest telemetry into orbit. At the same time, the Army would continue to develop the Jupiter intermediate-range ballistic missile, while the Air Force would work on its Atlas and Titan intercontinental ballistic missiles. Eisenhower didn't warm to the idea of a "missile czar," on the model of Gen. Leslie Groves during the Manhattan Project, to knock Army, Navy, and Air Force heads together; each service forged ahead independently of the others.

On July 31, 1955, American scientists, with the blessing of the White House, announced that the United States would launch a satellite during the International Geophysical Year (IGY), a resolutely peaceful eighteen-month (July 1957 through the end of 1958) multinational investigation of the planet and its resources. Within days of the American announcement, Soviet scientists revealed that they, too, were readying a satellite, also to be launched during IGY. American experts scoffed.

While the Navy worked to meet the IGY goal, von Braun's Army team launched a four-stage rocket on September 20, 1956. It reached a speed of 13,000 miles per hour and a record-setting altitude of 682 miles. The last stage might have been capable of achieving orbit, but because the Navy was in charge of satellites, the nose cone was filled with sand.

CASTING BLAME

To Eisenhower and one faction of his allies, *Sputnik* was noise signifying nothing. The President said, "We never considered ourselves to be in a race." The White House adviser Sherman Adams declared that the United States had no interest in "an outer-space basketball game." In *The New Republic* Richard Strout dryly saw a parallel to Ike's above-the-fray re-election campaign of 1956: "Mr. Eisenhower appeared prepared to treat the satellite as though it were Adlai Stevenson."

But some politicians took to bad-mouthing one another. A few Republicans, including Ike's Vice President, Richard M. Nixon, blamed Harry S. Truman, by then nearly five years out of office. Truman responded by writing a long article blaming Eisenhower and lamenting this "sorry chapter in the story of our defense." Distributed by the North American Newspaper Alliance, the article made its way to the front page of *The New York Times*. Evoking the memory of the "atomic spy couple," Julius and Ethel Rosenberg, *U.S. News & World Report* suggested that skulduggery explained the Soviet feat: "Did Russia Steal Satellite Secret from U.S.?"

Others faulted progressive educators, who, the critics claimed, had concentrated on children's feelings to the detriment of hard knowledge. *Life* devoted five issues to the "Crisis in Education," arguing in one article that the spartan Soviet system was producing students better equipped to cope with the Space Age. *Why Johnny Can't Read* rocketed up the bestseller lists. In an October 31 news conference, Eisenhower, while remaining unruffled by *Sputnik*'s military implications, declared himself "shocked" to learn the magnitude of the nation's education shortcomings. The following year he backed the National Defense Education Act, which funded laboratories and textbooks in public schools as well as loans for college-bound students—the federal government's first major steps into education. Like interstate highways, schooling had become a matter of national defense, endorsed by both the Republican White House and the Democratic-controlled Congress. The former Harvard president James Bryant Conant urged parents to tell children, "For your own sake and for the sake of the nation, do your homework."

Still others contended that the Soviets' lead in space reflected a deteriorating American spirit. Peace and prosperity, according to this line of argument, had produced an indolent self-satisfaction. "Our goal has become a life of amiable sloth," wrote the journalist Thomas Griffith. To the sharp-tongued playwright and Republican loyalist Clare Boothe Luce, *Sputnik*'s beeps represented "an intercontinental outer-space raspberry" aimed at American pretensions of superiority. *Sputnik*, then, might serve as a warning shot that would force "bland, gray-suited" America to contemplate national interest instead of self-interest. "We needed *Sputnik*," Adlai Stevenson said, calling the satellite "sure proof that God has not despaired of us."

Vice President Nixon recognized that the White House efforts to shrug off *Sputnik* were failing miserably. He deemed Adams's basketball remark "wrong in substance and disastrous in terms of public opinion." In a San Francisco speech the Vice President staked out his own ground, saying that "we could make no greater mistake than to brush off this event as a scientific stunt of more significance to the man in the moon than to men on earth." Privately Nixon urged Eisenhower to say that money was no object in the contest of freedom against slavery. Ignoring the advice, Ike instead cautioned against any "hasty and extraordinary effort under the impetus of sudden fear."

INCREASE IN MILITARY BUDGET

Nixon wasn't the only Republican up in arms. In early November a panel of defense experts delivered its previously commissioned report to Ike's National Security Council. The work of such Establishment bulwarks as John McCloy and Paul Nitze, the report argued that the United States could be "critically vulnerable" to a missile attack by the end of 1959, with likely casualties of up to 50 percent. Even if the Soviets chose not to wage cataclysmic war, the report suggested, they could conquer space, maybe militarize the moon. The panel's bottom line: Continued American security required *major* increases in the military budget, to be achieved by deficit spending. Called the Gaither Report (after the group's chair, the Ford Foundation's head, H. Rowan Gaither, Jr.), the document was leaked to *The New York Times* and the *Washington Post*. In his magisterial memoir *Danger and Survival*, McGeorge Bundy writes that Ike came to feel he'd been hit by a "double barrelled shock"—*Sputnik* and Gaither.

But the worst blast came a few weeks later. Along with portraying the *Sputnik*s as meaningless, the administration had been telling reporters that the United States was about to launch a satellite of its own. The Navy was still in charge of the program, though von Braun and the Army were quietly at work too. The day after *Sputnik I*'s launch, von Braun had told Defense Secretary Neil McElroy that the Navy rocket "will never make it," whereas the Army rocketeers could launch a satellite in sixty days. McElroy took it under advisement. A month later, amid the aftershocks of *Sputnik II*, von Braun was told to get to work.

The Navy's Vanguard program was also on an accelerated countdown. The original schedule called for a dozen meticulous test runs, each one involving additional hardware and equipment. Not until number seven was a full-scale "earnest try" for orbit to be attempted. But with two *Sputnik*s in orbit, as *Newsweek* put it, "the Vanguard test rocket with its grapefruit-sized satellite suddenly became the U.S. answer to the Soviet challenge."

"DUDNIK"

For four excruciating days beginning on December 2, the formerly sleepy (and off-limits) Cape Canaveral test site on Florida's Atlantic coast became media central. The Vanguard launch team sweated through a series of postponements that Navy spokesmen attributed to, at one time or another, "balky" guidance systems, "minor electrical troubles," and "sticky LOX" (liquid oxygen) valves. One countdown was aborted because of the "weariness of overworked technicians." Because this was nominally IGY "science," reporters received extraordinary cooperation: two Air Force flatbed trailers for photographers, schedules of launch times, viewing points on the beach outside the Cape gates.

Finally, at 11:45 A.M. on December 6, a rocket propulsion engineer flipped the firing toggle. As television recorded the scene, Vanguard's first-stage rocket roared, spewed flame and smoke, rose four feet—and fell back onto the steel launching pad and tumbled to the ground, exploding in a spectacular fireball. The satellite cargo, thrown clear, was damaged but still beeping. For Eisenhower, recovering from a late November stroke, the news couldn't get much worse. Headline writers around the world outdid each other: "Flopnik," "Stay-putnik," "Dudnik." A Russian delegate to the United Nations asked his American colleagues if they would be interested in applying for aid "under the Soviet program of technical assistance to backward nations."

Ike, his popularity plummeting (it had gone from almost 80 percent in late 1956 to just 50 percent in late 1957), bent a bit. His post-*Sputnik* budget increased military expenditures, a rise that mandated, in Eisenhower's words, "at least a token reduction in the 'butter' side of government," so spending on urban development and hospitals was cut. Still, the parsimonious President had little use for space exploration. "Look," he told his cabinet, "I'd like to know what's on the other side of the moon, but I won't pay to find out this year." Even so, he signed legislation creating NASA in 1958.

Through it all, though, while Ike bent, he never broke. He remained mostly, and bafflingly, unflappable in the eyes of many Americans. He had his reasons. He knew that *Sputnik* actually represented some good news. While it showed that the Soviets were ahead in rocketry thrust, it also showed that they were well behind in miniaturizing communications technology (the beeping *Sputnik I* weighed 184 pounds). Moreover, *Sputnik* settled practically a lingering question of international law: How high does a nation's airspace reach? That issue would have considerable bearing on the spy satellites then under development, a space venture that *did* interest Eisenhower. "The Russians," Assistant Defense Secretary Donald Quarles told the president, "have in fact done us a good turn, unintentionally, in establishing the concept of freedom of international space."

SECRET DEFENSE INFORMATION

Most important, Ike knew that the Russians were behind the United States militarily—so far behind on warhead production and ICBM development that a surprise attack on the United States would be suicidal. Since 1956 Ike had been seeing photographs taken by supersecret U-2 spy planes. These photos revealed the Soviet disadvantage in ICBMs and tellingly, they didn't show any preparations for a first strike. "We can still destroy Russia," Eisenhower told his cabinet. "We know it."

But the U-2 information was top secret. The Gaither Report authors didn't know about it. Neither did a thirty-four-year-old Harvard professor named Henry Kissinger, author of a sky-is-falling report for the Rockefeller Brothers Fund that was heavily publicized in early 1958, as brother Nelson positioned himself for 1960 presidential politics (when Nelson appeared on "Today" on NBC, Dave Garroway offered to send a free copy of the report to anyone who requested it. More than two hundred thousand people asked). Ike couldn't reveal the U-2 flights without disclosing American violations of Soviet airspace; at the altitudes at which the U-2s were flying, international law was very clear. This could jeopardize his attempts to achieve accommodation with Khrushchev over such flash points as Berlin and nuclear testing. (It later turned out that the Soviets already knew of the U-2 overflights but didn't have the missiles to shoot them down—yet.) Ike also didn't want to push the Soviets to escalate their military spending, as any revelation of American superiority would likely do. So mostly he tried to persuade the public to trust him on the basis of his own military record.

Historians tend to give Eisenhower high marks for *Sputnik.* In Stephen Ambrose's view, Ike's calm response to the Soviet satellite was "one of his finest hours," saving his country countless billions of dollars. In his book *Grand Expectations,* James Patterson agrees, noting that Ike presided over major gains in the U.S. nuclear capacity and did so quietly enough to allay Soviet fears.

Historians, though, do fault Ike for failing to grasp the public relations implications of *Sputnik.* The National Security Council recommended a greater emphasis on space-related projects "which, while having scientific or military value, are designed to achieve a favorable worldwide psychological impact," but Eisenhower responded coolly. As he later said, "I don't believe in spectaculars." When von Braun's Army team successfully launched the first American satellite (which weighed just thirty-one pounds) on January 31, 1958, Eisenhower downplayed what others were portraying as a great American triumph. Ike instructed his aides, "Let's not make too great a hullabaloo over this."

MISSILE GAP

History's verdict on Ike came slowly. Even after the U-2 flights became known, the Alsop brothers, columnists Joseph and Stewart, argued that because the photography was limited, it was not all that trustworthy. U-2 spy photography, they said, was confined to major Soviet railroad lines that would service ICBM launch complexes and thus skipped large parts of the Soviet land expanse. Later, by the time John Kennedy was in the Oval Office—

propelled to some extent by all the talk of the space and missile gaps—U.S. spy satellites covered all of the Soviet Union. These photos, in the summer of 1961, confirmed that there was indeed a missile gap all along—in America's favor. McBundy, a key player in the Kennedy White House, recalls the Soviet missile threat being steadily de-escalated from hundreds of ICBMs during the late 1950s to around thirty-five by the mid-1960s. The Alsops eventually confessed their error.

Such was the self-defeating effect of Soviet secrecy: In the absence of facts about Russian ICBMs, many Americans responded out of fear. By the late 1960s the American nuclear triad ensured invulnerability, reliability, and massive retaliatory capacity. By the 1990s the Communist state had collapsed, amid evidence that the Soviets had spent themselves into poverty trying to keep up in all the various races.

1960–1969

CHAPTER 3

THE DEATH OF PATRICE LUMUMBA: THE COLD WAR INVADES AFRICA

MADELAINE G. KALB

Throughout the Cold War era, the United States and the Soviet Union aggressively competed to spread their influence throughout the world and to "protect" nations from each other's influence. The Soviet Union invaded Eastern European nations. The United States trained foreign armies. Both countries overtly and covertly interfered in the struggles of developing nations that were teetering between communism and democracy.

Belgian Congo, the central African nation later renamed Zaire and more recently the Democratic Republic of Congo, was on that cusp in 1960. The nation had been a Belgian colony since the late nineteenth century. In 1960, citizens' rebellion forced Belgium to grant the nation independence. Nationalist leader Patrice Lumumba became its first prime minister. U.S. leaders who felt that Lumumba leaned toward communism preferred to see Joseph Mobutu, commander in chief of the Congolese army, as the emerging mineral-rich nation's leader. In September, with covert U.S. support, Mobutu seized power. His rival, Patrice Lumumba, was arrested and later murdered.

In the following article, *New York Times* reporter Madelaine G. Kalb discusses the U.S. role in Lumumba's death.

Reprinted, with permission, from "The CIA and Lumumba," by Madelaine G. Kalb, *The New York Times Magazine*, August 2, 1981. Copyright © 1981 Madelaine G. Kalb. Distributed by The New York Times Special Features/Syndication Sales.

On Sept. 19, 1960, the Central Intelligence Agency's station chief in Leopoldville, capital of the newly independent Congo, received a message through a top-secret channel from his superiors in Washington. Someone from headquarters calling himself "Joe from Paris" would be arriving with instructions for an urgent mission. No further details were provided. The station chief was cautioned not to discuss the message with anyone.

"Joe" arrived a week later. He proved to be the C.I.A.'s top scientist, and he came equipped with a kit containing an exotic poison designed to produce a fatal disease indigenous to the area. This lethal substance, he informed the station chief, was meant for Patrice Lumumba, the recently ousted pro-Soviet Prime Minister of the Congo, who had a good chance of returning to power.

The poison, the scientist said, was somehow to be slipped into Lumumba's food, or perhaps into his toothpaste. Poison was not the only acceptable method; any form of assassination would do, so long as it could not be traced back to the United States Government. Pointing out that assassination was not exactly a common C.I.A. tactic, the station chief asked who had authorized the assignment. The scientist indicated that the order had come from the "highest authority"—from Dwight D. Eisenhower, President of the United States. . . .

American Policy Out of Control

The plot against Lumumba is a classic example of American policy out of control—an assassination attempt launched by the C.I.A. without any known record of a Presidential order, merely on the assumption, which may or may not have been correct, that this was what the President wanted. The story of the plot, largely buried in the voluminous report of the Church committee, and now amplified by many hitherto classified cables, merits a searching examination before the safeguards now in effect are discarded as no longer necessary.

On July 27, 1960, Washington was host to an unusual visitor. Nowadays, with some 50 independent African states active on the world stage, it is routine for an African Prime Minister to call on an American Secretary of State, but two decades ago the arrival of the leader of a brand-new African republic was a novel and intriguing event—particularly when the Prime Minister was as controversial as this one.

Tall, thin, intense, his eyes flashing behind his spectacles, Patrice Lumumba was a spellbinding orator who had created a nationalist party and had led it to victory in the Congo's first election. Even before the former Belgian Congo became independent on June 30, 1960, he had figured in the C.I.A.'s reports as a radical who had accepted money from the Belgian Communist Party, appointed a leftist Cabinet and hinted that he might accept Soviet offers of financial aid. But there was no sense of urgency in Washington until two weeks after independence, when Belgian troops moved in to quell a Congolese mutiny against Belgian officers still holding their army posts and Lumumba appealed to the Soviet Union for military assistance against Belgian "imperialist aggression."

To Allen W. Dulles, Director of Central Intelligence and brother of Secretary of State John Foster Dulles, who had died in office the previous year, this was enough to make Lumumba "a Castro, or worse." At a meeting of the National Security Council on July 21, Allen Dulles described Lumumba's background as "harrowing." "It is safe," he said, "to go on the assumption that Lumumba has been bought by the Communists; this also, however, fits with his own orientation."

At the State Department, on the other hand, top officials were not convinced that Lumumba was a Communist and thought it might be possible to exert a moderating influence on him. When he came to New York for a meeting with United Nations Secretary General Dag Hammarskjold, they invited him to Washington. As Under Secretary of State Douglas Dillon was to testify before the Church committee 15 years later, "We hoped to see him and see what we could do to come to a better understanding with him."

Both for Lumumba and the United States, it was a decisive encounter. The new Secretary of State, Christian Herter, received him, and spent a frustrating half-hour trying to persuade him to rely exclusively on the United Nations and refrain from calling on outside powers for assistance. His arguments fell on deaf ears. Dillon, who was present at the meeting, testified that Lumumba had struck him and Herter as an "irrational, almost psychotic personality." "The impression that was left," Dillon said, "was . . . very bad, that this was an individual whom it was impossible to deal with. And the feelings of the Government as a result of this sharpened very considerably at that time."

On Aug. 1, Eisenhower presided at a National Security Council meeting at the Summer White House in Newport, R.I. The chief topic of discussion was the Congo. The Joint Chiefs were concerned about the possibility of Belgium's bases in the Congo falling into Soviet hands. The council decided that the United States should be prepared "at any time to take appropriate military action to prevent or defeat Soviet military intervention in the Congo."

QUESTION OF ASSASSINATION

It was at about this time, according to Dillon, that the possibility of assassinating Lumumba came up. The idea was broached at a Pentagon meeting he attended, along with representatives of the Defense Department, the Joint Chiefs of Staff and the C.I.A. As Dillon was to testify, "a question regarding the possibility of an assassination attempt against Lumumba was briefly raised," only to be "turned off by the C.I.A." The C.I.A. people present seemed reluctant to discuss the subject—not, Dillon believed, for any "moral" reason but because they either regarded the notion as unfeasible or thought the group was "too large for such a sensitive discussion." While this conference, in his opinion, "could not have served as authorization for an actual assassination effort against Lumumba," the C.I.A. officials "could have decided they wanted to develop the capability . . . just by knowing the concern that everyone had about Lumumba."

By the middle of August, the American strategy of using the United Nations to prevent Lumumba from turning to the Soviet Union was in trouble. Lumumba had broken relations with the Secretary General, claiming that Hammarskjold had yielded to Western pressure in refusing to suppress the Belgian-backed secession of mineral-rich Katanga Province, and he was threatening to expel the United Nations peacekeeping force. From Leopoldville, the C.I.A. station chief, Lawrence Devlin, summed up the situation in alarming terms:

"Embassy and station believe Congo experiencing classic Communist effort take over government. Many forces at work here: Soviets . . . Communist party, etc. Although difficult determine major influencing factors to predict outcome struggle for power, decisive period not far off. Whether or not Lumumba actually Commie or just playing Commie game to assist his solidifying power, anti-West forces rapidly increasing power Congo and there may be little time left in which take action avoid another Cuba."

To counter this threat, Devlin proposed an operation aimed at "replacing Lumumba with pro-Western group." Bronson Tweedy, head of the African division of the C.I.A.'s clandestine services, replied that he was seeking State Department approval.

The same day, C.I.A. and State Department officials raised the Congo issue with President Eisenhower at a meeting of the National Security Council. According to the minutes of the meeting, Dillon said it was essential to prevent Lumumba from forcing the United Nations contingent out of the Congo: "The elimination of the U.N. would be a disaster which, Secretary Dillon stated, we should do everything we could to prevent. If the U.N. were forced out, we might be faced by a situation where the Soviets intervened by invitation of the Congo." Dillon said Lumumba was serving the Soviet Union's purposes; Dulles said Lumumba was in Soviet pay.

UNITED NATIONS MUST NOT BE FORCED OUT

Eisenhower's reaction, the minutes made clear, was a forceful one:

"The President said that the possibility the U.N. would be forced out was simply inconceivable. We should keep the U.N. in the Congo even if we had to ask for European troops to do it. We should do so even if such action was used by the Soviets as the basis for starting a fight."

Dillon commented that that was how the State Department saw it, but that Hammarskjold and Henry Cabot Lodge, the American Ambassador to the United Nations, doubted the world body could keep its force in the Congo if the Congo put up determined opposition to its presence.

"In response, the President stated that Mr. Lodge was wrong to this extent—we were talking of one man forcing us out of the Congo; of Lumumba supported by the Soviets. There was no indication, the President stated, that the Congolese did not want U.N. support and the maintenance of order. Secretary Dillon reiterated that this was State's feeling about the matter. The situation that would be created by a U.N. withdrawal was altogether too ghastly to contemplate.". . .

Among those present at the meeting was a middle-level official, Robert H. Johnson, a member of the National Security Council staff, and in 1975 he testified before the Church committee as follows:

"At some time during that discussion, President Eisenhower said something—I can no longer remember his words—that came across to me as an order for the assassination of Lumumba. . . . There was no discussion; the meeting simply moved on. I remember my sense of that moment quite clearly because the President's statement came as a great shock to me."

Johnson added that "in thinking about the incident more recently" he had "had some doubts" about the accuracy of his impression; it was possible that what he had heard was an order for "political action" against Lumumba. Yet on further reflection, he said, he went back to feeling that his initial impression was correct. The minutes of the meeting did not contain any such assassination order, but that did not prove anything one way or the other, in Johnson's view. Under the procedures then in effect, he explained, a Presidential order of such a nature would either have been omitted from the minutes or "handled through some kind of euphemism."

Lumumba: Dangerous to the World?

The testimony of the other participants in the meeting was less dramatic. Marion Boggs, the council's acting executive secretary, could not remember hearing the President say anything that "could be interpreted as favoring action by the United States to bring about the assassination of Lumumba." Dillon said he did not recall a "clear-cut order" by Eisenhower for the assassination of Lumumba, but the circumstances themselves, he added, were ambiguous:

"It could have been—in view of this feeling of everybody that Lumumba was [a] very difficult if not impossible person to deal with, and was dangerous to the peace and safety of the world— that the President expressed himself, 'We will have to do whatever is necessary to get rid of him.' I don't know that I would have taken that as a clear-cut order, as Mr. Johnson apparently did. And I think perhaps others present may have interpreted it in other ways."

For instance, he said, it would be "perfectly plausible" to assume that Dulles would have taken such Presidential language as "implicit authorization" to proceed with an assassination plan. "[Dulles] felt very strongly that we should not involve the President directly in things of this nature," Dillon said. "And he was perfectly willing to take the responsibility personally."

In any case, the next recorded step was a cable sent to Devlin in Leopoldville the following day by Richard Bissell, the C.I.A.'s Deputy Director for Plans. Bissell, who was in charge of covert operations, authorized the station chief to proceed with his scheme for replacing Lumumba with a pro-Western group. Devlin, two days later, reported discouraging news: Anti-Lumumba leaders had approached the President of the Congo, Joseph Kasavubu, with a "plan to assassinate Lumumba," but Kasavubu had refused, explaining that he was reluctant to resort to violence and that there was no other leader of "sufficient stature to replace Lumumba."

At the same time, the American Ambassador in Leopoldville, Clare Timberlake, reported that about 100 Soviet and Czechoslovak "technicians" had arrived in the Congo and that more were expected shortly. Lodge reported from New York that United Nations sources were "worried about arms from 'certain quarters' being imported through the [Leopoldville] airport under guise of food consignments." The American Embassy in Athens reported that the Soviet Government had asked permission for 10 Russian cargo planes carrying food to Leopoldville to overfly Greece or land for refueling. Meanwhile, emboldened by the prospect of Soviet military aid, Lumumba started to move his troops south, in preparation for an assault on secessionist Katanga.

As these reports arrived in Washington, there was a growing sense of alarm in the top echelons of the State Department and the White House. On Aug. 25, Gordon Gray, the President's special assistant for national security, attended a meeting of the Special Group, a subcommittee of the National Security Council responsible for the planning of covert operations. Gray listened with interest as a C.I.A. representative, Thomas Parrott, outlined a plan to work through certain Congolese labor groups and arrange a vote of no confidence in Lumumba in the Congolese Senate. As stated in the minutes of the meeting, Gray interjected that "his associates had expressed extremely strong feelings on the necessity for very straightforward action in this situation, and he wondered whether the plans as outlined were sufficient to accomplish this."

Purely political intrigue against Lumumba was not, apparently, what the White House had in mind. Both Gray and Parrott told the Church committee that Gray's reference to his "associates" was a euphemism for the President, a way of maintaining the convention of "plausible deniability"—the ability to deny at some later time that the President had had any knowledge of the matter under discussion. Dulles, according to the minutes of the Special Group meeting, replied that he had taken the associates' views seriously and had every intention of proceeding as vigorously as he could, but that he had to interpret such instructions "within the bounds of necessity and capability." It was agreed that "planning for the Congo would not necessarily rule out 'consideration' of any particular kind of activity which might contribute to getting rid of Lumumba."

None of the participants, in their subsequent testimony, remembered hearing assassination mentioned. But John N. Irwin II, Assistant Secretary of Defense, thought the reference to "getting rid of Lumumba" was broad enough to cover that option. Dillon, who had not been at the meeting, said the minutes indicated that "assassination was within bounds." Bissell was even more specific:

"When you use the language that no particular means were ruled out, that is obviously what it meant, and it meant that to everybody in the room. . . . You don't use language of that kind except to mean, in effect, the Director is being told, get rid of the guy, and if you have to use extreme means up to and including assassination, go ahead."

In effect, Bissell testified, Dulles was being given a message by the President through Gray.

C.I.A. UNDER PRESSURE

The C.I.A. Director was obviously under pressure to produce results. The very next day he sent Devlin a cable stressing the view
"in high quarters here" that Lumumba's "removal must be an urgent and prime objective." He gave Devlin still "wider authority" to replace Lumumba with a pro-Western group, "including
even more aggressive action if it can remain covert," and authorized expenditure of up to $100,000 "to carry out any crash pro-
grams on which you do not have the opportunity to consult
headquarters."

The implications of this "wider authority" were spelled out by
Bissell to Tweedy, the chief of his African division. Tweedy described their conversation as follows: "What Mr. Bissell was saying to me was that there was agreement, policy agreement, in
Washington that Lumumba must be removed from the position
of control and influence in the Congo . . . and that among the possibilities of that elimination was indeed assassination."

It was now that the C.I.A.'s top scientist was brought into play.
His name was Sidney Gottlieb, he was Bissell's Special Assistant
for Scientific Matters, and he was asked by his superior to prepare biological materials and have them ready on short notice for
possible use in the assassination of an unspecified African leader,
"in case the decision was to go ahead." According to Gottlieb's
testimony, Bissell told him he "had direction from the highest authority . . . for getting into that kind of operation"; Gottlieb assumed he was referring to the President.

The scientist checked with the Army Chemical Corps at Fort
Detrick, Md., on substances that would "either kill the individual or incapacitate him so severely that he would be out of action," and he chose one that "was supposed to produce a disease
that was . . . indigenous to that area [of Africa] and that could be
fatal." He also assembled some "accessory materials," such as
hypodermic needles, rubber gloves and gauze masks. At about
that time, he was told that the African leader in question was Lumumba, that it had been decided to go ahead, and that he was to
take his deadly package to Leopoldville.

By the time he arrived there in September, the situation in the
Congo had changed. Disgusted by Lumumba's disastrous military campaign, which had degenerated into a massacre of more
than 1,000 civilians, and alarmed by his use of Soviet planes,
trucks, weapons and military advisers, President Kasavubu had
dismissed the Prime Minister. When Lumumba persuaded Parliament to reverse the dismissal, the Americans and their allies
persuaded a young colonel named Joseph Mobutu, the No. 2
man in the army, to take control. (Mobutu [later became] Presi-

dent Mobutu Sese Seko of Zaire, as the Congo was renamed in 1971.) Colonel Mobutu promptly ousted all the politicians and expelled the Soviet and Czechoslovak diplomats, along with the military advisers and their equipment. Yet Devlin in his cables put little stock in the stability of the new regime. He feared that the situation could be reversed at any moment, with Lumumba returning to power and inviting the Russians back in.

"Only solution," he concluded, "is to remove him from scene soonest." Dulles agreed. He told Eisenhower on Sept. 21 that the "danger of Soviet influence" was still present in the Congo and that Lumumba "remained a grave danger as long as he was not disposed of."

Five days later, Gottlieb ("Joe from Paris") arrived in Leopoldville with his poison kit. Ironically, the C.I.A. took its first concrete step toward the assassination of Lumumba three weeks after he was removed as Prime Minister, 12 days after Mobutu seized power and nine days after the expulsion of the Soviet diplomats and military advisers, whose arrival in Leopoldville had caused the panic in Washington and had set the assassination plot in motion.

OBJECTIONS TO ASSASSINATION

When Gottlieb reported to Devlin on his mission, the station chief, according to his later testimony, had an "emotional reaction of great surprise." As he put it:

"I looked upon the Agency as an executive arm of the Presidency. . . .Therefore, I suppose I thought that it was an order issued in due form from an authorized authority. On the other hand, I looked at it as a kind of operation that I could do without, that I thought that probably the Agency and the U.S. government could get along without.

> I didn't regard Lumumba as the kind of person who was going to bring on World War III. I might have had a somewhat different attitude if I thought that one man could bring on World War III and result in the deaths of millions of people or something, but I didn't see him in that light. I saw him as a danger to the political position of the United States in Africa, but nothing more than that.

Devlin also had practical objections to the assassination plot: "I looked on it as a pretty wild scheme professionally. . . . I explored it, but I doubt that I ever really expected to carry it out." Yet, like a good bureaucrat, he seems to have kept these doubts to himself, for he told headquarters that he and Gottlieb were on the "same wavelength," and he recommended a number of exploratory steps, such as infiltrating Lumumba's entourage. If headquarters approved, he would instruct one of his agents to "take refuge with Big Brother" (Lumumba) and "brush up details to razor edge." Headquarters told him to go ahead.

Over the next two months, Devlin sent a steady stream of progress reports to Washington through a top-secret channel set up for the assassination project. But, although he emphasized the need for haste, he apparently still had reservations about the scheme, for he kept stalling about putting it into effect. Finally, on Oct. 5, Gottlieb left Leopoldville, later recalling that he dumped the poison in the Congo River before his departure because it was "not refrigerated and unstable" and was probably no longer sufficiently "reliable."

By mid-October, headquarters was impatient. Tweedy asked Devlin what he thought of the idea of sending a senior C.I.A. officer to Leopoldville to concentrate on the assassination project, in view of the demands placed on Devlin by his other commitments. Tweedy also suggested using a "commando type group" to abduct Lumumba from the residence where he was under the protection of United Nations troops. Devlin thought that sending another man was an "excellent idea." As for alternative ways of disposing of Lumumba, he recommended that a "high-powered foreign-make rifle with telescopic scope and silencer" be sent to him by diplomatic pouch. "Hunting good here," he cabled cryptically, "when lights right."

The senior case officer selected for the task of getting the assassination project unstuck had his own reservations about the idea. The official, Justin O'Donnell, testified before the Church committee that he was called in by Bissell in mid-October and was asked to proceed to the Congo to "eliminate Lumumba." "I told him that I would absolutely not have any part of killing Lumumba," he said. However, O'Donnell was willing to go to Leopoldville and try to "neutralize" Lumumba "as a political factor." As he explained in his testimony, "I wanted . . . to get him out, to trick him out, if I could, and then turn him over . . . to the legal authorities and let him stand trial." He had "no compunction" about handing Lumumba over for trial by a "jury of his peers," although he realized there was a "very, very high probability" that he would be sentenced to death.

O'Donnell arrived in Leopoldville on Nov. 3. But he never had a chance to implement his plan to lure Lumumba out. Lumumba slipped away of his own accord on Nov. 27, after a United Nations vote to seat Kasavubu's delegation rather than his own. Fearing that he would lose the protection of the United Nations force, Lumumba headed for his own stronghold of Stanleyville, 1,000 miles to the east. He was arrested on the way by Colonel Mobutu's soldiers and was imprisoned in Thysville, 90 miles from Leopoldville.

On Jan. 13, 1961, the Thysville garrison mutinied, demanding higher pay and threatening to put Lumumba back in power. Devlin sent an alarming cable to Washington: "Station and embassy believe present government may fall within few days. Result would almost certainly be chaos and return [of Lumumba] to power." He added: "Refusal to take drastic steps at this time will lead to defeat of [U.S.] policy in Congo."

The next day, Devlin was informed that Mobutu was going to transfer Lumumba to a prison in a safer place. Three days later, Lumumba was flown to the province of Katanga, domain of his archenemy, the provincial leader Moise Tshombe. As he stumbled off the plane in the provincial capital of Elisabethville, blindfolded, his hands bound behind his back, he was kicked and beaten by Katangan soldiers, thrown into a jeep and driven off.

For the next few weeks, Lumumba's whereabouts were a matter of confusion and uncertainty. Two days after he was flown to Katanga, the C.I.A. station in Elisabethville cabled headquarters: "Thanks for Patrice. If we had known he was coming we would have baked a snake." On Feb. 13, the Katangan authorities announced that he had escaped; three days later they said he had been captured and killed by Congolese tribesmen. No one believed them. A United Nations investigation, while failing to establish the exact circumstances of Lumumba's death, concluded that he had been murdered by Katangan officials and Belgian mercenaries on the night of Jan. 17, immediately after his arrival in Elisabethville, with Tshombe's personal participation or approval.

WHAT ROLES DID U.S. PRESIDENT AND C.I.A. PLAY?

What was the role of the C.I.A. in Lumumba's death? What was the role of President Eisenhower?

The C.I.A. has stated that it had no hand in Lumumba's murder. But a review of the evidence suggests that over a period of four months American officials at the Embassy and the C.I.A. station in Leopoldville encouraged Lumumba's Congolese opponents to eliminate him before he turned the tables on them and invited the Russians back to the Congo. These officials were following a policy that had been set the previous summer, when Allen Dulles compared Lumumba to Fidel Castro and President Eisenhower agreed he was a threat to world peace. They were to get rid of Lumumba one way or another. If murder ordered by the United States Government and carried out by a C.I.A.-hired assassin was acceptable, then murder carried out by Lumumba's Congolese opponents, with the help of Belgian mercenaries, was not going to offend anyone's sensibilities.

As for the second question—did President Eisenhower actually order Lumumba's assassination?—there has been considerable controversy. Robert Johnson thought he did—implicitly. Douglas Dillon was not so sure. Several officials on President Eisenhower's staff denied knowledge of any Presidential consideration of assassination during their tenure. The Church committee found "reasonable inference" that the plot against Lumumba had been authorized by Eisenhower, though, because of the ambiguity of the evidence, it did not reach a conclusive finding to that effect.

But the people in charge of "dirty tricks," such as assassinations—from Allen Dulles right on down to Richard Bissell, Bronson Tweedy, the scientist who supplied the poison and the resourceful station chief who was certain there was a better way to dispose of Lumumba (and turned out to be right)—these people had no doubt they were acting on Presidential orders.

THE IMPACT OF THE COLD WAR ON ASIA

PATRICK G. MARSHALL

The actions and policies of the world's post–World War II superpowers—the United States and the Soviet Union—affected many countries not directly involved in the Cold War. Each power was determined to win as many countries as possible to its side, or at least, to keep countries out of the opposing power's camp. The superpowers did this overtly—by sending military forces and economic aid to countries they were wooing—and covertly—by secretly training the target country's armed forces and providing secret military or other aid.

The countries of Asia were major targets for the superpowers, who carried on various campaigns in Korea, Vietnam, Taiwan, Japan, and other countries. The following article, excerpted from an official congressional publication on foreign affairs, provides an overview of the superpowers' Cold War impact on Asia.

The beginnings of the Cold War between the Soviet Union and the United States had immediate and violent implications for the countries of Asia. Nowhere was the disruption greater than in Korea. Occupied by Japan before and during World War II, Korea at war's end was occupied by the Soviet Union in the North and U.S. forces in the South. The Soviets blocked Korean efforts at reunifying the country, and in 1948 the Democratic People's Republic of Korea, or North Korea, was officially formed under Kim Il Sung, who still holds power. The South responded by forming the Republic of Korea, with Syngman Rhee as president.

From "Superpower Battleground," by Patrick G. Marshall, *CQ Researcher*, November 27, 1992. Reprinted with permission from *CQ Researcher*.

On June 25, 1950, North Korea, armed primarily by the Soviet Union, invaded the South. With the backing of the U.N. Security Council, U.S. troops counterattacked and by the end of October had driven North Korean troops back almost to the Chinese border. At that point, China sent its troops across the Yalu River to support the North Koreans, eventually forcing a stalemate in the war with the country divided along its present border.

The conflict did have one beneficial side effect, particularly for South Korea: The dollars spent by the large U.S. military contingent that stayed behind helped to energize South Korea's economy—as did generous aid from America and preferential access to U.S. markets.

In the 40 years since the Korean War, South Korea has become one of the world's leading industrialized nations. North Korea, on the other hand, is one of the world's poorest countries, despite having a generous assortment of natural resources.

Both countries have devoted an inordinately large portion of their resources to defense. South Korea regularly spends 4–6 percent of its gross national product (GNP) on its military. North Korea spends at least 10 percent of its meager resources on defense. Some experts believe North Korea spends as much as 15–20 percent of its GNP on the military.

DISAGREEMENTS OVER TAIWAN

Korea was not the only site of superpower tensions in Northeast Asia in the years following World War II. The island of Taiwan, off the Chinese mainland, was one of the main sources of friction between the United States and China.

Ruled by Japan from 1895 until 1945, Taiwan was taken over by Chinese Nationalists in 1949. Led by Chiang Kai Shek, the Nationalists fled to the island after losing control of mainland China to the Communists. Both the Nationalist government on Taiwan and the Communist government on the mainland claimed to be the legitimate rulers of all of China. The United States backed the claim of the Nationalists.

When Chinese troops entered the Korean War in October 1950, the United States immediately sent the U.S. 7th Fleet to the Formosa Strait to protect Taiwan from an expected Chinese invasion. As it turned out, China did not press the Taiwan issue until after the Korean War ended.

In September 1954, the government in Beijing announced it was going to reclaim its territory from the Nationalists. In early 1955, the Communists pushed Nationalist forces—evacuated by the U.S. Navy—from two small island groups just off the coast of China. Over the next three years, the Communists repeatedly attacked the U.S.-armed Nationalists on two of the islands—Quemoy and Matsu.

While the Soviet Union did not get directly involved in this conflict, it did promise to use Soviet nuclear weapons against the United States if U.S. nuclear weapons were used against China, a move that was under active consideration by the Eisenhower administration. As a result of a firm U.S. statement in support of the Nationalists—backed up by a large buildup of U.S. naval forces—this U.S.-Soviet missile crisis ended in a standoff.

How Japan Benefited

The country of Northeast Asia that was least affected by the Cold War was, ironically, Japan. Following World War II, the former colonizer of Korea and Manchuria was occupied by a more benevolent power—the United States. Instead of punishing Japan, the Truman and Eisenhower administrations saw Japan as a potential bulwark against Soviet and Chinese encroachment and, as a result, the Americans sought to rebuild the Japanese economy.

The strategic importance of Japan became clearer with the outbreak of the Korean War. Japan—only 80 miles across the water from the southern coast of Korea—served as an excellent staging area for U.S. forces during the war.

Japan benefited from the conflict in two important ways: First, American spending on the war helped boost Japan's economy. Secondly, and more important over the long run, the United States relieved Japan of the need to provide for its own defense.

For the next several decades, Japan was able to focus on economic development and trade, aided both by concessionary access to U.S. markets and by American protection allowing Japan to divert only a fraction of its resources to defense. Indeed, under the new constitution written for Japan by the United States, Japan was forbidden to undertake military expeditions and was limited to spending no more than 1 percent of its gross national product on defense.

China's Role

China is the giant that ties Northern and Southern Asia together. And for most U.S. policymakers of the Cold War era, China was the political as well as the geographical center of the Far East.

"After the Korean War, the United States began to construct its overall strategy in the western Pacific around the containment of China," notes Harry Harding, a China specialist at the Brookings Institution. "Policy Planners in Washington regarded China's invasion of Tibet in 1950, its support for the Communist revolution in Vietnam, its involvement in the Korean conflict and its ties with revolutionary Communist parties in Southeast Asia as evidence enough that Peking's ultimate goal was the Communist seizure of power across Asia."

The initial U.S. response to this perceived threat was a series of mutual defense treaties. "Although some of these alliances were formally justified as efforts to deter the re-emergence of a military threat from Japan," Harding writes, "their real objective was to contain the expansion of Chinese influence in Asia."

Besides committing itself to protecting Taiwan, the United States signed defense agreements with Japan, South Korea, the Philippines and Thailand. The United States also tried in 1954 to create a Southeast Asian version of NATO—the Southeast Asian Treaty Organization (SEATO). But despite its name, the organization included only two countries in Southeast Asia—Thailand and the Philippines. SEATO never achieved the coherence of NATO, and the alliance was essentially abandoned in 1974.

During the Cold War period, relations between the United States and China often were determined by the wider conflict between the U.S. and the Soviet Union. In fact, for most of the 40 years following World War II, the United States continually sought to play the Chinese off against the Soviets.

Fears of Soviet expansionism and concerns about the continuing war in Vietnam—where U.S. troops were battling Soviet- and Chinese-supplied North Vietnamese—led President Richard M. Nixon to recognize China's Communist government in 1972, a move the United States had resisted since 1949. Nixon hoped Chinese pressure would force the North Vietnamese to the bargaining table, where some accommodation could be reached. The Nixon administration also felt closer U.S.- China ties would force the Soviet Union to pay more attention to its own borders and less attention to such places as Cuba, Angola and Vietnam.

China had its own reasons for responding to Nixon's overtures. With Soviet forces arrayed across the Sino-Soviet border, the Chinese were at least as interested as the Americans in containing Soviet power. And just as the United States sought Chinese cooperation on the issue of Vietnam, the Chinese sought U.S. cooperation on the issue of Taiwan. China's leaders also wanted access to U.S. markets and technology.

At first, it looked like both the United States and China might get what they wanted. By 1975, the United States was able to end its involvement in the Vietnam War—though it is not clear how much the Chinese helped with the disengagement. For its part, China received a rather vague commitment from the United States on Taiwan. In a communiqué released in Shanghai at the end of President Nixon's 1972 visit to China, the United States indicated that it would "not challenge" the idea that Taiwan was part of China—a proposition even the Nationalist government of Taiwan accepted. The United States also indicated its intention to withdraw all American forces from Taiwan at some point in the future.

In late 1978, the United States finally broke off diplomatic relations with Taiwan and agreed to pull out its remaining military forces. The following year, Washington and the Communist government in Beijing exchanged ambassadors for the first time.

Loyalty and Idealism

John F. Kennedy

In 1960, in one of the narrowest victories in a U.S. presidential election, John F. Kennedy was elected the thirty-fifth president over future president Richard Nixon. At forty-three, Kennedy was the youngest man to be elected to this office, and the first Roman Catholic. The Harvard-educated scion of a wealthy family had served with distinction in the U.S. Navy during World War II and then entered politics, where he served in both the House of Representatives and the Senate before running for president. Photogenic and charismatic, the young Democrat worked hard for labor reform, legal equality for minorities, and other liberal causes.

Kennedy was assassinated in November 1963 after only three years in office. His death was the first of four assassinations of U.S. leaders within only a few years. Malcolm X, one of the most outspoken and influential black separatist leaders, was shot in 1965. Martin Luther King Jr., the civil rights leader whose oratory and pacifist example were instrumental in achieving black civil rights, was assassinated in April 1968, and Kennedy's brother and attorney general, Robert Kennedy, himself a presidential candidate and vigorous upholder of civil rights laws, was assassinated only two months later. The nation reeled after each assassination, hardly believing such violence could occur in America.

Kennedy's 1961 inaugural address restates America's strong commitment to aiding countries being wooed or coerced by communist nations. At the same time, Kennedy calls on Americans to serve their country unselfishly. His ringing words, "Ask not what your country can do for you—ask what you can do for your country," inspired a generation.

From John F. Kennedy's Inaugural Address, January 20, 1961, in *Public Papers of the Presidents of the United States: John F. Kennedy* (Washington, DC: Government Printing Office, 1962–1964).

We observe today not a victory of party but a celebration of freedom—symbolizing an end as well as a beginning—signifying renewal as well as change. For I have sworn before you and Almighty God the same solemn oath our forebears prescribed nearly a century and three quarters ago.

The world is very different now. For man holds in his mortal hands the power to abolish all forms of human poverty and all forms of human life. And yet the same revolutionary beliefs for which our forebears fought are still at issue around the globe— the belief that the rights of man come not from the generosity of the state but from the hand of God.

We dare not forget today that we are the heirs of that first revolution. Let the word go forth from this time and place, to friend and foe alike, that the torch has been passed to a new generation of Americans—born in this century, tempered by war, disciplined by a hard and bitter peace, proud of our ancient heritage—and unwilling to witness or permit the slow undoing of those human rights to which this nation has always been committed, and to which we are committed today at home and around the world.

WE WILL PRESERVE LIBERTY

Let every nation know, whether it wishes us well or ill, that we shall pay any price, bear any burden, meet any hardship, support any friend, oppose any foe to assure the survival and the success of liberty.

This much we pledge—and more.

To those old allies whose cultural and spiritual origins we share, we pledge the loyalty of faithful friends. United, there is little we cannot do in a host of cooperative ventures. Divided, there is little we can do—for we dare not meet a powerful challenge at odds and split asunder.

To those new states whom we welcome to the ranks of the free, we pledge our word that one form of colonial control shall not have passed away merely to be replaced by a far more iron tyranny. We shall not always expect to find them supporting our view. But we shall always hope to find them strongly supporting their own freedom—and to remember that, in the past, those who foolishly sought power by riding the back of the tiger ended up inside.

To those peoples in the huts and villages of half the globe struggling to break the bonds of mass misery, we pledge our best efforts to help them help themselves, for whatever period is required— not because the communists may be doing it, not because we seek their votes, but because it is right. If a free society cannot help the many who are poor, it cannot save the few who are rich.

WE WILL OPPOSE FOREIGN AGGRESSION

To our sister republics south of our border, we offer a special pledge—to convert our good words into good deeds—in a new alliance for progress—to assist free men and free governments in casting off the chains of poverty. But this peaceful revolution of hope cannot become the prey of hostile powers. Let all our neighbors know that we shall join with them to oppose aggression or subversion anywhere in the Americas. And let every other power know that this Hemisphere intends to remain the master of its own house.

To that world assembly of sovereign states, the United Nations, our last best hope in an age where the instruments of war have far outpaced the instruments of peace, we renew our pledge of support—to prevent it from becoming merely a forum for invective—to strengthen its shield of the new and the weak—and to enlarge the area in which its writ may run.

Finally, to those nations who would make themselves our adversary, we offer not a pledge but a request: that both sides begin anew the quest for peace, before the dark powers of destruction unleashed by science engulf all humanity in planned or accidental self-destruction.

We dare not tempt them with weakness. For only when our arms are sufficient beyond doubt can we be certain beyond doubt that they will never be employed.

But neither can two great and powerful groups of nations take comfort from our present course—both sides overburdened by the cost of modern weapons, both rightly alarmed by the steady spread of the deadly atom, yet both racing to alter that uncertain balance of terror that stays the hand of mankind's final war.

So let us begin anew—remembering on both sides that civility is not a sign of weakness, and sincerity is always subject to proof. Let us never negotiate out of fear. But let us never fear to negotiate.

LET BOTH SIDES UNITE

Let both sides explore what problems unite us instead of belaboring those problems which divide us.

Let both sides, for the first time, formulate serious and precise proposals for the inspection and control of arms—and bring the absolute power to destroy other nations under the absolute control of all nations.

Let both sides seek to invoke the wonders of science instead of its terrors. Together let us explore the stars, conquer the deserts, eradicate disease, tap the ocean depths and encourage the arts and commerce.

Let both sides unite to heed in all corners of the earth the command of Isaiah—to "undo the heavy burdens . . . (and) let the oppressed go free."

And if a beach-head of cooperation may push back the jungle of suspicion, let both sides join in creating a new endeavor, not a new balance of power, but a new world of law, where the strong are just and the weak secure and the peace preserved.

All this will not be finished in the first one hundred days. Nor will it be finished in the first one thousand days, nor in the life of this Administration, nor even perhaps in our lifetime on this planet. But let us begin.

Ask What You Can Do for Your Country

In your hands, my fellow citizens, more than mine, will rest the final success or failure of our course. Since this country was founded, each generation of Americans has been summoned to give testimony to its national loyalty. The graves of young Americans who answered the call to service surround the globe.

Now the trumpet summons us again—not as a call to bear arms, though arms we need—not as a call to battle, though embattled we are—but a call to bear the burden of a long twilight struggle, year in and year out, "rejoicing in hope, patient in tribulation"—a struggle against the common enemies of man: tyranny, poverty, disease and war itself.

Can we forge against these enemies a grand and global alliance, North and South, East and West, that can assure a more fruitful life for all mankind? Will you join in that historic effort?

In the long history of the world, only a few generations have been granted the role of defending freedom in its hour of maximum danger. I do not shrink from this responsibility—I welcome it. I do not believe that any of us would exchange places with any other people or any other generation. The energy, the faith, the devotion which we bring to this endeavor will light our country and all who serve it—and the glow from that fire can truly light the world.

And so, my fellow Americans: ask not what your country can do for you—ask what you can do for your country.

My fellow citizens of the world: ask not what America will do for you, but what together we can do for the freedom of man.

Finally, whether you are citizens of America or citizens of the world, ask of us here the same high standards of strength and sacrifice which we ask of you. With a good conscience our only sure reward, with history the final judge of our deeds, let us go forth to lead the land we love, asking His blessing and His help, but knowing that here on earth God's work must truly be our own.

CRISIS IN THE CARIBBEAN

JOHN F. KENNEDY

In October 1962, the specter of worldwide nuclear war seemed a reality. The Soviet Union began to build nuclear missile bases on the Caribbean island of Cuba and to import nuclear weapons to furnish those bases, and the United States refused to allow it.

From the early twentieth century until 1959, Cuba, only ninety miles south of Florida's coast, had been ruled by a series of dictators friendly to the United States. But in 1959, under the leadership of Fidel Castro, the Cuban people rose up, overthrowing the last dictator, Fulgencio Batista, and establishing Communist rule. The Soviet Union was quick to support the new island nation, providing several billion dollars of aid annually.

As the Cold War heated up, the Soviet Union thought it saw a way to keep the United States at bay: If it could establish nuclear weapons launching locations that were clearly a threat to the United States, it would gain a significant strategic advantage. But the U.S. government, under the leadership of its youngest-ever elected president, John F. Kennedy, determined to keep the Soviet Union out of the Western Hemisphere.

In a bold and dangerous move, Kennedy demanded that Soviet leader Nikita Khrushchev remove all missiles and bases from Cuba. Kennedy backed up his demand by sending warships to the Caribbean to prevent Soviet ships from entering those waters. The following speech is Kennedy's radio address to the American people, explaining the need for his actions and confirming the U.S. commitment to fight Communist aggression. "Aggressive conduct, if allowed to go unchecked and unchallenged, ultimately leads to war," he argues.

From John F. Kennedy, radio and television broadcast, October 22, 1962, in *Public Papers of the Presidents of the United States: John F. Kennedy* (Washington, DC: Government Printing Office, 1962–1964).

For three days, the world held its breath. Would the Soviet Union back down? Would Kennedy's action start a war that would end life on earth?

Finally, on October 24, after a series of communications between Kennedy and Khrushchev, the Soviet Union did back down. Khrushchev agreed to remove the missiles and cease efforts to establish nuclear missile sites in the West. In return, Kennedy agreed to stop U.S. efforts to overthrow Castro.

G*ood evening, my fellow citizens:*
This Government, as promised, has maintained the closest surveillance of the Soviet military buildup on the island of Cuba. Within the past week, unmistakable evidence has established the fact that a series of offensive missile sites is now in preparation on that imprisoned island. The purpose of these bases can be none other than to provide a nuclear strike capability against the Western Hemisphere.

Upon receiving the first preliminary hard information of this nature last Tuesday morning at 9 A.M., I directed that our surveillance be stepped up. And having now confirmed and completed our evaluation of the evidence and our decision on a course of action, this Government feels obliged to report this new crisis to you in fullest detail.

TWO TYPES OF LETHAL MISSILES

The characteristics of these new missile sites indicate two distinct types of installations. Several of them include medium range ballistic missiles, capable of carrying a nuclear warhead for a distance of more than 1,000 nautical miles. Each of these missiles, in short, is capable of striking Washington, D.C., the Panama Canal, Cape Canaveral, Mexico City, or any other city in the southeastern part of the United States, in Central America, or in the Caribbean area.

Additional sites not yet completed appear to be designed for intermediate range ballistic missiles—capable of traveling more than twice as far—and thus capable of striking most of the major cities in the Western Hemisphere, ranging as far north as Hudson Bay, Canada, and as far south as Lima, Peru. In addition, jet bombers, capable of carrying nuclear weapons, are now being uncrated and assembled in Cuba, while the necessary air bases are being prepared.

This urgent transformation of Cuba into an important strategic base—by the presence of these large, long-range, and clearly offensive weapons of sudden mass destruction—constitutes an explicit threat to the peace and security of all the Americas, in flagrant and deliberate defiance of the Rio Pact of 1947, the traditions of this Nation and hemisphere, the joint resolution of the 87th Congress, the Charter of the United Nations, and my own public warnings to the Soviets on September 4 and 13. This action also contradicts the repeated assurances of Soviet spokesmen, both publicly and privately delivered, that the arms buildup in Cuba would retain its original defensive character, and that the Soviet Union had no need or desire to station strategic missiles on the territory of any other nation.

The size of this undertaking makes clear that it has been planned for some months. Yet only last month, after I had made clear the distinction between any introduction of ground-to-ground missiles and the existence of defensive antiaircraft missiles, the Soviet Government publicly stated on September 11 that, and I quote, "the armaments and military equipment sent to Cuba are designed exclusively for defensive purposes," that, and I quote the Soviet Government, "there is no need for the Soviet Government to shift its weapons . . . for a retaliatory blow to any other country, for instance Cuba," and that, and I quote their government, "the Soviet Union has no powerful rockets to carry these nuclear warheads that there is no need to search for sites for them beyond the boundaries of the Soviet Union." That statement was false.

Soviet Duplicity

Only last Thursday, as evidence of this rapid offensive buildup was already in my hand, Soviet Foreign Minister [Andrey] Gromyko told me in my office that he was instructed to make it clear once again, as he said his government had already done, that Soviet assistance to Cuba, and I quote, "pursued solely the purpose of contributing to the defense capabilities of Cuba," that, and I quote him, "training by Soviet specialists of Cuban nationals in handling defensive armaments was by no means offensive, and if it were otherwise," Mr. Gromyko went on, "the Soviet Government would never become involved in rendering such assistance." That statement also was false.

Neither the United States of America nor the world community of nations can tolerate deliberate deception and offensive threats on the part of any nation, large or small. We no longer live in a world where only the actual firing of weapons represents a sufficient challenge to a nation's security to constitute maximum peril. Nuclear weapons are so destructive and ballistic missiles are so swift, that any substantially increased possibility of their use or any sudden change in their deployment may well be regarded as a definite threat to peace.

For many years, both the Soviet Union and the United States, recognizing this fact, have deployed strategic nuclear weapons with great care, never upsetting the precarious status quo which insured that these weapons would not be used in the absence of some vital challenge. Our own strategic missiles have never been transferred to the territory of any other nation under a cloak of secrecy and deception; and our history—unlike that of the Soviets since the end of World War II—demonstrates that we have no desire to dominate or conquer any other nation or impose our system upon its people. Nevertheless, American citizens have become adjusted to living daily on the bull's-eye of Soviet missiles located inside the U.S.S.R. or in submarines.

CLEAR AND PRESENT DANGER

In that sense, missiles in Cuba add to an already clear and present danger—although it should be noted the nations of Latin America have never previously been subjected to a potential nuclear threat.

But this secret, swift, and extraordinary buildup of Communist missiles—in an area well known to have a special and historical relationship to the United States and the nations of the Western Hemisphere, in violation of Soviet assurances, and in defiance of American and hemispheric policy—this sudden, clandestine decision to station strategic weapons for the first time outside of Soviet soil—is a deliberately provocative and unjustified change in the status quo which cannot be accepted by this country, if our courage and our commitments are ever to be trusted again by either friend or foe.

The 1930's taught us a clear lesson: aggressive conduct, if allowed to go unchecked and unchallenged, ultimately leads to war. This nation is opposed to war. We are also true to our word. Our unswerving objective, therefore, must be to prevent the use of these missiles against this or any other country, and to secure their withdrawal or elimination from the Western Hemisphere.

Our policy has been one of patience and restraint, as befits a peaceful and powerful nation, which leads a worldwide alliance. We have been determined not to be diverted from our central concerns by mere irritants and fanatics. But now further action is required—and it is under way; and these actions may only be the beginning. We will not prematurely or unnecessarily risk the costs of worldwide nuclear war in which even the fruits of victory would be ashes in our mouth—but neither will we shrink from that risk at any time it must be faced.

STEPS TO END SOVIET AGGRESSION

Acting, therefore, in the defense of our own security and of the entire Western Hemisphere, and under the authority entrusted to me by the Constitution as endorsed by the resolution of the Congress, I have directed that the following *initial* steps be taken immediately:

First: To halt this offensive buildup, a strict quarantine on all offensive military equipment under shipment to Cuba is being initiated. All ships of any kind bound for Cuba from whatever nation or port will, if found to contain cargoes of offensive weapons, be turned back. This quarantine will be extended, if needed, to other types of cargo and carriers. We are not at this time, however, denying the necessities of life as the Soviets attempted to do in their Berlin blockade of 1948.

Second: I have directed the continued and increased close surveillance of Cuba and its military buildup. The foreign ministers of the OAS [Organization of American States], in their communique of October 6, rejected secrecy on such matters in this hemisphere. Should these offensive military preparations continue, thus increasing the threat to the hemisphere, further action will be justified. I have directed the Armed Forces to prepare for any eventualities; and I trust that in the interest of both the Cuban people and the Soviet technicians at the sites, the hazards to all concerned of continuing this threat will be recognized.

Third: It shall be the policy of this Nation to regard any nuclear missile launched from Cuba against any nation in the Western Hemisphere as an attack by the Soviet Union on the United States, requiring a full retaliatory response upon the Soviet Union.

Fourth: As a necessary military precaution, I have reinforced our base at Guantanamo, evacuated today the dependents of our personnel there, and ordered additional military units to be on a standby alert basis.

Fifth: We are calling tonight for an immediate meeting of the Organ of Consultation under the Organization of American States, to consider this threat to hemispheric security and to invoke articles 6 and 8 of the Rio Treaty in support of all necessary action. The United Nations Charter allows for regional security arrangements—and the nations of this hemisphere decided long ago against the military presence of outside powers. Our other allies around the world have also been alerted.

Sixth: Under the Charter of the United Nations, we are asking tonight that an emergency meeting of the Security Council be convoked without delay to take action against this latest Soviet threat to world peace. Our resolution will call for the prompt dismantling and withdrawal of all offensive weapons in Cuba, under the supervision of U.N. observers, before the quarantine can be lifted.

Seventh and finally: I call upon Chairman [Nikita] Khrushchev to halt and eliminate this clandestine, reckless, and provocative threat to world peace and to stable relations between our two nations. I call upon him further to abandon this course of world domination, and to join in an historic effort to end the perilous arms race and to transform the history of man. He has an opportunity now to move the world back from the abyss of destruction—by returning to his government's own words that it had no need to station missiles outside its own territory, and withdrawing these weapons from Cuba—by refraining from any action which will widen or deepen the present crisis—and then by participating in a search for peaceful and permanent solutions.

This Nation is prepared to present its case against the Soviet threat to peace, and our own proposals for a peaceful world, at any time and in any forum—in the OAS, in the United Nations, or in any other meeting that could be useful—without limiting our freedom of action. We have in the past made strenuous efforts to limit the spread of nuclear weapons. We have proposed the elimination of all arms and military bases in a fair and effective disarmament treaty. We are prepared to discuss new proposals for the removal of tensions on both sides—including the possibilities of a genuinely independent Cuba, free to determine its own destiny. We have no wish to war with the Soviet Union—for we are a peaceful people who desire to live in peace with all other peoples.

ATMOSPHERE OF INTIMIDATION

But it is difficult to settle or even discuss these problems in an atmosphere of intimidation. That is why this latest Soviet threat—or any other threat which is made either independently or in response to our actions this week—must and will be met with determination. Any hostile move anywhere in the world against the safety and freedom of peoples to whom we are committed—including in particular the brave people of West Berlin—will be met by whatever action is needed.

Finally, I want to say a few words to the captive people of Cuba, to whom this speech is being directly carried by special radio facilities. I speak to you as a friend, as one who knows of your deep attachment to your fatherland, as one who shares your aspirations for liberty and justice for all. And I have watched and the American people have watched with deep sorrow how your nationalist revolution was betrayed—and how your fatherland fell under foreign domination. Now your leaders are no longer

Cuban leaders inspired by Cuban ideals. They are puppets and agents of an international conspiracy which has turned Cuba against your friends and neighbors in the Americas—and turned it into the first Latin American country to become a target for nuclear war—the first Latin American country to have these weapons on its soil.

These new weapons are not in your interest. They contribute nothing to your peace and well-being. They can only undermine it. But this country has no wish to cause you to suffer or to impose any system upon you. We know that your lives and land are being used as pawns by those who deny your freedom.

Many times in the past, the Cuban people have risen to throw out tyrants who destroyed their liberty. And I have no doubt that most Cubans today look forward to the time when they will be truly free—free from foreign domination, free to choose their own leaders, free to select their own system, free to own their own land, free to speak and write and worship without fear or degradation. And then shall Cuba be welcomed back to the society of free nations and to the associations of this hemisphere.

A DIFFICULT AND DANGEROUS EFFORT

My fellow citizens: let no one doubt that this is a difficult and dangerous effort on which we have set out. No one can foresee precisely what course it will take or what costs or casualties will be incurred. Many months of sacrifice and self-discipline lie ahead—months in which both our patience and our will will be tested—months in which many threats and denunciations will keep us aware of our dangers. But the greatest danger of all would be to do nothing.

The path we have chosen for the present is full of hazards, as all paths are—but it is the one most consistent with our character and courage as a nation and our commitments around the world. The cost of freedom is always high—but Americans have always paid it. And one path we shall never choose, and that is the path of surrender or submission.

Our goal is not the victory of might, but the vindication of right—not peace at the expense of freedom, but both peace *and* freedom, here in this hemisphere, and, we hope, around the world. God willing, that goal will be achieved.

Thank you and good night.

POP ART TURNS THE ART WORLD UPSIDE DOWN

TONY SCHERMAN

Gigantic soup cans and comic strip panels; huge, sagging, canvas telephones, toilets, and French fries; "paintings" made up of a dozen prints of the same celebrity's face with only crude color variations—odd things to see in sophisticated Manhattan art galleries in the early 1960s. But odd as they might have seemed to some viewers, they were the masterpieces of a new art movement called pop art.

Pop art was a dramatic departure from abstract expressionism, the established art form that had reigned in the art world for two decades. Abstract expressionist art was often made up of stark slashes or drips or shapes of color on a plain canvas. It was about as far from realistic depiction of objects as art could get. In contrast, the practitioners of pop art often exactly copied actual objects. Pop art was widely influenced by post–World War II affluence and materialism, and by advertising. In fact, some critics claimed that it was no more than glorified commercial (advertising) art. But art critic Allan Kaprow disagreed. In a 1967 essay he wrote that "the difference between commercial art and pop art is that pop wrenches its commercial model from its normal context, isolating for contemplation an object that originally was not contemplative, just as we might bring home a pebble from the beach."[1] In a 1957 letter British pop artist Richard Hamilton noted several characteristics of pop art: It's "popular, transient, expendable, low-cost, mass-produced, young, witty, sexy, gimmicky, glamorous, [and] big business."[2]

Excerpted from "When Pop Turned the Art World Upside Down," by Tony Scherman, *American Heritage,* February 2001. Reprinted with permission from *American Heritage.*

The pop art movement started in England and the United States, and, although it influenced art in other areas of the world, American artists dominated. Journalist and historian Tony Scherman, author of the following article, writes for *Smithsonian* and other publications. He is also author of *Back Beat: The Earl Palmer Story.*

"I t was like a science fiction movie—," wrote the late curator and art critic Henry Geldzahler, "you Pop artists in different parts of the city, unknown to each other, rising up out of the muck and staggering forward with your paintings in front of you." Geldzahler's lines, with their playful lugubriousness, were apt. When the innovators of pop embarked on their mature work, much of which was uncannily similar and all of which explored the same terrain—American consumer culture—almost none knew what any of the others were doing, or even that they existed. Pop arose spontaneously, an authentic movement, an organic response to new realities.

Geldzahler's zombies-from-hell imagery, moreover, perfectly captured the art establishment's horrified reaction to pop's inexorable rise. Pop shocked the shockers: the avant-garde, the entrenched, self-appointed keepers of the gate between high and low culture. It was the first postmodernist art, its principles a departure from the tried-and-true humanism of even such a radical genre as its predecessor abstract expressionism. In its levelling instinct, it helped lay the groundwork for the upheavals that would define the sixties. Critically savaged as lightweight ("mindless" was the usual characterization), it was, in fact, knottily complex, its essence and nuances discernible only in retrospect.

The New Vulgarians

Unlike abstract expressionism, which had spent decades underground before winning widespread recognition, pop zoomed to pre-eminence within two or three years, climaxing its rise in the last two months of 1962. "The new vulgarians," as one hostile writer dubbed its practitioners, took the art world by storm.

In 1960, Andy Warhol, at 31 one of New York's most successful fashion illustrators, rebelled against the fey good taste of his advertising work and began filling his Upper East Side studio with big, stark, intentionally banal paintings. He took his subjects from the lower reaches of popular culture: comic books, and later tabloids like the New York *Daily News* and movie-star publicity photos. As clever as he was ambitious, Warhol knew that nothing would enrage the art world—and gain its full attention—more than imagery originally created for the base amusement of lowbrows.

Meanwhile, out in the Jersey suburbs, the 37-year-old Roy Lichtenstein, a Rutgers University art professor, was smuggling comic-strip characters into his otherwise unremarkable abstractions when it hit him: Why not make paintings that look *just like* comic books? And in a loft in lower Manhattan, a 27-year-old former North Dakotan named James Rosenquist came home every night from his job as a Times Square billboard painter, his mind reeling from staring at 50-foot Pepsodent smiles and whitewall tires from a foot away. He transferred his fragmentary images onto canvas, jarringly juxtaposed.

All around the city, artists were suddenly obsessed with popular culture. Claes Oldenburg, born in Sweden in 1929 and raised in Chicago, lived on the Lower East Side, a sculptor and onetime journalist. "I am for an art that is political-erotical-mystical, that does something other than sit on its ass in a museum," he declared in a 1961 manifesto, one of the great pieces of writing by a contemporary artist. In December of that year, he filled his East Second Street studio with brightly paint-splattered, eccentrically shaped plaster replicas of dime-store merchandise, christened it the Store, and declared it open for business.

EMBROILED WITH "EVERYDAY CRAP"

Everything in the Store—shoes, pants, shirts, dresses, hats, ladies' lingerie, ties, pies, cakes, fried eggs, sandwiches, candy bars and more—was for sale at prices ranging from $21.79 for an oval mirror to $899.95 for a statue of a bride. Behind its grubby facade, "the Store" was a complex entity, an indication of the metaphysical sleights of hand about art, life, and their interaction that would characterize pop. It was an art gallery filled with wonderful pieces; it was a neighborhood store—of sorts—where you could walk in, browse, buy, or shoot the breeze with the genial if opinionated proprietor; and it was a philosophical critique of the division between art and life, an effort to wrest art from its pedestal: "I am for an art that embroils itself with the everyday crap . . . [that is as] heavy and coarse and blunt and sweet and stupid as life itself."

Reviewing the Store for *Arts* magazine, Sidney Tillim wrote the first American article on the emerging tendency, coining a lofty name for its creators: "In mass man and his artifacts, . . . the New American Dreamer . . . finds the content that at once refreshes his visual experience and opens paths beyond the seemingly exhausted alternatives of abstraction. . . ." Almost at once, the names proliferated: Commonism, Popular Realism, Anti-Sensibility

Painting, the New Sign Painting, Factualism, Common Object Art. "Pop," which didn't come into use until later in 1962, had been coined in 1958 by an English critic. An English pop movement actually preceded America's but lacked the latter's fiery energy, just as a group of California pop-related artists never produced anything to rival the New Yorkers' powerful icons.

In February, a few weeks after Oldenburg closed the Store (owing his gallery $285), Roy Lichtenstein and James Rosenquist unveiled their new work in tony uptown galleries, Rosenquist at the Green, on West Fifty-seventh Street, Lichtenstein at the Castelli, on East Seventy-seventh.

What Rosenquist was after in early canvases like *The Lines Were Etched Deeply on the Map of Her Face* (1962) and *Pushbutton* (1961), was the way fragmentary images flash by us—the side of a woman's face, a streaking yellow taxi, a pair of staring eyes—discontinuous and alluring, when we hurry across a busy street or flip through a television's channels. Whereas Warhol and Lichtenstein strove for impersonality, Rosenquist's personal touch was always visible. He sought to dazzle. Of pop's major figures, he was the most likely to appeal to conventional tastes.

COMICS AS ART

A writer once asked Lichtenstein why he had started painting comic-book characters. "Desperation," he answered. "There were no spaces left between Milton Resnick and Mike Goldberg [two second-generation abstract expressionists]." He added on another occasion, equally mordantly, "It was hard to get a painting that was despicable enough so that no one would hang it. . . . It was almost acceptable to hang a dripping paint rag. . . . The one thing everyone hated was commercial art; apparently they didn't hate that enough either."

Newsweek came to Lichtenstein's opening: a remarkable coup for a relatively unknown artist, a sign of the buzz pop was already generating, and a portent of the role the media would play in its rise. The *Newsweek* writer, though clearly uneasy, refrained from judging Lichtenstein. Others would shortly be less reticent. "One of the worst artists in America," wrote Brian O'Doherty of *The New York Times* in 1963; *The New Yorker's* Harold Rosenberg called Lichtenstein "an academic draftsman retooled to blow up comic strips."

Lichtenstein's early pop subjects fell largely into three groups: war comics, romance comics, and everyday objects (golf balls, range ovens, etc.). At first, the comic-strip paintings seem to be mere copies—Lichtenstein was "making a sow's ear out of a sow's ear," wrote O'Doherty—but in fact the works depart sig-

nificantly from the originals. A comparison with, say, the source
that Lichtenstein used for *Takka Takka* (1962), shows that the differences are substantial. And the longer one looks at *Takka Takka*,
the more striking it is, at once elegant and vulgar, with a reso-
nance the original never had.

Artists from Picasso to Romare Bearden had appropriated others' work, but they had almost always made it part of a collage
or some other larger whole. For Lichtenstein (and Warhol), the
appropriated image *was* the whole. Lichtenstein was not a col-
lagist; he made second-generation pictures, which raised all sorts
of troubling questions. Was he ripping off the original artist? (He
and Warhol were both sued, Warhol successfully, for using others' work). What constitutes originality? In a culture glutted with
images, is originality not only impossible but beside the point?
When Warhol first saw Lichtenstein's work, in mid-1961, he was
distraught; Lichtenstein's comic-strip paintings were obviously
better than his own. "Right then I decided that since Roy was doing comics so well, that I would just stop comics altogether,"
Warhol wrote, "and go in other directions where I could come
out first." Serial repetition, for instance, a concept very much in
the air, largely thanks to the avant-garde composer John Cage.
Soon Warhol was producing row on row of dollar bills, S&H
Green Stamps, and bright red-and-white Campbell's soup cans.

RUBBER-STAMP ART

By the late summer of 1962, the rubber stamps Warhol was using
to imprint a repeated image began to feel "too homemade," as
he put it. He wanted something "that gave more of an assembly-
line effect," and he hit on the technique that became his trademark: photosilkscreening, or printing a silkscreened photograph
onto a painted canvas. ". . . You get the same image, slightly different each time. It was all so simple—quick and chancy," he
wrote in his memoir, *POPism*. Warhol's paintings aren't paintings
at all; they're hybrids, half painting, half photograph. . . .

SOFT SCULPTURES

Oldenburg introduced his enormous "soft sculptures" (a six-foot
hamburger, an eight-foot ice cream cone, and other majestically
inflated items) in September at the Green Gallery. A half-dozen
other pop shows were scheduled for the fall, all at prestigious
venues. "The art galleries are being invaded by the pinheaded
and contemptible style of gumchewers, bobby-soxers and worse,
delinquents," wrote Max Kozloff in *Arts International*.

Until pop arrived, vanguard American art had fought its battles in private. "Up through the fifties and even in the early six-

ties," Hilton Kramer says, "the New York galleries showing serious art you could count on the fingers of two hands. By the end of the sixties, the number of galleries had increased by four or five hundred percent. Pop art not only changed the tone of the art world, it changed its size."

Mass-circulation magazines may have peered under abstract expressionism's lid from time to time, as *Life* did with its famous 1949 Jackson Pollock article, but the passions of Mark Rothko, Barnett Newman, or Pollock, for that matter, were too arcane for steady coverage. Pop, on the other hand, lent itself easily to glib phrasemaking. The national magazines and big newspapers picked up on it as soon as, or even sooner than, the art journals. But their response was overwhelmingly disparaging; if the mass media helped pop to prominence, it was through their energetic contempt. After a few tentative forays, *Time* and *Newsweek* roared out in high, superficial dudgeon, scandalized and loving it, and long after pop had entered the mainstream, the newsmagazines lost few opportunities to pillory these . . . these . . . these . . . *Who the hell* are *these guys?* They're artists all right—con artists!

The new art was a response to two forces, abstract expressionism and the postwar explosion of popular culture. Rebelling against the first, it embraced the second. In the mid-fifties, after years of rejection, the abstract expressionists, or New York school—Jackson Pollock, Willem de Kooning, Mark Rothko, Franz Kline, Barnett Newman, Robert Motherwell, and their colleagues—had finally prevailed. For the first time in history, American painters were recognized as the dominant force in international art. As the art historian and critic Leo Steinberg puts it, the New York school "was the first American cultural product after jazz to really conquer the world.". . .

BAITING THE ESTABLISHMENT

Against this backdrop, Warhol's famous remark that he wanted to be a machine takes on its proper meaning. It's not a statement of alienation, or a death wish; it was Warhol, the young Turk, baiting the New York school. Nor was it just talk. Warhol's found imagery infuriated the abstract expressionists, with their stress on originality. He made multiple copies of a painting—another outrage, this time against the emphasis on uniqueness. Taking on spontaneity, he planned everything ahead of time. What mattered was choosing the right image; as Warhol often said, anyone could do the actual work on his paintings. Almost all his ideas—ready-made imagery, mechanical procedures, mass production, de-emphasis of spontaneity, and an emphasis on impersonality—were darts hurled at abstract expressionism.

Lichtenstein, too, rebelled into impersonality. Copying a comic-strip frame by hand, he put the copy into a projector and traced the magnified image onto a canvas for the outline of his painting. His trademark Ben Day dots (the tiny dots used by printers and cartoonists for shading) made his canvases look printed, not painted. "I wanted to look programmed," he told an interviewer. The hand, bearer of individuality, was fetishized by abstract expressionism. Pop slapped it away. . . .

DISCOVERING AMERICA

Clement Greenberg and most of the abstract expressionists had always maintained a rigidly elitist stance toward vernacular culture. In his most famous essay, "Avant-Garde and Kirsch," Greenberg called pop culture "ersatz culture . . . destined for those who are insensible to the value of genuine culture." By 1960 Greenberg's kitsch—television, advertising, magazines, movies, and other mass media—had lodged itself deeply in America's consciousness. Media-generated imagery was too urgent, too omnipresent, for artists to ignore. Like the Beats a few years earlier, the pop artists were discovering America. Driving through the commercial bustle of the Lower East Side's Orchard Street in 1960, Claes Oldenburg felt "that I had discovered a new world. I began wandering through stores—all kinds and all over—as though they were museums. I saw the objects displayed in windows and on counters as precious works of art." But the best pop passage about encountering America comes from that unlikely wanderer in the heartlands, Warhol.

"The farther West we drove," he wrote, describing an early-sixties cross-country trip, "the more Pop everything looked on the highways. Suddenly we all felt like insiders because even though Pop was everywhere—that was the thing about it, most people still took it for granted, whereas we were dazzled by it—to us, it was the new Art. Once you 'got' Pop, you could never see a sign the same way again. And once you thought Pop, you could never see America the same way again. . . . I was lying on the mattress in the back of our station wagon looking up at the lights and wires and telephone poles zipping by, and the stars and the blue-black sky. . . . I didn't ever want to live anyplace where you couldn't drive down the road and see drive-ins and giant ice cream cones and walk-in hot dogs and motel signs flashing!" Pop reveled in America, but not, like Whitman, in the nobility of the multitudes. Pop reveled in America's supermarkets. In its magazines and TV shows, in its rising tide of commodities.

Pop arrived on October 31, 1962. This is only a slight exaggeration, for not only was the big "New Realists" show, which opened on that day, spectacular in itself, but the show's location had special significance. The Sidney Janis Gallery on East Fifty-seventh Street was, as Harold Rosenberg put it, "the leading emporium of American abstract art." Less than a decade earlier, it had been Sidney Janis's backing that had legitimized the New York school in the eyes of the world. In 1962 the gallery still represented most of the major abstract expressionists, including Rothko, de Kooning, Motherwell, Adolf Gottlieb, and Philip Guston. Depending on one's perspective, the "New Realists" show was either a betrayal or a housecleaning; in either case, "the show was an implicit proclamation," as Thomas Hess, editor of *Art News*, wrote, "that the new had arrived and it was time for the fogies to pack."

Janis, a hot-jazz enthusiast, one-time vaudeville dancer, and self-taught art scholar with several books to his credit, invited a whopping 54 artists: 12 were American (including Lichtenstein, Oldenburg, Rosenquist, Warhol, Wesselmann, Jim Dine, Robert Indiana, Wayne Thiebaud, and George Segal), 7 French, 5 Italian, 3 English, and 2 Swedish. His gallery couldn't hold all this art, so he rented an empty store across Fifty-seventh Street and filled the window with Oldenburg's garishly painted ladies' underwear from the Store, a touch of dumpy Orchard Street on soigné Fifty-seventh.

Of Janis's abstract expressionist artists, only de Kooning came to the opening, pacing up and down in front of the paintings for two hours and leaving without a word. Later that evening, at an opening-night soirée thrown by the wealthy collector Burton Tremaine, Warhol, Lichtenstein, Wesselmann, Rosenquist, and Indiana were all being served drinks by uniformed maids when de Kooning appeared in the doorway. "Oh, so nice to see you," said Tremaine, who owned a number of de Koonings. "But please, at any other time."

"It was a shock to see de Kooning turned away," Rosenquist recalled. "At that moment I thought, something in the art world has definitely changed." Within days of the opening, Janis's abstract expressionists held a meeting, at which all but de Kooning voted to leave.

It was a classic Oedipal situation, the pop upstarts eager to supplant their elders. When a *Newsweek* reporter asked Warhol how he felt about abstract expressionism, the painter responded with an exquisite put-down: "I love the New York school, but I never did any abstract expressionism—I don't know why, it's so easy." Oh so innocently, Warhol was waving a red flag at the abstract expressionists, whose fury lasted. Years after pop's heyday, Warhol spotted de Kooning at a party in the Hamptons. Approaching the older man, Warhol held out his hand. "You're a killer of art," de Kooning screamed. "You're a killer of beauty, and you're even a killer of laughter! I can't bear your work!"....

POP ART GETS ITS NAME

On December 13, the term "pop art" was officially introduced. The occasion was a "Symposium on Pop Art" organized by the Museum of Modern Art. Present in the packed house were, as Henry Geldzahler said, "many idols and sacred monsters": John Cage, Robert Rauschenberg, Warhol, Lichtenstein, Leo Castelli (soon to become pop's leading dealer), Janis, the collectors Robert and Ethel Scull, and a figure many were blaming for pop: Marcel Duchamp, the founder of Dada. The audience was more hostile than sympathetic; Ivan Karp said he felt "surrounded by Apaches."

To have begun the year as a nameless rumor and end it as the focus of a packed event at the world's leading modern art institution was remarkable. Still, it's hard to avoid seeing the symposium as a setup. How could the temple of pure, difficult abstract art afford to ignore the hottest thing going? The solution: Rather than plan an exhibit (as the Guggenheim was already doing), hold a one-night discussion with a stacked panel. The event's organizer and moderator, Peter Selz, the museum's curator of painting and sculpture exhibitions, loathed pop and invited three more detractors: Dore Ashton, Hilton Kramer, and the poet Stanley Kunitz. This left Leo Steinberg, who was ambivalent about pop, and Geldzahler, an assistant curator at the Metropolitan Museum of Art and the panel's only out-and-out pop advocate.

Despite the uneven sides, the symposium produced sparks. Listening to a tape recording of the evening feels like eavesdropping on history; even the printed proceedings have a palpable electricity. "Like many people at that time," says Kramer today, "I had to wonder whether the art world was coming to an end. Certainly the whole abstract expressionist circle, Rothko, Motherwell, Gottlieb, looked upon this as the end of the world. Whether you were for it or against it, everybody felt that an enormous change had occurred."....

Pop, Kramer argued, was significant only as a reaction to abstract expressionism. On its own, it amounted to almost nothing; it was art "by default, only because [it is] nothing else." What especially irritated him (and Ashton, Selz, and Kunitz) was its failure to transform its subject matter, its "shanghaiing of the recognizable," as Kramer put it. . . .

The art's lack of transformation, its "poverty of visual invention," as one critic put it, was of course an aesthetic choice, part of pop's effort to close the gap between art and life. "There is something very beautiful in putting art back into the present world. . . ." Oldenburg said. "This process of humbling [art] is a testing of the definition of art. You reduce everything to the same level and then see what you get." Pop was a stunt pilot flying as close to life as he could without crashing. Moreover, it did transform its subjects, although not in the way traditional critics had in mind. "Transpose" may be a better word, following the philosopher Umberto Eco's analysis of how pop put its subjects through any of several alterations—in context, size, number, physical composition—in order to render the familiar striking.

Consider a sculpture by Lichtenstein, eight feet high by five feet wide. Made of four concentrically stacked, irregularly shaped steel sheets brightly painted in red, yellow, black and white, it looks like a striking abstract design. Suddenly its identity declares itself: It's an immense, three-dimensional rendering of the explosions you've seen hundreds of times in old fighter-pilot comics—*Explosion No. 1* (1965). Lichtenstein's transformations of his "original," the generic comic-book explosion, are twofold. He has removed it from its familiar comic-book context (in which it was barely noticed), and he has given it a three-dimensional shape and a size that make it look strange and new, demanding contemplation. Cancelling our automatic reactions to a staple of comic-book imagery, Lichtenstein prompts us to appreciate its formal beauty and the creativity of its originators.

When Warhol displayed hundreds of near-perfect replicas of Brillo soap-pad cartons in the spring of 1964, he made only one alteration to his banal subjects aside from painting on plywood instead of cardboard: a change of context from a supermarket to a classy New York art gallery. What the boxes provoked, aside from endless jokes and scowls, was the question, What makes these art, but their look-alikes plain old cardboard boxes? The answer: Nothing. No merely visual criterion can distinguish art from non-art, as Warhol demonstrated with his Brillo boxes. This revelation, simple but inspired enough for the critic Arthur Danto to call Warhol "the nearest thing to a philosophical genius the history of art has produced," was the last in an 80-year series of self-diminutions by Western art. First, art had declared it didn't have to be beautiful, then that it didn't have to be realistic, then that it didn't need a pictorial subject, and on down to the logical conclusion reached by Warhol: Art doesn't have to be *anything*.

Conversely, anything can be art. For Danto, Warhol's Brillo boxes meant the end of art, not in the sense that art could no longer be made but in the sense that it had exploded all of its presumably necessary conditions. Warhol himself expressed this in

1963: "How can you say one style is better than another? You ought to be able to be an Abstract-Expressionist next week, or a Pop artist, or a realist, without feeling you've given up something." Indeed, the swarm of genres and styles that exists in today's art world, none with any apparent necessity, is the result of Warhol's remorseless logic.

UNDERMINING ELITISM

With the insight that everyday things were works of art, pop changed American culture, undermining elitism and awakening serious art to the vernacular resources—from comic strips to movies to rock 'n' roll—that now enliven it. But that basic insight remains problematic. "Pop Art is liking things," said Warhol, and the remark points up the acquiescence, even collusion, as some critics have said, at the genre's core. Happily adrift in a sea of products, pop was unable to look beneath their gleaming surfaces to ask where they came from, how they were produced, and whose interests they served. Despite the vast stylistic difference between the illustrations of his advertising years and his work after 1960, there was no break in Andy Warhol's career. Even after he left advertising, he was still pushing products.

In the first half of 1963, pop swiftly consolidated its position at the forefront of American art. Museum after museum—in New York, Kansas City, Houston, Washington, D.C., and Los Angeles—mounted shows. But the critical phase, winning pre-eminence among New York's dealers and collectors, was over. The hegemony of abstract expressionism was broken, the divide between fine art and mass culture crossed. In its embrace of the vernacular, pop was a breath of fresh air, an indication of the redefinitions and fresh starts the sixties would bring.

Abstract expressionism had drawn the artist's gaze inward, to a purely subjective realm. What was hard for its artists and ideologues to accept about pop was its reversal of this gaze, its redirection of the artist's awareness outward: to the teeming, exciting, vulgar new world of early-sixties America. Pop argued that the world was worth looking at—and it won the argument.

NOTES

1. Allan Kaprow, "Pop Art: Past, Present, and Future," *The Malahat Review*, July 1967.
2. Quoted in John Russell, "Pop Reappraised," *Art in America*, July–August 1969.

SEGREGATION FOREVER

GEORGE C. WALLACE

In a nation still reeling from the bitter aftermath of the Civil War, the 1896 Supreme Court decision in *Plessy v. Ferguson* ruled that the Constitution guaranteed political equality, but not necessarily social equality, to all citizens. This ruling unleashed widespread segregation policies and laws, particularly in the southern states, covering everything from separate railcar facilities, restaurants, and drinking fountains to separate schools for blacks and whites. In 1954 the Supreme Court's unanimous decision in *Brown v. Board of Education of Topeka, Kansas*, overturned *Plessy* and set off discord that reverberated through the nation for the next two decades. *Brown* unequivocally declared that school segregation was unconstitutional. After *Brown* it was no longer legal for any state to have segregated schools.

This ruling was not only an affront to southerners who had never fully recovered from losing the Civil War, but it was an affront to those who believed that states' rights took precedence over those of the federal government. Pitched battles took place not only between debaters in state legislatures, but on the streets of the United States between those for and against segregation.

George C. Wallace was a newly elected Alabama governor and ambitious rising politician in January 1963. In 1958, he had lost his first gubernatorial bid to an extreme segregationist who had the support of the Ku Klux Klan, a rabidly racist organization. Wallace vowed he would not lose to such a man again, and his 1962 campaign was based on an anti–big government and pro-segregation platform. His victory was resounding, and in his inaugural address he pledged to his constituents to uphold the values on which he had campaigned. An excerpt from that address follows.

Excerpted from George C. Wallace's Inaugural Address, January 14, 1963, Alabama Department of Archives and History, Montgomery, Alabama.

Today I have stood, where once Jefferson Davis stood, and took an oath to my people. It is very appropriate then that from this Cradle of the Confederacy, this very Heart of the Great Anglo-Saxon Southland, that today we sound the drum for freedom as have our generations of forebears before us done, time and time again through history. Let us rise to the call of freedom-loving blood that is in us and send our answer to the tyranny that clanks its chains upon the South. In the name of the greatest people that have ever trod this earth, I draw the line in the dust and toss the gauntlet before the feet of tyranny, and I say, segregation today, segregation tomorrow, segregation forever.

The Washington, D.C., school riot report is disgusting and revealing. We will not sacrifice our children to any such type school system—and you can write that down. The federal troops in Mississippi could be better used guarding the saftey of the citizens of Washington, D.C., where it is even unsafe to walk or go to a ballgame—and that is the nation's capital. I was safer in a B-29 bomber over Japan during the war in an air raid, than the people of Washington are walking to the White House neighborhood. A closer example is Atlanta. The city officials fawn for political reasons over school integration and THEN build barricades to stop residential integration—what hypocrisy!

WE WILL FIGHT FOR OUR FREEDOM

Let us send this message back to Washington by our representatives who are with us today: that from this day we are standing up, and the heel of tyranny does not fit the neck of an upright man; that we intend to take the offensive and carry our fight for freedom across the nation, wielding the balance of power we know we possess in the Southland; that WE, not the insipid bloc of voters of some sections will determine in the next election who shall sit in the White House of these United States. That from this day, from this hour, from this minute, we give the word of a race of honor that we will tolerate their boot in our face no longer, and let those certain judges put that in their opium pipes of power and smoke it for what it is worth.

Hear me, Southerners! You sons and daughters who have moved north and west throughout this nation, we call on you from your native soil to join with us in national support and vote, and we know, wherever you are, away from the hearths of the Southland, that you will respond, for though you may live in the fartherest reaches of this vast country, your heart has never left Dixieland.

And you native sons and daughters of old New England's rock-ribbed patriotism, and you sturdy natives of the great Mid-

West, and you descendants of the far West flaming spirit of pioneer freedom, we invite you to come and be with us, for you are of the Southern spirit and the Southern philosophy, you are Southerners too and brothers with us in our fight.

What I have said about segregation goes double this day and what I have said to or about some federal judges goes TRIPLE this day.

Alabama has been blessed by God as few states in this Union have been blessed. Our state owns ten percent of all the natural resources of all the states in our country. Our inland waterway system is second to none and has the potential of being the greatest waterway transport system in the entire world. We possess over thirty minerals in usable quantities and our soil is rich and varied, suited to a wide variety of plants. Our native pine and forestry system produces timber faster than we can cut it and yet we have only pricked the surface of the great lumber and pulp potential.

With ample rainfall and rich grasslands our livestock industry is in the infancy of a giant future that can make us a center of the big and growing meat packing and prepared foods marketing. We have the favorable climate, streams, woodlands, beaches, and natural beauty to make us a recreational mecca in the booming tourist and vacation industry. Nestled in the great Tennessee Valley, we possess the Rocket center of the world and the keys to the space frontier.

While the trade with a developing Europe built the great port cities of the east coast, our own fast developing port of Mobile faces as a magnetic gateway to the great continent of South America, well over twice as large and hundreds of times richer in resources, even now awakening to the growing probes of enterprising capital with a potential of growth and wealth beyond any present dream for our port development and corresponding results throughout the connecting waterways that thread our state.

THE CENTRALIZED GOVERNMENT IS TRYING TO USURP OUR FREEDOM

And while the manufacturing industries of free enterprise have been coming to our state in increasing numbers, attracted by our bountiful natural resouces, our growing numbers of skilled workers and our favorable conditions, their present rate of settlement here can be increased from the trickle they now represent to a stream of enterprise and endeavor, capital and expansion that can join us in our work of development and enrichment of the educational futures of our children, the opportunities of our citizens and the fulfillment of our talents as God has given them to us. To realize our ambitions and to bring to fruition our dreams, we as Alabamians must take cognizance of the world about us. We must re-define our heritage, re-school our thoughts in the lessons our forefathers knew so well, first hand, in order to function and to grow and to prosper. We can no longer hide our head in the sand and tell ourselves that the ideology of our free fathers is not being attacked and is not being threatened by another idea, for it is. We are faced with an idea that if a centralized government assumes enough authority, enough power over its people, that it can provide a utopian life, that if given the power to dictate, to forbid, to require, to demand, to distribute, to edict and to judge what is best and enforce that will produce only "good," and it shall be our father, and our God. It is an idea of government that encourages our fears and destroys our faith, for where there is faith, there is no fear, and where there is fear, there is no faith. In encouraging our fears of economic insecurity it demands we place that economic management and control with government; in encouraging our fear of educational development it demands we place that education and the minds of our children under management and control of government, and even in feeding our fears of physical infirmities and declining years, it offers and demands to father us through it all and even into the grave. It is a government that claims to us that it is bountiful as it buys its power from us with the fruits of its rapaciousness of the wealth that free men before it have produced and builds on crumbling credit without responsibilities to the debtors—our children. It is an ideology of government erected on the encouragement of fear and fails to recognize the basic law of our fathers that governments do not produce wealth, people produce wealth, free people; and those people become less free as they learn there is little reward for ambition, that it requires faith to risk, and they have none, as the government must restrict and penalize and tax incentive and endeavor and must increase its expenditures of bounties, then this government must assume more and more police powers and we find we are become government-fearing people, not God-fearing people. We find we have replaced faith with fear, and though we may give lip service to the Almighty, in reality, government has become our god. It is, therefore, a basically ungodly government and its appeal to the pseudo-intellectual and the politician is to change their status from servant of the people to master of the people, to play at being God without faith in God and without the wisdom of God. It is a system that is the very opposite of Christ for it feeds and encourages everything degenerate and base in our people as it assumes the responsibilities that we ourselves should assume. Its pseudo-liberal spokesmen and some Harvard advocates have never examined the logic of its substitution of what it calls "human rights" for individual rights, for its propaganda play on words has appeal for the unthinking. Its logic is totally material and irresponsible as it runs the full gamut of human desires, including the theory that everyone has voting rights without the spiritual responsibility of preserving freedom. Our founding fathers recognized those rights, but only within the framework of those spiritual responsibilities. But the strong, simple faith and sane reasoning of our founding fathers has long since been forgotten as the so-called "progressives" tell us that our Constitution was written for "horse and buggy" days, so were the Ten Commandments.

LIBERALISM IS DEGENERATE AND DECADENT

Not so long ago men stood in marvel and awe at the cities, the buildings, the schools, the autobahns that the government of Hitler's Germany had built, just as centuries before they stood in wonder of Rome's building, but it could not stand, for the system that built it had rotted the souls of the builders, and in turn, rotted the foundation of what God meant that men should be. Today that same system on an international scale is sweeping the world. It is the "changing world" of which we are told, it is called "new" and "liberal." It is as old as the oldest dictator. It is degenerate and decadent. As the national racism of Hitler's Germany persecuted a national minority to the whim of a national majority, so the international racism of the liberals seeks to persecute the international white minority to the whim of the international colored majority, so that we are footballed about according to the favor of the Afro-Asian bloc. But the Belgian survivors of the Congo cannot present their case to a war crimes commission, nor the Portuguese of Angola, nor the survivors of Castro, nor the citizens of Oxford, Mississippi.

It is this theory of international power politic that led a group of men on the Supreme Court for the first time in American history to issue an edict, based not on legal precedent, but upon a volume, the editor of which said our Constitution is outdated and must be changed and the writers of which, some had admittedly belonged to as many as half a hundred communist-front organizations. It is this theory that led this same group of men to briefly bare the ungodly core of that philosophy in forbidding little school children to say a prayer. And we find the evidence of that ungodliness even in the removal of the words "in God we trust" from some of our dollars, which was placed there as like evidence by our founding fathers as the faith upon which this system of government was built. It is the spirit of power thirst that caused a President in Washington to take up Caesar's pen and with one stroke of it make a law. A Law which the law making body of Congress refused to pass—a law that tells us that we can or cannot buy or sell our very homes, except by his conditions, and except at HIS discretion. It is the spirit of power thirst that led the same President to launch a full offensive of twenty-five thousand troops against a university, of all places, in his own country, and against his own people, when this nation maintains only six thousand troops in the beleaguered city of Berlin. We have witnessed such acts of "might makes right" over the world as men yielded to the temptation to play God, but we have never before witnessed it in America. We reject such acts as free men. We do not defy, for there is nothing to defy, since as free men we do not recognize any government right to give freedom, or deny freedom. No government erected by man has that right. As Thomas Jefferson said, "The God who gave us life, gave us liberty at the same time; no King holds the right of liberty in his hands." Nor does any ruler in American government.

WE INTEND TO PRACTICE OUR HERITAGE

We intend, quite simply, to practice the free heritage as bequeathed to us as sons of free fathers. We intend to re-vitalize the truly new and progressive form of government that is less that two hundred years old, a government first founded in this nation simply and purely on faith: that there is a personal God who rewards good and punishes evil, that hard work will receive its just desserts, that ambition and ingenuity and incentiveness, and profit of such, are admirable traits and goals; that the individual is encouraged in his spiritual growth and from that growth arrives at a character that enhances his charity toward others and from that character and that charity so is influenced business, and labor and farmer and government. We intend to renew our faith as God-fearing men, not government-fearing men nor any other kind of fearing-men. We intend to roll up our sleeves and pitch in to develop this full bounty God has given us—to live full and useful lives and in absolute freedom from all fear. Then can we enjoy the full richness of the Great American Dream.

We have placed this sign, "In God We Trust," upon our State Capitol on this Inauguration Day as physical evidence of determination to renew the faith of our fathers and to practice the free heritage they bequeathed to us. We do this with the clear and solemn knowledge that such physical evidence is evidently a direct violation of the logic of that Supreme Court in Washington, D.C., and if they or their spokesmen in this state wish to term this defiance, I say, then let them make the most of it.

This nation was never meant to be a unit of one, but a united of the many, that is the exact reason our freedom loving forefathers established the states, so as to divide the rights and powers among the states, insuring that no central power could gain master government control.

THE RIGHT TO BE SEPARATE

In united effort we were meant to live under this government—whether Baptist, Methodist, Presbyterian, Church of Christ, or whatever one's denomination or religious belief—each respecting the others' right to a separate denomination; each, by working to develop his own, enriching the total of all our lives through united effort. And so it was meant in our political lives—whether Republican, Democrat, Prohibition, or whatever political party—each striving from his separate political station, respecting the rights of others to be separate and work from within their political framework, and each separate political station making its contribution to our lives. . . .

And so it was meant in our racial lives—each race, within its own framework has the freedom to teach, to instruct, to develop, to ask for and receive deserved help from others of separate racial stations. This is the great freedom of our American founding fathers, but if we amalgamate into the one unit as advocated by the communist philosophers, then the enrichment of our lives, the freedom for our development, is gone forever. We become, therefore, a mongrel unit of one under a single all powerful government, and we stand for everything, and for nothing.

The true brotherhood of America, of respecting the separateness of others and uniting in effort has been so twisted and distorted from its original concept that there is a small wonder that communism is winning the world.

We invite the negro citizen of Alabama to work with us from his separate racial station as we will work with him to develop, to grow in individual freedom and enrichment. We want jobs and a good future for BOTH races, the tubercular and the infirm. This is the basic heritage of my religion, of which I make full practice, for we are all the handiwork of God.

But we warn those, of any group, who would follow the false doctrine of communistic amalgamation that we will not surrender our system of government, our freedom of race and religion. That freedom was won at a hard price and if it requires a hard price to retain it, we are able and quite willing to pay it.

The liberals' theory that poverty, discrimination and lack of opportunity is the cause of communism is a false theory. If it were true the South would have been the biggest single communist bloc in the western hemisphere long ago, for after the great War Between the States, our people faced a desolate land of burned universities, destroyed crops and homes, with man-power depleted and crippled, and even the mule, which was re-quired to work the land, was so scarce that whole communities shared one animal to make the spring plowing. There were no government handouts, no Marshall Plan aid, no coddling to make sure that our people would not suffer; instead the South was set upon by the vulturous carpetbagger and federal troops, all loyal Southerners were denied the vote at the point of bayo-net, so that the infamous, illegal 14th Amendment might be passed. There was no money, no food and no hope of either. But our grandfathers bent their knee only in church and bowed their head only to God.

SOUTHERNERS FOUGHT FOR FREEDOM

Not for a single instant did they ever consider the easy way of federal dictatorship and amalgamation in return for fat bellies. They fought. They dug sweet roots from the ground with their bare hands and boiled them in iron pots. They gathered poke salad from the woods and acorns from the ground. They fought. They followed no false doctrine. They knew what they wanted and they fought for freedom! They came up from their knees in the greatest display of sheer nerve, grit and guts that has ever been set down in the pages of written history, and they won! The great writer, Rudyard Kipling wrote of them, that: "There in the Southland of the United States of America, lives the greatest fighting breed of man in all the world!"

And that is why today, I stand ashamed of the fat, well-fed whimperers who say that it is inevitable that our cause is lost. I am ashamed of them and I am ashamed for them. They do not represent the people of the Southland.

And may we take note of one other fact, with all trouble with communists that some sections of this country have, there are not enough native communists in the South to fill up a telephone booth. And THAT is a matter of public FBI record.

We remind all within hearing of this Southland that a South-erner, Peyton Randolph, presided over the Continental Congress in our nation's beginning; that a Southerner, Thomas Jefferson, wrote the Declaration of Independence; that a Southerner, George Washington, is the Father of our country; that a South-erner, James Madison, authored our Constitution; that a South-erner, George Mason, authored the Bill of Rights and it was a Southerner who said, "Give me liberty . . . or give me death," Patrick Henry.

Southerners played a most magnificent part in erecting this great divinely inspired system of freedom, and as God is our witness, Southerners will save it.

Let us, as Alabamians, grasp the hand of destiny and walk out of the shadow of fear and fill our divine destination. Let us not simply defend but let us assume the leadership of the fight and carry our leadership across this nation. God has placed us here in this crisis. Let us not fail in this, our most historical moment.

You are here today, present in this audience, and to you over this great state, wherever you are in sound of my voice, I want to humbly and with all sincerity, thank you for your faith in me.

I promise you that I will try to make you a good governor. I promise you that, as God gives me the wisdom and the strength, I will be sincere with you. I will be honest with you.

I will apply the old sound rule of our fathers, that anything worthy of our defense is worthy of one hundred percent of our defense. I have been taught that freedom meant freedom from any threat or fear of government. I was born in that freedom, I was raised in that freedom. I intend to live in that freedom and God willing, when I die, I shall leave that freedom to my children as my father left it to me.

STAND UP FOR ALABAMA

My pledge to you to "Stand up for Alabama" is a stronger pledge today than it was the first day I made that pledge. I shall "Stand up for Alabama," as Governor of our State. You stand with me and we, together, can give courageous leadership to millions of people throughout this nation who look to the South for their hope in this fight to win and preserve our freedoms and liberties.

So help me God.

And my prayer is that the Father who reigns above us will bless all the people of this great sovereign State and nation, both white and black.

I thank you.

BLACKS WANT SEPARATION, NOT INTEGRATION

MALCOLM X

Not all black activists believed in Martin Luther King Jr.'s goal of attaining equal rights for blacks through peaceful demonstrations. Malcolm X was one of the best-known advocates of black equality "by any means necessary," including violence, as he stated in one of his speeches.

Born Malcolm Little, the son of a Baptist minister, the future Malcolm X acquired a criminal record as a teenager. While in prison, he converted to the Black Muslim faith, an American variation of Islam led by Elijah Muhammad and devoted to the upraising of blacks through devotion and a return to African roots. This religion, far more radical in its stance on black-white relations than the beliefs of Martin Luther King Jr., gave Malcolm a reason to turn his life around, and its influence led him to drop his "slave" surname and adopt the letter X. After his release from prison in 1953, Malcolm X traveled the United States promoting Black Muslim ideology and black pride and decrying American treatment of its black citizens.

Eventually, his views began to conflict with Elijah Muhammad's, and in 1964 he left the organization and founded his own group, Muslim Mosque, Inc., and later, the Organization of Afro-American Unity.

Conflict between Elijah Muhammad's and Malcolm X's followers sometimes became violent, and possibly led to Malcolm's assassination in 1965, allegedly by Black Muslims. Malcolm's charismatic leadership left a lasting legacy of black pride.

Excerpted from "Twenty Million Black People in a Political, Economic, and Mental Prison," by Malcolm X, in *Malcolm X: The Last Speeches*, edited by Bruce Perry. Copyright © 1989 by Betty Shabazz and Pathfinder Press. Reprinted with permission.

Malcolm X gave the following speech in 1963, while he was still a follower of Elijah Muhammad. In it he disparages blacks who want to be like whites, or even live among whites in an integrated society. He preaches the need for a separate black society. After splitting from the Black Muslims, his views became less extreme than those expressed here.

N ow in speaking as a—professing to speak for Black people by representing the Honorable Elijah Muhammad, you want to know who does he represent. Who does he speak for? There are two types of Negroes in this country. There's the bourgeois type who blinds himself to the condition of his people, and who is satisfied with token solutions. He's in the minority. He's a handful. He's usually the handpicked Negro who benefits from token integration. But the masses of Black people who really suffer the brunt of brutality and the conditions that exist in this country are represented by the leadership of the Honorable Elijah Muhammad.

So when I come in here to speak to you, I'm not coming in here speaking as a Baptist or a Methodist or a Democrat or a Republican or a Christian or a Jew or—not even as an American. Because if I stand up here—if I could stand up here and speak to you as an American we wouldn't have anything to talk about. The problem would be solved. So we don't even profess to speak as an American. We are speaking as—I am speaking as a Black man. And I'm letting you know how a Black man thinks, how a Black man feels, and how dissatisfied Black men should have been 400 years ago. So, and if I raise my voice you'll forgive me or excuse me, I'm not doing it out of disrespect. I'm speaking from my heart, and you get it exactly as the feeling brings it out.

Two Types of Negroes

When I pointed out that there are two kinds of Negroes—some Negroes don't want a Black man to speak for them. That type of Negro doesn't even want to be Black. He's ashamed of being Black. And you'll never hear him refer to himself as Black. Now that type we don't pretend to speak for. You can speak for him. In fact you can have him. [*Laughter*]

But the ones that the Honorable Elijah Muhammad speaks for are those whose pattern of thinking, pattern of thought, pattern of behavior, pattern of action is being changed by what the Honorable Elijah Muhammad is teaching throughout America. These are that mass element, and usually when you hear the press refer to the Honorable Elijah Muhammad, they refer to him as a teacher of hate or an advocator of violence or—what's this other thing?—Black supremacist.

Actually this is the type of propaganda put together by the press, thinking that this will alienate masses of Black people from what he's saying. But actually the only one whom that type of propaganda alienates is this Negro who's always up in your face begging you for what you have or begging you for a chance to live in your neighborhood or work on your job or marry one of your women. Well that type of Negro naturally doesn't want to hear what the Honorable Elijah Muhammad is talking about. But the type that wants to hear what he's saying is the type who feels that he'll get farther by standing on his own feet and doing something for himself towards solving his own problem, instead of accusing you of creating the problem and then, at the same time, depending upon you to do something to solve the problem.

NEW UNCLE TOMS

So you have two types of Negro. The old type and the new type. Most of you know the old type. When you read about him in history during slavery he was called "Uncle Tom." He was the house Negro. And during slavery you had two Negroes. You had the house Negro and the field Negro. The house Negro usually lived close to his master. He dressed like his master. He wore his master's secondhand clothes. He ate food that his master left on the table. And he lived in his master's house—probably in the basement or the attic—but he still lived in the master's house. So whenever that house Negro identified himself, he always identified himself in the same sense that his master identified himself.

When his master said, "We have good food," the house Negro would say, "Yes, we have plenty of good food." "We" have plenty of good food. When the master said that "we have a fine home here," the house Negro said, "Yes, we have a fine home here." When the master would be sick, the house Negro identified himself so much with his master he'd say, "What's the matter boss, we sick?" His master's pain was his pain. And it hurt him more for his master to be sick than for him to be sick himself. When the house started burning down, that type of Negro would fight harder to put the master's house out than the master himself would.

But then you had another Negro out in the field. The house Negro was in the minority. The masses—the field Negroes were the masses. They were in the majority. When the master got sick, they prayed that he'd die. [*Laughter*] If his house caught on fire, they'd pray for a wind to come along and fan the breeze.

If someone came to the house Negro and said, "Let's go, let's separate," naturally that Uncle Tom would say, "Go where? What could I do without boss? Where would I live? How would I dress? Who would look out for me?" That's the house Negro. But if you went to the field Negro and said, "Let's go, let's separate," he wouldn't even ask you where or how. He'd say, "Yes, let's go." And that one ended right there.

So today you have a twentieth-century-type of house Negro. A twentieth-century Uncle Tom. He's just as much an Uncle Tom today as Uncle Tom was 100 or 200 years ago. Only he's a modern Uncle Tom. That Uncle Tom wore a handkerchief around his head. This Uncle Tom wears a top hat. He's sharp. He dresses just like you do. He speaks the same phraseology, the same language. He tries to speak it better than you do. He speaks with the same accents, same diction. And when you say, "your army," he says, "our army." He hasn't got anybody to defend him, but anytime you say "we" he says "we." "Our president," "our government," "our Senate," "our congressmen," "our this and our that." And he hasn't even got a seat in that "our" even at the end of the line. So this is the twentieth-century Negro. Whenever you say "you," the personal pronoun in the singular or in the plural, he uses it right along with you. When you say you're in trouble, he says, "Yes, we're in trouble."

THE NEW NEGRO

But there's another kind of Black man on the scene. If you say you're in trouble, he says, "Yes, you're in trouble." [*Laughter*] He doesn't identify himself with your plight whatsoever.

And this is the thing that the white people in America have got to come to realize. That there are two types of Black people in this country. One who identifies with you so much so he will let you brutalize him and still beg you for a chance to sit next to you. And then there's one who's not interested in sitting next to you. He's not interested in being around you. He's not interested in what you have. He wants something of his own. He wants to sit someplace where he can call his own. He doesn't want a seat in your restaurant where you can give him some old bad coffee or bad food. He wants his own restaurant. And he wants some land where he can build that restaurant on, in a city that it can go in. He wants something of his own.

And when you realize that this type of thinking is existing and developing fastly or swiftly behind the teachings of the Honorable Elijah Muhammad among the so-called Negroes, then I think that you'll also realize that this whole phony effort at integration is no solution. Because the most you can do with this phony effort toward integration is to put out some token integration. And whereas this Uncle Tom will accept your token effort, the masses of Black people in this country are no more interested in token integration than they would be if you offered them a chance to sit inside a furnace somewhere. The only one who'll do that is this twentieth-century Uncle Tom. And you can always tell him because he wants to be next to you. He wants to eat with you. He wants to sleep with you. He wants to marry your woman, marry your mother, marry your sister, marry your daughter. And if you watch him close enough he's even after your wife. [*Laughter*]

DESIRE TO BE WHITE

This type has blind faith—in your religion. He's not interested in any religion of his own. He believes in a white Jesus, white Mary, white angels, and he's trying to get to a white heaven. When you listen to him in his church singing, he sings a song, I think they call it, "Wash me white as snow." He wants to be—he wants to be turned white so he can go to heaven with a white man. It's not his fault; it's actually not his fault. But this is the state of his mind. This is the result of 400 years of brainwashing here in America. You have taken a man who is black on the outside and made him white on the inside. His brain is white as snow. His heart is white as snow. And therefore, whenever you say, this is ours, he thinks he's white, the same as you, so what's yours he thinks is also his. Even right on down to your woman.

Now many of them will take offense at my implying that he wants your woman. They'll say, "No, this is what Bill Bowen, Talmadge, and all of the White Citizens' Councils say." They say that to fool you. If this is not what they want, watch them. And if you find evidence to the contrary, then I'll take back my words. But all you have to do is give him the chance to get near you, and you'll find that he is not satisfied until he is sitting next to your woman, or closer to her than that.

And this type of Negro, usually he hates Black and loves white. He doesn't want to be Black, he wants to be white. And he'll get on his bended knees and beg you for integration, which means he would rather live—rather than live with his own kind who love him, he'll force himself to live in neighborhoods around white people whom he knows don't mean him any good. And again I say, this is not his fault. He is sick. And as long as America listens to this sick Negro, who is begging to be integrated into American society despite the fact that the attitude and actions of whites are sufficient proof that he is not wanted, why then you are actually allowing him to force you into a position where you look just as sick as he looks.

If someone holds a gun on a white man and makes him embrace me—put his hand, arm, around me—this isn't love nor is it brotherhood. What they are doing is forcing the white man to be a hypocrite, to practice hypocrisy. But if that white man will put his arm around me willingly, voluntarily, of his own volition, then that's love, that's brotherhood, that's a solution to the problem.

Likewise, as long as the government has to get out here and legislate to force Negroes into a white neighborhood or force Negroes into a white school or force Negroes into white industry—and make white people pretend that they go for this—all the government is doing is making white people be hypocrites. And rather than be classified as a bigot, by putting a block, the average white person actually would rather put up a hypocritical face, the face of a hypocrite, than to tell the Black man, "No, you stay over there and let me stay over here." So that's no solution.

As long as you force people to act in a hypocritical way, you will never solve their problem. It has to be—the Honorable Elijah Muhammad teaches us that a solution has to be devised that will be satisfactory, completely satisfactory to the Black man and completely satisfactory to the white man. And the only thing that makes white people completely satisfied and Black people completely satisfied, when they're in their right mind, is when the Black man has his own and the white man has his own. You have what you need; we have what we need. Then both of us have something, and even the Bible says, "God bless the child that has his own." And the poor so-called Negro doesn't have his own name, doesn't have his own language, doesn't have his own culture, doesn't have his own history. He doesn't have his own country. He doesn't even have his own mind. And he thinks that he's Black 'cause God cursed him. He's not Black 'cause God cursed him. He's Black because—rather he's cursed because he's out of his mind. He has lost his mind. He has a white mind instead of the type of mind that he should have.

New Uncle Tom and White Liberals Cause the Race Problem

So, when these so-called Negroes who want integration try and force themselves into the white society, which doesn't solve the problem—the Honorable Elijah Muhammad teaches us that that type of Negro is the one that creates the problem. And the type of white person who perpetuates the problem is the one who poses as a liberal and pretends that the Negro should be integrated, as long as he integrates someone else's neighborhood. But all these whites that you see running around here talking about how liberal they are, and we believe everybody should have what they want and go where they want and do what they want, as soon as a Negro moves into that white liberal's neighborhood, that white liberal is—well he moves out faster than the white bigot from Mississippi, Alabama, and from someplace else.

So we won't solve the problem listening to that Uncle Tom Negro, and the problem won't be solved listening to the so-called white liberal. The only time the problem is going to be solved is when a Black man can sit down like a Black man and a white man can sit down like a white man. And make no excuses whatsoever with each other in discussing the problem. No offense will stem from factors that are brought up. But both of them have to sit down like men, on one side and on the other side, and look at it in terms of Black and white. And then take some kind of solution based upon the factors that we see, rather than upon that which we would like to believe. . . .

Also this type of so-called Negro, by being intoxicated over the white man, he never sees beyond the white man. He never sees beyond America. He never looks at himself or where he fits into things on the world stage. He only can see himself here in America, on the American stage or the white stage, where the white man is in the majority, where the white man is the boss. So this type of Negro always feels like he's outnumbered or he's the underdog or he's the minority. And it puts him in the role of a beggar—a cowardly, humble, Uncle Tomming beggar on anything that he says is—that should be his by right. [*Commotion*]

SICK NEGRO IN WHITE AMERICA

Whereas there is—he wants to be an American rather than to be Black. He wants to be something other than what he is. And knowing that America is a white country, he knows he can't be Black and be an American too. So he never calls himself Black. He calls himself an American Negro—a Negro in America. And usually he'll deny his own race, his own color, just to be a second-class American. He'll deny his own history, his own culture. He'll deny all of his brothers and sisters in Africa, in Asia, in the East, just to be a second-class American. He denies everything that he represents or everything that was in his past, just to be accepted into a country and into a government that has rejected him ever since he was brought here.

For this Negro is sick. He has to be sick to try and force himself amongst some people who don't want him, or to be accepted into a government that has used its entire political system and educational system to keep him relegated to the role of a second-class citizen. Therefore he spends a lifetime begging for acceptance into the same government that made slaves of his people. He gives his life for a country that made his people slaves and still confines them to the role of second-class citizens. And we feel that he wastes his time begging white politicians, political hypocrites, for civil rights or for some kind of first-class citizenship.

He is like a watchdog or a hound dog. You may run into a dog—no matter how vicious a dog is, you find him out in the street, he won't bite you. But when you get him up on the porch, he will growl, he'll take your leg. Now that dog, when he's out in the street, only his own life is threatened, and he's never been trained to protect himself. He's only been trained by his master to think in terms of what's good for his master. So when you catch him in the street and you threaten him, he'll go around you. But when you come up on the—through the gate when he's sitting on the master's porch, then he'll bare his fangs and get ready to bite you. Not because you're threatening him, but because you threaten his master who has trained him not to protect himself but to protect the property of the master.

And this type of twentieth-century Uncle Tom is the same way. He'll never attack you, but he'll attack me. I can run into him out on the street and blast him; he won't say a word. But if I look like I'm about to blast you in here, he'll open up his mouth and put up a better defense for you than you can put up for yourself. Because he hasn't been trained to defend himself. He has only been trained to open up his mouth in defense of his master. He hasn't been educated, he's been trained. When a man is educated, he can think for himself and defend himself and speak for himself.

Malcolm X (center) was a charismatic activist who fought for black equality. He was assassinated in 1965.

But this twentieth-century Uncle Tom Negro never opens up his mouth in defense of a Black man. He opens up his mouth in defense of the white man, in defense of America, in defense of the American government. He doesn't even know where his government is, because he doesn't know that he ever had one. He doesn't know where his country is, because he doesn't know that he ever had one.

NEW UNCLE TOM DOESN'T REALIZE NEGROES' RICH HISTORY

He believes in exactly what he was taught in school. That when he was kidnapped by the white man, he was a savage in the jungle someplace eating people and throwing spears and with a bone in his nose. And the average American Negro has that concept of the African continent. It is not his fault. This is what has been given to him by the American educational system.

He doesn't realize that there were civilizations and cultures on the African continent at a time when the people in Europe were crawling around in the caves, going naked. He doesn't realize that the Black man in Africa was wearing silk, was wearing slippers— that he was able to spin himself, make himself at a time when the people up in Europe were going naked.

He doesn't realize that he was living in palaces on the African continent when the people in Europe were living in caves. He doesn't realize that he was living in a civilization in Africa where science had been so far advanced, especially even the astronomical sciences, to a point where Africans could plot the course of the stars in the universe when the people up in Europe still thought the earth was round, the planet was round—or flat.

He doesn't realize the advancement and the high state of his own culture that he was living in before he was kidnapped and brought to this country by the white man. He knows nothing about that. He knows nothing about the ancient Egyptian civilization on the African continent. Or the ancient Carthaginian civilization on the African continent. Or the ancient civilizations of Mali on the African continent. Civilizations that were highly developed and produced scientists. Timbuktu, the center of the Mali Empire, was the center of learning at a time when the people up in Europe didn't even know what a book was. He doesn't know this because he hasn't been taught. And because he doesn't know this, when you mention Africa to him, why he thinks you're talking about a jungle. . . .

So you're familiar with that type of Negro. And the Black man that you're not familiar with is the one that we would like to point out now.

New Black Wants Separation

He is the new—he is the new type. He is the type that the white man seldom ever comes in contact with. And when you do come in contact with him, you're shocked, because you didn't know that this type of Black man existed. And immediately you think, well here's one of those Black supremacists or racists or extremists who believe in violence and all of that kind of—well that's what they call it. [*Laughter*]

This new type of Black man, he doesn't want integration; he wants separation. Not segregation, separation. To him, segregation, as we're taught by the Honorable Elijah Muhammad, means that which is forced upon inferiors by superiors. A segregated community is a Negro community. But the white community, though it's all white, is never called a segregated community. It's a separate community. In the white community, the white man controls the economy, his own economy, his own politics, his own everything. That's his community. But at the same time while the Negro lives in a separate community, it's a segregated community. Which means it's regulated from the outside by outsiders. The white man has all of the businesses in the Negro community. He runs the politics of the Negro community. He controls all the civic organizations in the Negro community. This is a segregated community.

We don't go for segregation. We go for separation. Separation is when you have your own. You control your own economy; you control your own politics; you control your own society; you control your own everything. You have yours and you control yours; we have ours and we control ours.

They don't call Chinatown in New York City or on the West Coast a segregated community, yet it's all Chinese. But the Chinese control it. Chinese voluntarily live there, they control it. They run it. They have their own schools. They control their own politics, control their own industry. And they don't feel like they're being made inferior because they have to live to themselves. They choose to live to themselves. They live there voluntarily. And they are doing for themselves in their community the same thing you do for yourself in your community. This makes them equal because they have what you have. But if they didn't have what you have, then they'd be controlled from your side; even though they would be on their side, they'd be controlled from your side by you.

So when we who follow the Honorable Elijah Muhammad say that we're for separation, it should be emphasized we're not for segregation; we're for separation. We want the same for ourselves as you have for yourself. And when we get it, then it's possible to think more intelligently and to think in terms that are along peaceful lines. But a man who doesn't have what is his, he can never think always in terms that are along peaceful lines.

No Peaceful Suffering for New Negro

This new type rejects the white man's Christian religion. He recognizes the real enemy. That Uncle Tom can't see his enemy. He thinks his friend is his enemy and his enemy is his friend. And he usually ends up loving his enemy, turning his other cheek to his enemy. But this new type, he doesn't turn the other cheek to anybody. He doesn't believe in any kind of peaceful suffering. He believes in obeying the law. He believes in respecting people. He believes in doing unto others as he would have done to himself. But at the same time, if anybody attacks him, he believes in retaliating if it costs him his life. And it is good for white people to know this. Because if white people get the impression that Negroes all endorse this old turn-the-other-cheek cowardly philosophy of Dr. Martin Luther King, then whites are going to make the mistake of putting their hands on some Black man, thinking that he's going to turn the other cheek, and he'll end up losing his hand and losing his life in the try. [*Commotion and laughter*]

So it is always better to let someone know where you stand. And there are a large number of Black people in this country who don't endorse any phase of what Dr. Martin Luther King and these other twentieth-century religious Uncle Toms are putting in front of the public eye to make it look like this is the way, this is the behavior, or this is the thought pattern of most of our people.

Also this new type, you'll find, he doesn't look upon it as being any honor to be in America. He knows he didn't come here on the *Mayflower*. He knows he was brought here in a slave ship. But this twentieth-century Uncle Tom, he'll stand up in your face and tell you about when his fathers landed on Plymouth Rock. His father never landed on Plymouth Rock; the rock was dropped on him [*Laughter*] but he wasn't dropped on it. [*Applause*]

Problem Was Created by Whites

So this type doesn't make any apology for being in America, nor does he make any apology for the problem his presence in America presents for Uncle Sam. He knows he was brought here in chains, and he knows he was brought here against his will. He knows that the problem itself was created by the white man and that it was created because the white man brought us here in chains against our will. It was a crime. And the one who committed that crime is the criminal today who should pay for the crime that was committed. You don't put the crime in jail, you put the criminal in jail. And kidnapping is a crime. Slavery is a crime. Lynching is a crime. And the presence of 20 million Black people in America against their will is a living witness, a living testimony of the crime that Uncle Sam committed, your forefathers committed, when our people were brought here in chains.

And the reason the problem can't be solved today is you try and dress it up and doctor it up and make it look like a favor was done to the Black man by having brought the Black man here. But when you realize that it was a crime that was committed, then you approach the solution to that problem in a different light and then you can probably solve it. And as long as you think Negroes are running around here of the opinion that you're doing them a favor by letting them have some of this and letting them have some of that, why naturally every time you give a little bit more justice or freedom to the Black man, you stick out your chest and say, "See, we're solving the problem."

You're not doing the Black man any favor. If you stick a knife in my back, if you put it in nine inches and pull it out six inches, you haven't done me any favor. If you pull it all the way out, you haven't done me any favor. And this is what you have to realize. If you put a man in jail against his will—illegally, he's not guilty—you frame him up, and then because he resents what you've done to him, you put him in solitary confinement to break his spirit, then after his spirit is broken, you let him out a little bit and give him the general run of the prison, you haven't done him any favor. If you let him out of prison completely, you haven't done him any favor, because you put him in there unjustly and illegally in the first place.

AMERICA IS A PRISON FOR BLACKS

Now you have 20 million Black people in this country who were brought here and put in a political, economic, and mental prison. This was done by Uncle Sam. And today you don't realize what a crime your forefathers have committed. And you think that when you open the door a few cracks, and give this little integration-intoxicated Negro a chance to run around in the prison yard—that's all he's doing—that you're doing him a favor. But as long as he has to look up to someone who doesn't represent him and doesn't speak for him, that person only represents the warden, he doesn't represent some kind of president or mayor or governor or senator or congressman or anything else.

So this new type—the fact has to be faced that he exists. Especially since he's in the house. And he didn't come here because it was his will. So you have to take the blame for his being here.

And once you take the blame, then it's more easy. It's easier for you to approach the problem more sensibly and try and get a solution. And the solution can never be based upon hypocrisy. The Honorable Elijah Muhammad says that this solution has to be based upon reality. Tokenism is hypocrisy. One little student in the University of Mississippi, that's hypocrisy. A handful of students in Little Rock, Arkansas, is hypocrisy. A couple of students going to school in Georgia is hypocrisy. . . .

THE NEW NEGRO SEES BEYOND AMERICA

We don't think as Americans any more, but as a Black man. With the mind of a Black man, we look beyond America. And we look beyond the interests of the white man. The thinking of this new type of Negro is broad. It's more international. This integrationist always thinks in terms of an American. But you find the masses of Black people today think in terms of Black. And this Black thinking enables them to see beyond the confines of America. And they look all over the world. They look at the happenings in the international context.

By this little integrationist Negro thinking locally, by his thinking and desires being confined to America, he's limited. He's the underdog. He's a minority. But the masses of Black people who have been exposed to the teachings of the Honorable Elijah Muhammad, their thinking is more international. They look on this earth and they see that the majority of the people on this earth are dark. And by seeing that the majority of the people on this earth are dark, they don't regard themselves as a minority in America, but rather they regard themselves as part of that vast, dark majority.

So therefore, when you run into that type of Black man, he doesn't speak as an underdog. He doesn't speak like you outnumber him, or he doesn't speak like there's any harm that you can do to him. He speaks as one who outnumbers you. He sees that the dark world outnumbers the white world. That the odds have turned today and are in his favor, are on his side. He sees that the people of this earth are on his side. That time is on his side. That history is on his side. And most important of all, he sees that God is on his side toward getting him some kind of solution that's immediate, and that's lasting, and that is no way connected or concerned or stems from the goodwill or good conscience in any way, shape, 'soever of the man who created—who committed the crime and created the problem in the first place.

Why the United States Is in Vietnam

Lyndon B. Johnson

As the Cold War progressed, U.S. foreign policy became more actively interventionist when an international conflict involved a Communist combatant. The United States and many of its allies were determined that communism not be allowed to make any more headway in the world, and the United States, as the strongest, largest, richest nation, viewed itself as the natural defender of democracy in nations under Communist siege. This perspective dominated American policy for decades as the United States aided anti-Communist forces in Asia, Central and South America, and Africa.

Beginning in 1954, the United States took on a greater role in the conflict between North (Communist) and South (Democratic) Vietnam, but much of its involvement was economic, advisory, and passively threatening through its lurking presence in warships patrolling the waters surrounding the two countries. In 1964, North Vietnamese patrol boats allegedly attacked an American destroyer. That was all that was needed for President Lyndon B. Johnson to begin sending American troops to fight alongside the South Vietnamese.

Not all Americans believed American involvement was justified. A vocal antiwar movement protested. In 1965 Johnson delivered the following response, justifying American participation in the war. He reiterates America's commitment to preserving democracy not only in the United States, but elsewhere when it is challenged by Communists. He also gives voice to the "domino theory"—the belief that if one nation falls to communism, others will follow.

From "Pattern for Peace in Southeast Asia," by Lyndon B. Johnson, *Department of State Bulletin*, April 26, 1965.

Last week 17 nations sent their views to some two dozen countries having an interest in Southeast Asia. We are joining those 17 countries and stating our American policy tonight, which we believe will contribute toward peace in this area of the world.

I have come here to review once again with my own people the views of the American Government.

Tonight Americans and Asians are dying for a world where each people may choose its own path to change. This is the principle for which our ancestors fought in the valleys of Pennsylvania. It is a principle for which our sons fight tonight in the jungles of Viet-Nam.

Viet-Nam is far away from this quiet campus. We have no territory there, nor do we seek any. The war is dirty and brutal and difficult. And some 400 young men, born into an America that is bursting with opportunity and promise, have ended their lives on Viet-Nam's steaming soil.

A PAINFUL ROAD

Why must we take this painful road? Why must this nation hazard its ease, its interest, and its power for the sake of a people so far away?

We fight because we must fight if we are to live in a world where every country can shape its own destiny, and only in such a world will our own freedom be finally secure.

This kind of world will never be built by bombs or bullets. Yet the infirmities of man are such that force must often precede reason and the waste of war, the works of peace. We wish that this were not so. But we must deal with the world as it is, if it is ever to be as we wish.

The world as it is in Asia is not a serene or peaceful place.

The first reality is that North Viet-Nam has attacked the independent nation of South Viet-Nam. Its object is total conquest. Of course, some of the people of South Viet-Nam are participating in attack on their own government. But trained men and supplies, orders and arms, flow in a constant stream from North to South.

This support is the heartbeat of the war.

And it is a war of unparalleled brutality. Simple farmers are the targets of assassination and kidnaping. Women and children are strangled in the night because their men are loyal to their government. And helpless villages are ravaged by sneak attacks. Large-scale raids are conducted on towns, and terror strikes in the heart of cities.

The confused nature of this conflict cannot mask the fact that it is the new face of an old enemy.

Over this war—and all Asia—is another reality: the deepening shadow of Communist China. The rulers in Hanoi are urged on by Peiping. This is a regime which has destroyed freedom in Tibet, which has attacked India, and has been condemned by the United Nations for aggression in Korea. It is a nation which is helping the forces of violence in almost every continent. The contest in Viet-Nam is part of a wider pattern of aggressive purposes.

WHY ARE WE IN SOUTH VIET-NAM?

Why are these realities our concern? Why are we in South Viet-Nam?

We are there because we have a promise to keep. Since 1954 every American President has offered support to the people of South Viet-Nam. We have helped to build, and we have helped to defend. Thus, over many years, we have made a national pledge to help South Viet-Nam defend its independence.

And I intend to keep that promise.

To dishonor that pledge, to abandon this small and brave nation to its enemies, and to the terror that must follow, would be an unforgivable wrong.

We are also there to strengthen world order. Around the globe, from Berlin to Thailand, are people whose well-being rests in part on the belief that they can count on us if they are attacked. To leave Viet-Nam to its fate would shake the confidence of all these people in the value of an American commitment and in the value of America's word. The result would be increased unrest and instability, and even wider war.

We are also there because there are great stakes in the balance. Let no one think for a moment that retreat from Viet-Nam would bring an end to conflict. The battle would be renewed in one country and then another. The central lesson of our time is that the appetite of aggression is never satisfied. To withdraw from one battlefield means only to prepare for the next. We must say in Southeast Asia—as we did in Europe—in the words of the Bible: "Hitherto shalt thou come, but no further."

There are those who say that all our effort there will be futile—that China's power is such that it is bound to dominate all Southeast Asia. But there is no end to that argument until all of the nations of Asia are swallowed up.

RESPONSIBILITY FOR FREEDOM

There are those who wonder why we have a responsibility there. Well, we have it there for the same reason that we have a responsibility for the defense of Europe. World War II was fought in both Europe and Asia, and when it ended we found ourselves with continued responsibility for the defense of freedom.

Our objective is the independence of South Viet-Nam and its freedom from attack. We want nothing for ourselves—only that the people of South Viet-Nam be allowed to guide their own country in their own way. We will do everything necessary to reach that objective, and we will do only what is absolutely necessary.

In recent months attacks on South Viet-Nam were stepped up. Thus it became necessary for us to increase our response and to make attacks by air. This is not a change of purpose. It is a change in what we believe that purpose requires.

We do this in order to slow down aggression.

We do this to increase the confidence of the brave people of South Viet-Nam who have bravely borne this brutal battle for so many years with so many casualties.

And we do this to convince the leaders of North Viet-Nam— and all who seek to share their conquest—of a simple fact:

We will not be defeated.

We will not grow tired.

We will not withdraw, either openly or under the cloak of a meaningless agreement.

We know that air attacks alone will not accomplish all of these purposes. But it is our best and prayerful judgment that they are a necessary part of the surest road to peace.

The Path of Peaceful Settlement

We hope that peace will come swiftly. But that is in the hands of others besides ourselves. And we must be prepared for a long continued conflict. It will require patience as well as bravery— the will to endure as well as the will to resist.

I wish it were possible to convince others with words of what we now find it necessary to say with guns and planes: armed hostility is futile—our resources are equal to any challenge—because we fight for values and we fight for principle, rather than territory or colonies, our patience and our determination are unending.

Once this is clear, then it should also be clear that the only path for reasonable men is the path of peaceful settlement. Such peace demands an independent South Viet-Nam—securely guaranteed and able to shape its own relationships to all others—free from outside interference—tied to no alliance—a military base for no other country.

These are the essentials of any final settlement.

We will never be second in the search for such a peaceful settlement in Viet-Nam.

There may be many ways to this kind of peace: in discussion or negotiation with the governments concerned; in large groups or in small ones; in the reaffirmation of old agreements or their strengthening with new ones.

We have stated this position over and over again 50 times and more to friend and foe alike. And we remain ready with this purpose for unconditional discussions.

And until that bright and necessary day of peace we will try to keep conflict from spreading. We have no desire to see thousands die in battle—Asians or Americans. We have no desire to devastate that which the people of North Viet-Nam have built with toil and sacrifice. We will use our power with restraint and with all the wisdom that we can command.

But we will use it.

A COOPERATIVE EFFORT FOR DEVELOPMENT

This war, like most wars, is filled with terrible irony. For what do the people of North Viet-Nam want? They want what their neighbors also desire—food for their hunger, health for their bodies, a chance to learn, progress for the country, and an end to the bondage of material misery. And they would find all these things far more readily in peaceful association with others than in the endless course of battle.

These countries of Southeast Asia are homes for millions of impoverished people. Each day these people rise at dawn and struggle through until the night to wrest existence from the soil. They are often wracked by diseases, plagued by hunger, and death comes at the early age of 40.

Stability and peace do not come easily in such a land. Neither independence nor human dignity will ever be won, though, by arms alone. It also requires the works of peace. The American people have helped generously in times past in these works, and now there must be a much more massive effort to improve the life of man in that conflict-torn corner of our world.

The first step is for the countries of Southeast Asia to associate themselves in a greatly expanded cooperative effort for development. We would hope that North Viet-Nam would take its place in the common effort just as soon as peaceful cooperation is possible.

The United Nations is already actively engaged in development in this area, and as far back as 1961 I conferred with our authorities in Viet-Nam in connection with their work there. And I would hope tonight that the Secretary-General of the United Nations could use the prestige of his great office and his deep knowledge of Asia to initiate, as soon as possible, with the countries of that area, a plan for cooperation in increased development.

AMERICAN INVESTMENT

For our part I will ask the Congress to join in a billion-dollar American investment in this effort as soon as it is under way. And I would hope that all other industrialized countries, including the Soviet Union, will join in this effort to replace despair with hope and terror with progress.

The task is nothing less than to enrich the hopes and existence of more than a hundred million people. And there is much to be done.

The vast Mekong River can provide food and water and power on a scale to dwarf even our own TVA [Tennessee Valley Authority, an extensive power-generating project]. The wonders of modern medicine can be spread through villages where thousands die every year from lack of care. Schools can be established to train people in the skills needed to manage the process of development. And these objectives, and more, are within the reach of a cooperative and determined effort.

Lyndon B. Johnson

I also intend to expand and speed up a program to make available our farm surpluses to assist in feeding and clothing the needy in Asia. We should not allow people to go hungry and wear rags while our own warehouses overflow with an abundance of wheat and corn and rice and cotton.

So I will very shortly name a special team of outstanding, patriotic, and distinguished Americans to inaugurate our participation in these programs. This team will be headed by Mr. Eugene Black, the very able former President of the World Bank.

THE DREAM OF OUR GENERATION

This will be a disorderly planet for a long time. In Asia, and elsewhere, the forces of the modern world are shaking old ways and uprooting ancient civilizations. There will be turbulence and struggle and even violence. Great social change—as we see in our own country—does not always come without conflict.

We must also expect that nations will on occasion be in dispute with us. It may be because we are rich, or powerful, or because we have made some mistakes, or because they honestly fear our intentions. However, no nation need ever fear that we

desire their land, or to impose our will, or to dictate their institutions.

But we will always oppose the effort of one nation to conquer
another nation.

We will do this because our own security is at stake.

But there is more to it than that. For our generation has a
dream. It is a very old dream. But we have the power, and now
we have the opportunity to make that dream come true.

For centuries nations have struggled among each other. But
we dream of a world where disputes are settled by law and
reason. And we will try to make it so.

For most of history men have hated and killed one another in
battle. But we dream of an end to war. And we will try to make
it so.

For all existence most men have lived in poverty, threatened
by hunger. But we dream of a world where all are fed and
charged with hope. And we will help to make it so.

The ordinary men and women of North Viet-Nam and South
Viet-Nam, of China and India, of Russia and America, are brave
people. They are filled with the same proportions of hate and
fear, of love and hope. Most of them want the same things for
themselves and their families. Most of them do not want their
sons to ever die in battle, or to see their homes, or the homes of
others, destroyed.

Well, this can be their world yet. Man now has the knowledge—
always before denied—to make this planet serve the real needs
of the people who live on it.

I know this will not be easy. I know how difficult it is for reason to guide passion, and love to master hate. The complexities
of this world do not bow easily to pure and consistent answers.

But the simple truths are there just the same. We must all try
to follow them as best we can.

POWER, WITNESS TO HUMAN FOLLY

We often say how impressive power is. But I do not find it impressive at all. The guns and the bombs, the rockets and the warships, are all symbols of human failure. They are necessary symbols. They protect what we cherish. But they are witness to
human folly.

A dam built across a great river is impressive.

In the countryside where I was born, and where I live, I have
seen the night illuminated, and the kitchen warmed, and the
home heated, where once the cheerless night and the ceaseless
cold held sway. And all this happened because electricity came
to our area along the humming wires of the REA [Rural Electri-

fication Administration]. Electrification of the countryside—yes, that, too, is impressive.

A rich harvest in a hungry land is impressive.

The sight of healthy children in a classroom is impressive.

These—not mighty arms—are the achievements which the American nation believes to be impressive. And if we are steadfast, the time may come when all other nations will also find it so.

Every night before I turn out the lights to sleep I ask myself this question: Have I done everything that I can do to unite this country? Have I done everything I can to help unite the world, to try to bring peace and hope to all the peoples of the world? Have I done enough?

Ask yourselves that question in your homes—and in this hall tonight. Have we, each of us, all done all we can do? Have we done enough?

We may well be living in the time foretold many years ago when it was said: "I call heaven and earth to record this day against you, that I have set before you life and death, blessing and cursing: therefore choose life, that both thou and thy seed may live."

This generation of the world must choose: destroy or build, kill or aid, hate or understand. We can do all these things on a scale that has never been dreamed of before.

Well, we will choose life. And so doing, we will prevail over the enemies within man, and over the natural enemies of all mankind.

WESTERN DECADENCE THREATENS THE COMMUNIST IDEAL

HUNG TSIN-TA AND NAN HSUEH-LIN

In 1949, after decades of conflict between Nationalists and Communists, the Communist People's Republic of China was formed under the leadership of dictator Mao Zedong (Mao Tse-tung). Under Mao's radical Communist philosophy, the country underwent massive changes, forced to conform to his strict view of a revolutionary Communist society. Agricultural collectives and national industries replaced private enterprise. Literature and art depicting workers supporting the state replaced traditional Chinese culture.

From 1966 to 1976 Mao promoted the Cultural Revolution, a youth movement that worked to eradicate all remaining remnants of bourgeois and bureaucratic culture, including religion. Expression of all kinds was strictly regulated. Intellectuals and artists in many fields were "re-educated" to conform to the Communist ideal of all people working together as one for the good of the nation as a whole. Individualist and materialist views were regarded as treasonous affronts to the nation. American culture was viewed as particularly pernicious.

The selection below was published during the Cultural Revolution in an English-language magazine that promoted Chinese communism. The authors, adherents of Chairman Mao's policies, accuse the Soviet Union of being willingly corrupted by U.S. culture and conclude that the people of the world will eventually

From "Salesmen of Reactionary Western Culture," by Hung Tsin-ta and Nan Hsueh-lin, in *Chinese Literature*, vol. 11 (Beijing: Foreign Languages Press, 1968).

see the light of communism and overthrow decadent Western culture.

T he so-called "Western culture" is nothing but imperialist culture, which is most reactionary, decadent and vicious. With the imperialist system heading for total collapse, its culture, like the sun setting beyond the Western hills resembles a dying person who is sinking fast. Since Khrushchev and his successors came to power they have gone all out to carry out "cultural co-operation" with U.S. imperialism and thrown the door wide open to "Western culture," which has thus found a new market in the Soviet Union. Amid the fanfare of their all-round reactionary collaboration, a new sinister deal was made between the Soviet Union and the United States not long ago— the Soviet-U.S. cultural exchange agreement for 1968–1969 signed in Moscow.

This agreement covers many fields, ranging from science, technology, literature, art, education, medicine and physical culture to the exchange of "artists," "experts," periodicals, exhibitions and films, and so on. More than twenty departments are involved in the exchange of visits by "experts" alone.

If the United States only "made a breach" in 1958 when the arch-renegade Khrushchev signed the first "cultural agreement" with it, then today, ten years later, when the sixth "cultural agreement" has been signed, the world's most reactionary, decadent and vicious "Western culture" has flooded Soviet Union like the muddy water rushing through a breached dyke. The Soviet revisionist renegade clique's efforts to go in for wholesale "Westernization" have earned it the plaudits of its master. In a recent speech, U.S. imperialist chief [President Lyndon] Johnson gleefully said that no other period in history has been more productive in promoting co-operation between the two countries.

Let us see how "productive" Soviet-U.S. "cultural co-operation" is at present.

Not only has Soviet revisionist literature become increasingly decadent under the impact of Soviet-U.S. "cultural co-operation," but the most reactionary and rotten American literature has been translated and published in large quantities in the Soviet Union. The chief editor of the Soviet revisionist *Literaturnaya Gazeta* confessed in a statement that American novels were the best sellers in the foreign book market in the Soviet Union.

Disguised as "cultural co-operation," degenerate Western music, commercialized jazz, has become the rage in the Soviet revisionist musical, dancing and theatrical world. The rock-'n'-roll, the twist and other similar vulgar dances are executed more madly than before. The Soviet revisionist renegade clique has not only spent big sums of money to invite large numbers of night club jazz bands from the West to perform in different parts of the Soviet Union, it has also sent its own musicians to take part in "international contests" so as to learn from Western jazz bands. As a result, various weird-named American and British jazz bands have performed in the Soviet Union. . . . The Soviet revisionist Central Television Station started a monthly series of lectures on "Jazz Music, Yesterday and Today" in its fourth programme. In these lectures, American commercialized jazz was unctuously described as the "real music" and the "sacred music" and was lauded as helping to "understand the world." Seven disgusting "jazz music festivals" have been held in Moscow and six other Soviet cities this year to give such vulgar music a big boost. And as before, the Soviet revisionist clique has given the green light to performances of many vulgar American plays on the Soviet stage.

SOVIET CULTURE HANDED OVER TO HOLLYWOOD

As a result of Soviet-U.S. "cultural co-operation," Soviet revisionist screens have been turned into an instrument for publicizing "Western culture." As it did previously, the Soviet revisionist clique has spared no efforts to lavish praise on American films through its newspapers and magazines, and it has printed many books to publicize these reactionary American films. Moreover, in January this year, the Soviet revisionist Central Television Station began obsequiously introducing American film stars to its viewers. The Soviet revisionists in effect, have handed over a large part of the Soviet screen to Hollywood. S.K. Romanovsky, Chairman of the Soviet Committee for Cultural Relations with Foreign Countries, admitted that often "there are several hundred copies of American films being shown in our country." Even this cannot satisfy the Soviet revisionist clique. The new "cultural agreement" explicitly provides for "the widest possible distribution" of American films.

Under the signboard of "cultural co-operation," the Soviet revisionist clique has thrown the door wide open to Voice of America [radio programming], an instrument of U.S. imperialism for opposing communism, China, the people and revolution. The notorious V.O.A., as former U.S. President Kennedy said, is an "arm" of the U.S. Government. But the Soviet revisionist clique loves it as dearly as flies love muck. As far back as soon after the 20th Congress of the C.P.S.U. [the Soviet Union's Communist

Party], the revisionist clique intermittently stopped jamming V.O.A. broadcasts to the Soviet Union. Later, an agreement was reached between the Soviet Union and the United States under which the former formally and completely stopped jamming and provided facilities for V.O.A. transcription programmes to be broadcast in the Soviet Union. After [Leonid] Brezhnev and [Aleksey] Kosygin came to power, they gave V.O.A. the go-ahead signal, allowing it to be heard all over the country. With great exultation, the U.S. press said that in content, form and technique, the Soviet revisionist radio and television programmes had been "radically reformed" after the fashion of the West.

SOVIETS CURRY FAVOR WITH U.S.

Soviet revisionism's television is the same as the radio. Last year the Soviet revisionist clique racked its brains making a television newsreel called "Chronicle of Half Century" in the name of "celebrating" the 50th anniversary of the October Revolution and "reviewing" the history of the Soviet Union over the past half century. On the one hand, the newsreel frantically attacks China; on the other hand, it nauseatingly advocates "Soviet-U.S. friendship" to curry favour with its master. A good number of shots of Soviet revisionists embracing and kissing Americans were produced to show Soviet-U.S. "friendship" and "co-operation." Even the coming to power and the death of the U.S. imperialist chief Kennedy was shamelessly brought into the "chronicle" as a "big event" in the Soviet Union. The commentary flatters Kennedy as a "clear-headed" and "practical" man and sadly "mourns" his death.

It is also under the camouflage of Soviet-U.S. "cultural co-operation" that the decadent way of life of the Western bourgeoisie penetrates the Soviet Union everywhere. Not long ago, a so-called "Soviet fashion design show" was held in Washington. On display were "outstanding fashions" by Soviet revisionism's "top contemporary designers," including so-called "space age" fashions and "revolutionized" clothing designed by "the Soviet Union's best-known avant-garde designer" who copied the cowboy pants and mini-skirts of the West. The marked trends of "Westernization" in the fashion show won praise and applause from their U.S. master who cheered it as "inspiring." The Soviet revisionists also put on dog shows in Moscow similar to those in New York and London and went so far as to make this thing fashionable. All this is absolutely the height of rottenness.

To speed up the "Westernization" of the Soviet Union, the Soviet revisionist clique is becoming more and more open in utilizing "international tourism" to attract by all possible means "tourists" of all descriptions from the Western capitalist countries, allowing them to spread the dissipated Western way of life in the Soviet Union. The Soviet revisionists recently announced that more than one hundred cities in all fifteen union republics will be opened to large numbers of pleasure-seeking foreign bourgeois gentlemen and ladies coming to the Soviet Union. In addition, the Soviet revisionists are developing "cultural co-operation" with U.S. imperialism in a big way so as to surrender completely to the latter and bring on a wholesale "Westernization" of the Soviet Union through such channels as setting up "night clubs," free "distribution" of the U.S. magazine *America,* holding rotating U.S. exhibitions, introduction of American experience, exchanging students, commendation of scholars, sponsoring pen clubs and reprinting articles of the reactionary U.S. press, etc.

COUNTER-REVOLUTIONARY UNHOLY ALLIANCE

The above mentioned facts are but a few examples of this "co-operation." All these "fruits" fully show that since the confidential Glassboro talks by the chieftains of Soviet revisionism and U.S. imperialism in June 1967, U.S.-Soviet counter-revolutionary collaboration has shown a new striking development. It has developed in many fields—on earth, and under the sea and in the sky, by the "hot line" contact between the White House and Kremlin and through the opening of the New York–Moscow direct airline, and in political, economic and military fields as well as in the cultural realm. Soviet revisionism and U.S. imperialism have entered into an out-and-out counter-revolutionary unholy alliance.

Our great leader Chairman Mao teaches us: "In the world today all culture, all literature and art belong to definite classes and are geared to definite political lines." The large-scale importation of "Western culture" by the Soviet revisionist clique today wholly aimed at serving the all-round restoration of capitalism in the Soviet Union and the comprehensive Soviet-U.S. counter-revolutionary collaboration. In other words, to serve its counter-revolutionary revisionist political line. The so-called Soviet-U.S. "cultural co-operation," like their collaboration in the political, economic and military fields, is the product of the capitulationist line of "peaceful co-existence" carried out by the Soviet revisionist clique of renegades, and it is a big betrayal of the people of the Soviet Union and of the world.

Why is Soviet-U.S. "cultural co-operation" carried out so unscrupulously and so feverishly in this period? The U.S. magazine *Newsweek* in its July 15, 1968, issue admits outright that Soviet revisionism and U.S. imperialism "have often found themselves undergoing many of the same internal and external stresses and strains in the rapidly changing world of the 1960s." What are these "internal and external stresses and strains"? First of all, in this period, under the leadership of our great leader Chairman Mao himself, China has victoriously unfolded the great prole-tarian cultural revolution which has tremendous influence on the whole world and deals a heavy blow to imperialism, revisionism and reaction. The radiance of Mao Tse-tung's thought lights up the road for liberation of the world's revolutionary people. The news of victories from the hills of the Truong Son Range, the war drums on the equator, the red flags fluttering in the Pu Pan Mountains, the roar of the raging tide along the Mississippi River, and the revolutionary storm in West Europe and North America . . . all these converged into an irresistible revolutionary torrent which is rapidly breaching the dam of global Soviet-U.S. counter-revolutionary collaboration. The drastically deepening political and economic crises in imperialist countries headed by the United States have become an incurable disease. Modern re-visionism with the Soviet revisionist clique as its centre, which is daily disintegrating, is in a shaky state. Such an excellent revo-lutionary situation naturally means "stresses and strains" for U.S. imperialism and the Soviet revisionist clique. It is in these days that they have to depend on each other to bolster up their totter-ing bourgeois dictatorships and use decadent "Western culture" as a talisman in a vain effort to prevent the surging tide of the world revolution and save themselves from being drowned in it.

USURPED BY REVISIONISTS

Our great leader Chairman Mao wisely points out: "The Soviet Union was the first socialist state and the Communist Party of the Soviet Union was created by Lenin. Although the leadership of the Soviet Party and state has now been usurped by revision-ists, I would advise comrades to remain firm in the conviction that the masses of the Soviet people and of Party members and cadres are good, that they desire revolution and that revisionist rule will not last long." It can be asserted that the Soviet people who have a glorious revolutionary tradition will by no means let their country be ruined by these renegades of the Soviet Union in such a way. No matter how reckless and unbridled their out-rageous acts, the U.S. imperialists and Soviet revisionists can never change the law of historical development, nor can they hold back the victory of socialism in the Soviet Union and the world over. U.S. imperialism and Soviet revisionism together with the decadent "Western culture" they treasure will eventu-ally be buried by the people of the Soviet Union, the United States and the whole world.

A Dream of Racial Equality

Martin Luther King Jr.

In 1955, Rosa Parks, a Montgomery, Alabama, seamstress, was arrested when she refused to give up her bus seat to a white man. In response to her arrest, a group of fifty black community leaders, including Martin Luther King Jr., met and organized the Montgomery bus boycott. They urged all black Montgomerians, and indeed, all people of conscience, to refuse to ride the city buses until the bus company ended its discriminatory policy of allowing blacks to sit only in the back of the bus and only after all whites had seats. The boycott cost King a $500 fine, but it sparked the modern civil rights movement.

Until his assassination in 1968, King was one of the main spokesmen for the movement, which took all avenues to bring political and civil equality to black people in the United States. Bus boycotts, lunch counter sit-ins, political rallies, prayers, and voter-registration campaigns were all part of the movement. Although people in the movement had different views of how equality should be achieved, King's brand of passive resistance, inspired by actions of Mahatma Gandhi decades earlier in India, were predominant. King and his cohorts urged their followers to nonviolently demonstrate against injustice and assert their rights.

One of the most gifted and eloquent speakers of his time, Martin Luther King Jr. influenced not only civil rights activists, but also generations of blacks and whites alike through his ideas and his expression. The civil rights movement may have been sparked by a tired black woman's decision to not move to the back of the bus, but it was sustained by King's leadership. The son of a Southern Baptist minister and a minister himself, King

"I Have a Dream," by Martin Luther King Jr., 1963. Reprinted by arrangement with the Estate of Martin Luther King Jr., c/o Writers House as sole agent of the proprietor.

was a founder of Atlanta's National Association for the Advancement of Colored People (NAACP) and the Southern Christian Leadership Conference (SCLC). In 1964, he was awarded the Nobel Peace Prize for his role in the civil rights movement.

Few who heard the charismatic King speak could fail to be moved. One of his most lasting and influential speeches was one he gave during the 1963 March on Washington, a protest march that drew 250,000 people to the nation's capital to demand equal rights for all Americans. That speech is reprinted below.

F ive score years ago, a great American, in whose symbolic shadow we stand today, signed the Emancipation Proclamation. This momentous decree came as a great beacon of light of hope to millions of Negro slaves who had been seared in the flames of withering injustice. It came as a joyous daybreak to end the long night of their captivity.

NEGRO STILL NOT FREE

But one hundred years later, the Negro still is not free. One hundred years later, the life of the Negro is still sadly crippled by the manacles of segregation and the chains of discrimination.

One hundred years later, the Negro lives on a lonely island of poverty in the midst of a vast ocean of material prosperity. One hundred years later, the Negro is still languished in the corners of American society and finds himself an exile in his own land. So we have come here today to dramatize a shameful condition.

In a sense we have come to our nation's capital to cash a check. When the architects of our republic wrote the magnificent words of the Constitution and the Declaration of Independence, they were signing a promissory note to which every American was to fall heir. This note was a promise that all men, yes, black men as well as white men, would be granted the unalienable rights of life, liberty, and the pursuit of happiness.

It is obvious today that America has defaulted on this promissory note insofar as her citizens of color are concerned. Instead of honoring this sacred obligation, America has given the Negro people a bad check; which has come back marked "insufficient funds."

But we refuse to believe that the bank of justice is bankrupt. We refuse to believe that there are insufficient funds in the great vaults of opportunity of this nation. So we have come to cash this check—a check that will give us upon demand the riches of freedom and the security of justice.

The Promises of Democracy

We have also come to this hallowed spot to remind America of the fierce urgency of now. This is no time to engage in the luxury of cooling off or to take the tranquilizing drug of gradualism. Now is the time to make real the promises of democracy. Now is the time to rise from the dark and desolate valley of segregation to the sunlit path of racial justice. Now is time to lift our nation from the quick sands of racial injustice to the solid rock of brotherhood. Now is the time to make justice a reality for all of God's children.

It would be fatal for the nation to overlook the urgency of the movement and to underestimate the determination of the Negro. This sweltering summer of the Negro's legitimate discontent will not pass until there is an invigorating autumn of freedom and equality. 1963 is not an end but a beginning. Those who hope that the Negro needed to blow off steam and will now be content will have a rude awakening if the nation returns to business as usual.

There will be neither rest nor tranquility in America until the Negro is granted his citizenship rights. The whirlwinds of revolt will continue to shake the foundations of our nation until the bright day of justice emerges.

But there is something that I must say to my people who stand on the warm threshold which leads into the palace of justice. In the process of gaining our rightful place we must not be guilty of wrongful deeds.

Let us not seek to satisfy our thirst for freedom by drinking from the cup of bitterness and hatred. We must forever conduct our struggle on the high plane of dignity and discipline. We must not allow our creative protest to degenerate into physical violence. Again and again we must rise to the majestic heights of meeting physical force with soul force.

The marvelous new militancy which has engulfed the Negro community must not lead us to a distrust of all white people, for many of our white brothers, as evidenced by their presence here today, have come to realize that their destiny is tied up with our destiny and they have come to realize that their freedom is inextricably bound to our freedom. This offense we share mounted to storm the battlements of injustice must be carried forth by a bi-racial army. We cannot walk alone.

We Cannot Turn Back

And as we walk, we must make the pledge that we shall always march ahead. We cannot turn back. There are those who are asking the devotees of civil rights, "When will you be satisfied?" We can never be satisfied as long as the Negro is the victim of the unspeakable horrors of police brutality.

We can never be satisfied as long as our bodies, heavy with fatigue of travel, cannot gain lodging in the motels of the highways and the hotels of the cities. We cannot be satisfied as long as the Negro's basic mobility is from a smaller ghetto to a larger one.

We can never be satisfied as long as our children are stripped of their selfhood and robbed of their dignity by signs stating "for whites only." We cannot be satisfied as long as a Negro in Mississippi cannot vote and a Negro in New York believes he has nothing for which to vote. No, we are not satisfied, and we will not be satisfied until justice rolls down like waters and righteousness like a mighty stream.

I am not unmindful that some of you have come here out of excessive trials and tribulation. Some of you have come fresh from narrow jail cells. Some of you have come from areas where your quest for freedom left you battered by the storms of persecution and staggered by the winds of police brutality. You have been the veterans of creative suffering. Continue to work with the faith that unearned suffering is redemptive.

Go back to Mississippi; go back to Alabama; go back to South Carolina; go back to Georgia; go back to Louisiana; go back to the slums and ghettos of the Northern cities, knowing that somehow this situation can, and will be changed. Let us not wallow in the valley of despair.

I Have a Dream

So I say to you, my friends, that even though we must face the difficulties of today and tomorrow, I still have a dream. It is a dream deeply rooted in the American dream that one day this nation will rise up and live out the true meaning of its creed—we hold these truths to be self evident, that all men are created equal.

I have a dream that one day on the red hills of Georgia, sons of former slaves and sons of former slave-owners will be able to sit down together at the table of brotherhood.

I have a dream that one day, even the state of Mississippi, a state sweltering with the heat of injustice, sweltering with the heat of oppression, will be transformed into an oasis of freedom and justice.

I have a dream my four little children will one day live in a nation where they will not be judged by the color of their skin but by the content of their character. I have a dream today!

I have a dream that one day, down in Alabama, with its vicious racists, with its governor having his lips dripping with the words of interposition and nullification, that one day, right there in Alabama, little black boys and black girls will be able to join hands with little white boys and white girls as sisters and brothers. I have a dream today!

I have a dream that one day every valley shall be exalted, every hill and mountain shall be made low, the rough places shall be made plain, and the crooked places shall be made straight and the glory of the Lord will be revealed and all flesh shall see it together.

This is our hope. This is the faith that I go back to the South with.

With this faith we will be able to hear out of the mountain of despair a stone of hope. With this faith we will be able to transform the jangling discords of our nation into a beautiful symphony of brotherhood.

LET FREEDOM RING

With this faith we will be able to work together to pray together, to struggle together, to go to jail together, to stand up for freedom together, knowing that we will be free one day. This will be the day when all of God's children will be able to sing with new meaning—"my country 'tis of thee; sweet land of liberty; of thee I sing; land where my fathers died, land of the pilgrim's pride; from every mountain side, let freedom ring"—and if America is to be a great nation, this must become true.

So let freedom ring from the prodigious hilltops of New Hampshire.

Let freedom ring from the mighty mountains of New York.

Let freedom ring from the heightening Alleghenies of Pennsylvania.

Let freedom ring from the snow-capped Rockies of Colorado.

Let freedom ring from the curvaceous slopes of California.

But not only that.

Let freedom ring from Stone Mountain of Georgia.

Let freedom ring from Lookout Mountain of Tennessee.

Let freedom ring from every hill and molehill of Mississippi, from every mountainside, let freedom ring.

And when we allow freedom to ring, when we let it ring from every village and hamlet, from every state and city, we will be able to speed up that day when all of God's children—black men and white men, Jews and Gentiles, Catholics and Protestants—will be able to join hands and to sing in the words of the old Negro spiritual. "Free at last, free at last; thank God Almighty, we are free at last."

The Chinese Cultural Revolution: The Red Guards

Teresa Poole

Following World War II, after years of conflict between Chinese Communists and Nationalists, civil war broke out in earnest. The Communists, under the leadership of Mao Zedong, won the battle in 1949, forcing the Nationalist contingent, led by Chiang Kai-shek, to Formosa, an island off China's southeast coast. Mao declared China the People's Republic on October 1, 1949.

Mao immediately began to collectivize the country's farms and to nationalize industry. He instituted five-year plans and other strategies to improve the country's economic status and make the country more socially equitable. Ideologically opposed to class superiority, which he ascribed to intellectuals, party leaders, and virtually all others but peasants, Mao instituted the decade-long Cultural Revolution in 1966. The Cultural Revolution was a mass movement carried out at first by the youth of the Red Guard, who fanatically set to the task of cutting down to size those who offended Mao's sense of what a Chinese Communist should be. The Red Guards beat and killed intellectuals and other political offenders and destroyed schools and religious temples. By 1968 even Mao could see that the Red Guards had gotten out of hand, and he disbanded them, sending many of them to the country to be "re-educated."

From "Mao's Frenzy of Mass Violence," by Teresa Poole, *Independent on Sunday*, May 12, 1996. Reprinted with permission.

The repressive nature of the Cultural Revolution continued, but on a less violent level. Nonconformists were imprisoned. Traditional Chinese culture was forbidden, and a new culture of art, drama, and music, all based on and dedicated to the Chinese Communist revolution, was born.

As Mao's health began to fail in the early 1970s, the Gang of Four—four Mao loyalists including his wife—took over more control of the country, but after Mao's death in 1976, the Gang of Four was imprisoned and the Cultural Revolution ended.

Journalist Teresa Poole interviewed former members of the Red Guard for the following article.

I n May 1966, Lu Chen, Yao Zhongyong, and Li Jiang were 12-year-old schoolboys in Beijing. Today, like people in their early 40s all over China, they have at least one thing in common: The defining experience of their lives began that month and, three decades later, remains vivid. For Lu Chen, it is still almost too painful to talk about. "It happened a long time ago," he says—and starts to sob.

From 1966 to 1968, his father was detained as a "Capitalist Roader." Lu's mother was away at the time, and Lu was left to fend for himself. "I just ate noodles," he remembers. "But one day, I had a meat sausage. The Red Guards saw me eating it in the courtyard." Not long afterward, his father was allowed home for a brief visit. "One night, father came and knelt down by my bed," Lu recalls. "He begged me not to eat in front of other people any longer. It was so shocking. For a very long time, when I picked up a bowl of food, I felt scared."

Yao Zhongyong remembers how he and his brother wandered the streets of Beijing. "We could go to Houhai Lake to see people committing suicide. Some wrote their wills in chalk on the ground. One could often see corpses in the lake."

Li Jiang is haunted by one particular afternoon. "Near our school, there was a wife of a landlord," he says. The Red Guards went to the house to take the property. "But the old lady was quite tough. At first she screamed and tried to push the Red Guards out of the house. . . . We pushed the old lady on the ground and beat her for one hour with our belts. And she died. I was one of the beaters."

MOBILIZATION OF THE MASSES

Thirty years ago, Chairman Mao launched China's Cultural Revolution. The "16 May Circular" called for the unrestrained mobilization of the masses against the "bourgeoisie" who had "sneaked" into the Communist Party as "counterrevolutionary revisionists." Ostensibly, Mao's aim was to purify the revolution; in reality, his goal was to reassert control over the party and purge his political rivals.

To this end, he unleashed a decade of savagery and chaos, encouraging a whole generation of teenagers to run riot in a frenzy of mass violence so fanatical as to be scarcely credible. Soon schools and universities had suspended all classes, and Red Guards were taking to the city streets in an uncontrolled fury of righteousness. Teachers were often the first victims, locked up in schools and in many cases tortured. "Bad elements" were beaten to death by teenagers wielding metal-buckled belts. No one knew who would be targeted next as neighbors and work mates turned on each other in vicious denunciations and "criticism sessions." Over the next decade, hundreds of thousands—probably more than 1 million—died.

Yao's most vivid memory is of the scene in the garden of an old Qing Dynasty palace where a group of Red Guards was dumping belongings ransacked from people's homes: "At the back door was a pile of books, all very precious. There was a line of 'bad factor' people, also known as 'cow ghosts' and 'snake spirits.' They were beaten by the Red Guards along the way and forced to carry the ransacked things. Pages from these books were blowing in the wind."

What was going on in the minds of these teenagers? "There were two kinds of feeling," says Li, whose parents were party officials. "I thought that the beatings were correct, and in order to express that we were revolutionary, we must beat other people. But this kind of thinking contradicted the moral education I had previously been given. In our hearts we also felt frightened. Because of this fear we were eager to take part in the revolution. The main feeling then was fear."

FEAR AND CONFUSION

Fear was compounded by confusion as the Cultural Revolution spread through society. No one could be sure they were safe. Toward the end of 1966, Li's parents fell from grace and were attacked as rightists, and he could no longer be officially classified as a Red Guard. This was common; of the 100 youths in his Red Guard group, he says, 80 saw their families turned upon. Such teenagers then formed their own gangs.

The chaos gave free rein to personal vendettas and settling of old grudges. Standard humiliation rituals evolved for the public criticism sessions. Li's father was forced to stand for hours in the crippling "airplane position," bent over with arms stretched out behind, and made to wear a dunce's hat and a placard detailing his crimes around his neck. "In 1968, after a criticism meeting, my father had heart failure and died," says Li. Women often had half their heads shaved.

By this time, the whole country was engulfed in violence. Armed battles between Red Guard factions took place in major cities across China. Many factories had closed, and foreign trade collapsed. Food was in short supply.

REEDUCATION OF THE RED GUARDS

In mid-1968, alarmed that he was losing control of the situation, Mao disbanded the Red Guards. Over the next year or so, 16 million urban teenagers were sent into the countryside for "reeducation" by the peasants. This highly organized logistical feat illustrates one of the most striking aspects of the Cultural Revolution. The rule of law had completely broken down, yet the Communist Party apparatus could still exert complete control over the population.

Among those who boarded trains were Lu, Li, and Yao. "We were very happy because we thought we were responding to appeals from Mao," says Lu, who was dispatched to Shuangyashan village in the far northeastern province of Heilongjiang. His group included 12 boys and 12 girls from Beijing. "We were sent in equal numbers, with the idea that we could build a family there."

On arrival, the urban teenagers were shocked at the living conditions and physical work. Lu was set to work planting vast acreages of wheat and corn by hand, herding cattle, and laboring. "The psychological hardship was worse than the physical pain," Lu says. "There was only work, no schooling. But we had to read Mao's works every day."

The persecutions continued, Lu says: "We used to be called on by local party officials to join in criticism sessions against local 'bad factors.' I remember one engineer, Ye Tingchang. The group planned to hold a criticism meeting against him and went looking for him. We found him and beat him. Ye said: 'I should be beaten. I deserve that.' I can never forget this incident."

Li and Yao were dispatched, separately, to the opposite corner of China, an impoverished Yunnan province town called Ruili on the border with Burma (now Myanmar). "Living conditions were very poor, quite different from what the propaganda had taught us," says Li.

DOUBTS ABOUT MAO

Li's first doubts about Mao started in September 1971, when, on a visit to Beijing, he heard about the downfall and death of Lin

Biao, Mao's second in command. He recalls, "In the past, I had adored Mao without limit. But by that time I had lived in the countryside, and I found the difference between the reality and what we had learned in school was enormous. So the death of Lin Biao aroused all my feelings and suspicions and made me think."

As the years passed, the Cultural Revolution started to wind down. In 1974, Lu and Li were allowed to return to Beijing. After Mao's death in 1976 and the subsequent arrest of the Gang of Four, China finally set about a process of material and spiritual repair. Lu now works as a private investigator and is trying to qualify as a lawyer. He married one of the 12 girls in his reeducation group: "One good thing to come out of the experience," he smiles.

When the universities reopened in 1978, Li studied history in Beijing, went on to be a journalist and publisher, and is now in property development. Yao, at that point still in Yunnan, passed the exams for teachers' training college, where he met his wife. He did not return to live in Beijing until 1990. He now works for the *City Environment Paper*. Lu and Yao joined the Communist Party; Li did not.

Lu is the one most visibly still pained by his family's experiences. As we sit in his office, he expresses sadness about lost opportunity. Li, on the other hand, sits poised and confident in his book-lined study, an intellectual trying to make the most of business opportunities in modern China. But he reflects: "I feel that there is no real authority in the world. In that period, all the teachers, officials, parents whom I respected, all lost their dignity. My respect for humanity was totally smashed."

Yao, who spent by far the longest time out of Beijing, is the most tense and serious on first meeting. He says: "I can face any cruel reality without being astonished. But that does not mean I am numb to life. It also wasted a lot of time and made me miss a lot of chances. . . . Most of my generation is not very successful."

WOUND ON A GENERATION'S HEART

Just as significant to them is the legacy of the Cultural Revolution to Chinese society as a whole. "The wound on the heart of my generation is too deep," says Lu. He points out how everyone had to mouth slogans to have any chance of surviving. "Everybody learned how to lie," he says.

During the turbulent years, the persecutors often became the persecuted, and there were no easy divisions between the guilty and the innocent. Few are honest enough to recall publicly their roles as protagonists or victims. Do the three men feel that more people should have been punished for their crimes? Lu says:

"The influence of the Cultural Revolution was too wide. Almost everybody has some black mark in their history. It is not possible to punish them all." Yao agrees. "The crimes were witnessed by a lot of people, but it is not practical to punish all the murderers." With Mao still lying in state in Tiananmen Square, the history of that period is still politically sensitive. Even in private, people do not usually talk very openly about their experiences. Lu says, "That period is a kind of scar on Chinese history. Like a scar on somebody's body, they do not want to expose it."

In Beijing's curio markets, foreign tourists browse through Cultural Revolution memorabilia, bargaining over old copies of Mao's Little Red Book or kitsch statuettes of revolutionary opera characters. These are not mementos locals want to buy.

WOMEN MUST BE RESPECTED AS PEOPLE

BETTY FRIEDAN

The 1963 publication of *The Feminine Mystique* by suburban housewife and former journalist Betty Friedan galvanized the modern women's movement. The book explored women's role in American life. It exposed the frustrations of American women who had felt unprecedented social and economic freedom and responsibility during World War II when they had had to take over many jobs in the American workforce. Then, once the war was over, women were expected to return to the almost solely domestic roles they had assumed prior to the war. Friedan's book argues that this situation was detrimental not only to women but to the nation as a whole, which was losing the talents of intelligent, educated, ambitious, and capable people who made up more than half of the country's population. Friedan's book was the voice of a generation of women who had been unable to name, let alone express, their discontent. Other factors, such as the civil rights movement, combined with the impact of Friedan's book to make the women's movement and the underlying theory of feminism, a vocal force in American society.

One issue that unified women with otherwise diverse politics was the legalization of abortion. Those who believed that women should have control over their own bodies—that they should have the right to decide whether to bear a child or not, even after conception—sought to overturn American laws of the time, which in most states made abortion illegal. Friedan was asked to speak at the First National Conference for Repeal of Abortion Laws held in Chicago in 1969. Although her topic was abortion rights, most of her fiery speech declaimed the role of women in American society. The following article is excerpted from that speech.

Betty Friedan was a founder and first president of the National Organization for Women (NOW), an organization dedicated to equal rights for women in employment, housing, politics, and other areas. The group campaigned vigorously for the Equal Rights Amendment, a proposed amendment to the U.S. Constitution that would formally guarantee women equality under law in all areas of American life. Despite feminists' efforts, only thirty-five of the required thirty-eight states ratified the amendment by the end of the ten-year deadline. Friedan also founded the National Women's Political Caucus, which focused on electing women to political office.

W omen, even though they're almost too visible as sex objects in this country, are invisible people. As the Negro was the invisible man, so women are the invisible people in America today: women who have a share in the decisions of the mainstream of government, of politics, of the church—who don't just cook the church supper, but preach the sermon; who don't just look up the ZIP codes and address the envelopes, but make the political decisions; who don't just do the housework of industry, but make some of the executive decisions. Women, above all, who say what their own lives and personalities are going to be, and no longer listen to or even permit male experts to define what "feminine" is or isn't.

WOMEN AS SEX OBJECTS

The essence of the denigration of women is our definition as sex object. To confront our inequality, therefore, we must confront both society's denigration of us in these terms and our own self-denigration as people.

Am I saying that women must be liberated from sex? No. I am saying that sex will only be liberated to be a human dialogue, sex will only cease to be a sniggering, dirty joke and an obsession in this society, when women become active self-determining people, liberated to a creativity beyond motherhood, to a full human creativity.

Am I saying that women must be liberated from motherhood? No. I am saying that motherhood will only be a joyous and responsible human act when women are free to make, with full conscious choice and full human responsibility, the decisions to become mothers. Then, and only then, will they be able to embrace motherhood without conflict, when they will be able to de-

fine themselves not just as somebody's mother, not just as ser-
vants of children, not just as breeding receptacles, but as people
for whom motherhood is a freely chosen part of life, freely cele-
brated while it lasts, but for whom creativity has many more dimensions, as it has for men.

Then, and only then, will motherhood cease to be a curse and
a chain for men and for children. For despite all the lip service
paid to motherhood today, all the roses sent on Mother's Day, all
the commercials and the hypocritical ladies' magazines' celebration of women in their roles as housewives and mothers, the fact
is that all television or night-club comics have to do is go before
a microphone and say the words "my wife," and the whole audience erupts into gales of guilty, vicious and obscene laughter.

Hostility Between the Sexes

The hostility between the sexes has never been worse. The image of women in avant-garde plays, novels and movies, and behind the family situation comedies on television is that mothers
are man-devouring, cannibalistic monsters, or else Lolitas, sex
objects—and objects not even of heterosexual impulse, but of
sadomasochism. That impulse—the punishment of women—is
much more of a factor in the abortion question than anybody
ever admits.

Motherhood is a bane almost by definition, or at least partly
so, as long as women are forced to be mothers—and only mothers—against their will. Like a cancer cell living its life through
another cell, women today are forced to live too much through
their children and husbands (they are too dependent on them,
and therefore are forced to take too much varied resentment, vin-
dictiveness, inexpressable resentment and rage out on their husbands and children).

Perhaps it is the least understood fact of American political life:
the enormous buried violence of women in this country today.
Like all oppressed people, women have been taking their violence out on their own bodies, in all the maladies with which
they plague the M.D.'s and the psychoanalysts. Inadvertently,
and in subtle and insidious ways, they have been taking their violence out, too, on their children and on their husbands, and
sometimes they're not so subtle.

The battered-child syndrome that we are hearing more and
more about from our hospitals is almost always to be found in
the instance of unwanted children, and women are doing the bat-
tering, as much or more than men. In the case histories of psychologically and physically maimed children, the woman is always the villain, and the reason is our definition of her: not only

as passive sex object, but as mother, servant, someone else's mother, someone else's wife.

Am I saying that women have to be liberated from men? That men are the enemy? No. I am saying the *men* will only be truly liberated to love women and to be fully themselves when women are liberated to have a full say in the decisions of their lives and their society.

Until that happens, men are going to bear the guilty burden of the passive destiny they have forced upon women, the suppressed resentment, the sterility of love when it is not between two fully active, joyous people, but has in it the element of exploitation. And men will not be free to be all they can be as long as they must live up to an image of masculinity that disallows all the tenderness and sensitivity in a man, all that might be considered feminine. Men have enormous capacities in them that they have to repress and fear in order to live up to the obsolete, brutal, bear-killing, Ernest Hemingway, crew-cut Prussian, napalm-all-the-children in-Vietnam, bang-bang-you're-dead image of masculinity. Men are not allowed to admit that they sometimes are afraid. They are not allowed to express their own sensitivity, their own need to be passive sometimes and not always active. Men are not allowed to cry. So they are only half-human, as women are only half-human, until we can go this next step forward. All the burdens and responsibilities that men are supposed to shoulder alone makes them, I think, resent women's pedestal, much as that pedestal may be a burden for women.

THE REAL SEXUAL REVOLUTION

This is the real sexual revolution. Not the cheap headlines in the papers about at what age boys and girls go to bed with each other and whether they do it with or without the benefit of marriage. That's the least of it. The real sexual revolution is the emergence of women from passivity, from the point where they are the easiest victims for all the seductions, the waste, the worshiping of false gods in our affluent society, to full self-determination and full dignity. And it is the emergence of men from the stage where they are inadvertent brutes and masters to sensitive, complete humanity.

This revolution cannot happen without radical changes in the family as we know it today; in our concepts of marriage and love, in our architecture, our cities, our theology, our politics, our art. Not that women are special. Not that women are superior. But these expressions of human creativity are bound to be infinitely more various and enriching when women and men are allowed to relate to each other beyond the strict confines of the *Ladies'*

Home Journal's definition of the Mamma and Papa marriage.

If we are finally allowed to become full people, not only will children be born and brought up with more love and responsibility than today, but we will break out of the confines of that sterile little suburban family to relate to each other in terms of all of the possible dimensions of our personalities—male and female, as comrades, as colleagues, as friends, as lovers. And without so much hate and jealousy and buried resentment and hypocrisies, there will be a whole new sense of love that will make what we call love on Valentine's Day look very pallid.

1970–1980

CHAPTER 4

Apartheid in South Africa

William S. Ellis

From the seventeenth century until nearly the end of the twentieth, most of the continent of Africa was colonized by one European power or another, most of which wished to exploit Africa's human and natural resources. The continent was rich in coal, gold, diamonds, and other minerals, and its substantial native populations were considered by Europeans mere sources of cheap slave labor. South Africa, by contrast, was atypically established as a homeland for the Boers—Dutch for *peasants*—who first came to the area in the mid–seventeenth century.

French Huguenots escaping religious persecution in France settled in the area about the same time, and soon the French and Dutch intermingled, the Dutch gradually distancing themselves from the Dutch East India Company, the powerful trading monopoly that had sent them to this new land to establish a restocking station for Dutch ships traveling from Europe and Asia. Over the next two and one-half centuries, the Boers engaged in periodic struggles with native populations, and in the early nineteenth century, they came into conflict with the British, who had established a coastal colony nearby. The British banned slavery and wrote laws allowing blacks to take their Boer masters to court. The unyielding Boers set out on the so-called Great Trek through the dry interior country to the area of Transvaal and the Orange River, where they reestablished themselves as farmers.

When diamonds and gold were discovered in the area in 1867, the British attacked the Boers under the guise of liberating Africans from slavery. The British won, and the country became a British colony. In 1910, the Union of South Africa was formed from two former Boer republics, Transvaal and Orange Free State. It remained a part of the British Commonwealth until 1961, when its Prime Minister, Hendrik F. Verwoerd, declared the nation—an area three times the size of California, covering the entire southern tip of Africa—a republic.

Following the formation of the union, the Boers, now called Afrikaners, struggled to keep their nation a white enclave within a black continent. In 1948, South Africa officially adopted the policy of apartheid—"apartness." Stringent laws were designed to keep the races apart in almost every way—except that blacks could work for whites. Apartheid strictly defined racial designations—"white," "black," "coloured," "Indian," or "Asian"—and the laws treated each group differently. Every person over age sixteen had to carry an identity card that stated his or her official race, which determined where the person could live, what hours he or she could be in certain areas, and how other laws applied to that individual. Apartheid gave whites virtually all political and economic power even though they made up less than 15 percent of the country's population. It gave whites the best land and designated poor, leftover spots for communities where blacks had to live. Blacks and whites were forbidden to marry outside their race. Separate schools, hospitals, and other facilities were designated for blacks, whites, coloureds, and Indians.

The African National Congress (ANC), an organization representing black South Africans, began a campaign of nonviolent protest, modeled on the campaign for independence Mahatma Gandhi waged in India. But in 1960, when government security forces broke up a rally in the black township of Sharpeville by shooting and killing sixty-seven people and wounding almost two hundred, the ANC became more militant. Violence broke out many times over the next years, perpetrated by both sides.

Eventually, in the 1970s, under both internal and international pressure, South Africa began to grant some political rights to blacks by establishing four black "homelands" (*bantustans*), which some people compared to American Indian reservations. Blacks had full citizenship rights in the homelands, which were small areas with poor resources widely separated from one another so that the white minority would be less fearful of black unification and revolt.

In the following article, William S. Ellis describes the history and effect of apartheid, as observed by him during a several-week journey through South Africa. Ellis was a senior editor and writer for *National Geographic* for twenty-four years.

I n the course of six weeks in that tense and troubled, but still lovely, land at the bottom of the African Continent, I would encounter nightmares. There was raging anger and riot, fear and confusion. And there were young people falling—dying— in the streets of Soweto.

It is called a township, but Soweto is more than that. It is Fortress Black Africa in a nation grown wealthy on black labor and white-minority rule. It was in Soweto that the troubles started last June with a student protest. It was in Soweto that a black workers' strike was organized. It was in Soweto, more than any other place, that youngsters gave form and expression to a new militancy that has astounded their parents.

Perhaps a million people live in Soweto. All are black, with the largest single tribal group being Zulu. Most of those who work do so in Johannesburg, 15 miles away, and in the suburbs of that largest of South African cities. At night, when they return to the workers' dormitories and small houses, there is outrageous crime. Indeed, few cities, if any, in the world have a higher crime rate than Soweto (in September 1976 there were 145 reported murders), and certainly none is more tightly primed for combustive mob violence.

"It's like having a bomb in your backyard," a white businessman said. "But what can we do? Without the manpower we draw from there, Johannesburg would not survive."

CREATURE OF APARTHEID

Soweto is a creature of apartheid, which means "apartness" in Afrikaans, the language of the Afrikaners whose Dutch forebears settled this land. Apartheid: keeping the whites in one place and the nonwhites in others. The word has become a linguistic melanoma. It had brought widespread condemnation down on South Africa, but not enough to crush the resolve of Balthazar John Vorster, Prime Minister of South Africa, who once said to me, "Thank God I sleep well."

Many Afrikaners say that apartheid—it is now sometimes referred to as "plural democracy"—is not fully understood outside the country. There is truth in that. For one thing, apartheid, as official government policy, is less than thirty years old. It was with a mandate to institute the practice that the National Party came to power in 1948. Since that time, in order to give legality to almost all forms of racial separation, the government has legislated as heavily as any government in history. South Africans of all colors order their lives from a catalog of acts.

Thus there are complexities, and they are compounded by certain anomalies involving the role of the white man in early South

African history. The Dutch came to the Cape—empty then except for a scattering of Hottentots and Bushmen—not as 19th-century colonialists, but as 17th-century settlers. They regard themselves as no less an African tribe than, say, the Zulus. From their ancestors, the Voortrekkers who pushed northeast from Cape Colony to claim the land with its wealth of beauty and natural resources, they have drawn lessons in strength and courage.

Most Nationalist Afrikaners of today are convinced that those hard-won gains must be preserved, just as many are convinced that what they do to preserve them carries the seal of Biblical righteousness. It was the Lord, they say, who planted this new nation in Africa, and it was He who decreed that there be racial purity within its bounds.

Allied with Deity or not, the white stewardship of South Africa and its 16.5 million blacks (white population: 4.3 million) is now faced with a serious internal challenge. It may be that developments over the past year have set the stage for the last stand of racial-minority rule in Africa. This is a voice from Soweto: "We are the last generation [of blacks] . . . who will ask for dialogue, and if it does not come about, we can expect something worse than the riots."

VIOLENT STUDENT PROTESTS

The first riot occurred last June 16 when black students protested against the use of Afrikaans as an additional teaching language. It didn't stop with that, even after the government rescinded the requirement. After bullets from police guns tore into the ranks of demonstrating teenagers, buses and buildings took fire from petrol bombs. Work stoppages were called, and some of those who chose to ignore them returned to Soweto after a day on the job to find nothing but smoldering rubble where their houses had stood.

On the first day of the first strike the trains and buses that shuttle more than 250,000 persons daily between Soweto and Johannesburg ran all but empty. The job absentee rate reached 70 percent. The great, gleaming city built on gold slowed. The streets, suddenly, were devoid of the mass of blacks sweeping sidewalks, washing windows, moving from building to building as bearers of goods and messages, waiting, always waiting, for slow-moving freight elevators and dispatchings of boss men.

Appraisals of the impact varied. Some businessmen admitted to hardships. Prime Minister Vorster said the action served only to harm the black worker. "Not only did businessmen and industrialists find they were over-staffed, but they started to make changes," he told me. "And that is the danger as far as the black is concerned. If he doesn't look after his work, employers will make changes."

Black labor is cheap in South Africa, and some employers use it in saturation quantities. Without question, jobs could be abolished in rather large numbers before the economy would start to totter. Such a move would affect not only South Africa's blacks but also many from neighboring countries. There are 150,000 citizens of Lesotho employed in South Africa, together with 60,000 from Mozambique and additional thousands from Botswana and Rhodesia.

"For generations to come," Vorster said, "the main export of African countries will be labor, because they cannot create the job opportunities in their own countries. At the moment they can find work only in South Africa. If we were to tell Lesotho tomorrow, 'You must take back your 150,000 workers here,' can you imagine what would happen to the economy there?"

NO CLEAR BLACK LEADERSHIP

Whatever harm or good they caused, the fact that strikes came off at all was something of a triumph for those who participated, for the protest movement among blacks in South Africa is without clearly defined leadership. No Shaka exists around whom tens of thousands rally for the soul-firing fuel of his words and presence—no one, even, to cast saintly spells over the downtrodden with the magic of the liturgy. Attorneys Nelson Mandela and Robert Sobukwe are two South African blacks who might have assumed such leadership roles, but the government has imprisoned the former and banned all political activity by the latter.

There are only shadows of leadership. And they are cast, more often than not, by teenagers assembled in casual conspiracies. Their generation is the first to grow up in an Africa no longer completely dominated by whites. They themselves, however, like their counterparts in Rhodesia, have lived under the harsh restrictions of white-minority rule since birth. The thought of living under them until death gives rise to a certain desperation. That in turn has made them militant, and they have become that way without parental blessing.

"The parents in Soweto have lost control," Mrs. Esline Shuenyane said. "They do not understand the grievances of their children." Mrs. Shuenyane is a social worker, and the burden of her activities since the disturbances began has at times been difficult to bear. Talking with her, I sensed despair, as if she had gone through her manual of case studies and failed to find precedents for dealing with revolution as a puberty rite.

Many of the parents were born in rural villages where there

were no jobs, no way for a man to earn money for the cattle he would need to become someone of importance. There was little to eat, and surviving marasmus as a child brought no immunity against tuberculosis as an adult. So the men left. More and more of them went away to the cities, until today there are maleless societies along the back roads of South Africa—along a road, for example, that leads out of Nqutu.

VILLAGE LIFE

It's good that I knew the way to Nqutu and didn't have to ask for directions. The name is difficult to pronounce. It's done with a click of the tongue against the roof of the mouth, as one might do to urge a horse to move. *Nuh*(click)*tu*.

The town is in Zululand, in northern Natal. It is a brown and parched place most of the year. And noisy too, with the gassy wheezings of the old buses that come and go through most of the day. There is a small, but clean and comfortable, hotel run by whites for whites only. There is also a hospital, and that is for blacks only. Though the law suspends apartheid in dire emergencies, it is not unknown for a person to die in South Africa because hospital personnel let their fears of violating the law override medical concerns.

The hospital, which provides treatment for a basic, minimal fee, serves an area of almost 700 square miles in which 95,000 persons live. One of them is Khathazile Thusini, a 65-year-old woman whose home is among a group of traditional Zulu huts that sit on a slight rise a hundred yards or so back from a dirt road. When I first saw her, she was hunkered down, chipping at a large stone with a mallet. Her five daughters were there, and grandchildren too, one of whom, a young boy, clung to her neck in a throttling embrace.

Of the 15 members of the family present, not one was an adult male. The husbands and brothers of the daughters were away in the cities, working. They wouldn't be home until Christmas, if then. Meanwhile, money was being sent back, but, most likely, the letters would become more and more infrequent with the passage of time. And also with the passage of time, the seductiveness of the city would spread like lichen, choking off loneliness and the longing for home.

STRINGENT SEPARATION LAWS

Under the plan of things for South Africa, as drafted or amended by the Nationalist government, the more than five million blacks living in urban areas are not to be in permanent residence there. The government holds the power to order the urban black back to the native homeland of his or her tribe. It's all legal under Section 10 of the Bantu Urban Areas Consolidation Act. (Bantu is the government's name for tribes, such as the Zulu and Xhosa, who first came to southern Africa as migrants from the north.) Of all the laws of apartheid, none is more feared by blacks with city jobs than Section 10.

It is South African law that a black who is 16 or older must carry a passbook at all times. The information on those few grimy, well-fingered pages is meant to establish the right of the bearer to be in the area. There is no winking by authorities at Section 10; in some years arrests for violations of the passbook laws have averaged more than 1,500 a day. If found guilty, the person is "endorsed out"—ordered back to the tribal homeland.

"They have the right to appeal within seven days," Mrs. Sheena Duncan said. "We help them do that." Mrs. Duncan, a white woman, is president of Black Sash, an organization that has been helping nonwhites and bedeviling the Nationalist government for more than twenty years. "At first we were known as the Women's Defense of the Constitution," she said, "but the press gave us the name Black Sash. That was because we wore black sashes as a sign of mourning for the rape of the constitution."

Black Sash headquarters is in an office building on Marshall Street in Johannesburg. On most days blacks are there in large numbers to seek assistance. Mrs. Duncan pointed to one, a young, frail woman, and said:

"She comes from Amersfoort in the Transvaal. She has no legal right to be in Johannesburg, and there is no way we can get around it. She's unmarried but has two children to support. She must work. She can either go back to Amersfoort or stay illegally in Johannesburg. I would be very surprised if she went back, because she can't afford to do that. She can't afford to go back and sit there and watch her children starve."

It is an ugly truth that children have starved in South Africa because of this herdlike control of people. At Dimbaza, it is only when you come close that you see the narrow, short mounds spread out in rows. Each has a steel rod at one end, bearing a name and a number. The last rod in the last row is number 908. And that's the number of children buried in a field behind the houses of Dimbaza.

They started dying in the late 1960s, shortly after Dimbaza was created as a resettlement area for thousands of blacks. It was a forced move. Uprooted and thrown into a new environment where there was no way to make a living—where, at first, there wasn't even a supply of drinking water—the people experienced hunger and suffering. Fresh graves were dug for the children each day, and sometimes, when one was buried and the last spadeful of earth was added to the mound, the mother would kneel and place one of the child's toys on the site. Most times it was a doll. A white doll.

A puppy lurched along at my side as I walked through the field, reminding myself that I mustn't be maudlin when writing about the graves of Dimbaza. So rather than say that I wept when I set a toppled toy straight, I'll say that I laughed when the puppy tried to spear a butterfly with his art gum eraser of a nose.

AMID THE TURMOIL, BEAUTY

Riots, hunger, uncertainty. . . . Yes, all of that, but the jacarandas continue to bloom in Pretoria, and the blue-purple shawl that falls over the city is a distraction from the unpleasantries. South Africa is like that, like a zitherist plucking on the emotions to draw chords of pain and delight. If there is a Soweto, there is also a Cape Town, in a setting often called one of the most spectacular in the world. There is the Drakensberg range and the coast at Durban, where the Indian Ocean rolls in with a fierce and wonderful slap of surf. The gold of the Witwatersrand, and diamonds in the earth at Kimberly. And Kruger National Park in the north, where impalas are everywhere, thousands of tawny-skinned impalas dancing on the veld.

There is nothing quite like it in the rest of Africa. The Afrikaner has become one with this land, and that is why peace is not likely to come soon to South Africa. More than three hundred years of history have laminated soul to soil. Any loosening of the bind, even for purposes of reason and fairness, is both painful and frightening.

In April of 1652, the first mate of the Dutch ship *Drommedaris,* three and a half months out of Texel, sighted Table Mountain at today's Cape Town. On board was Jan van Riebeeck. His mission was to establish a waystop at the Cape of Good Hope for the Dutch East India Company. It would be a station where trading vessels could put in for provisions and medical care. Other people were there before the *Drommedaris* docked. They were called Hottentots and Bushmen.

Before the turn of the century many new Dutch settlers had arrived, as well as black and Malay slaves and French Protestant Huguenots. Also, a new color classification had been added. Lighter than black and darker than white, offspring of master and slave, they would become known as Cape Coloureds. Today there are nearly 2.5 million Coloureds in South Africa, most of them in the Cape Town area. They too have become militant in demanding changes. . . .

LOVE OF COUNTRY

Soon after my arrival in South Africa, I went to where it all began, to Cape Town. There are few cities in the world, to my way of thinking, with depth of both character and visual appeal. Cape Town is one. It sits at the bottom of that great continent, a city cleansed with the sparkle of seas and rouged with the shadow of mountains. It is where proteas bloom in a convention of floral splendor unsurpassed on earth.

Atop Table Mountain I watched a woman, a white South African with hints of Teutonic ancestry, as she looked down on the city and then out to the Cape of Good Hope. She stood there for the better part of an hour, unspeaking, and when she turned to leave, her face carried an expression that seemed to have been singed by the fires of emotion. We talked as the cable car, lurching like a wind-kicked kite, started down the mountain.

"I can't tell you how I feel when I'm up there," she said. "The views bring my love of this country into sharp focus. And I *do* love it—as much as any black, as much as any Coloured, and as much as any *verkrumpte* [close-minded one] Afrikaner. There is enough time left to work out peaceful solutions to our problems. There has to be."

But time seemed to be running short in Cape Town. Only a few weeks earlier crowds of Coloureds had stormed through the center of the city, breaking windows, setting fires, challenging police guns with rocks and bottles. In days to follow, tension in the Coloured townships flared into violence. In one 24-hour period, the death toll reached 16.

The troubles came as something of a surprise to the whites. Passivity, apparently, had been misread as contentment. In 1968 representation for the Coloureds in Parliament was abolished, and that, I was to hear over and over, was one of the most damaging mistakes the Nationalist government has made. For one thing, the number of Coloureds in South Africa will probably double by the end of the century, to approximately 4.7 million.

Acting quickly to deflate Coloured unrest, the government announced certain concessions it was willing to make, such as the opening of previously closed areas to Coloured businessmen and entrepreneurs. Meanwhile, the whites of Cape Town were lining up at gun shops to purchase weapons, and thus boost their distinction as the world's most heavily armed civilian population. . . .

BLAMING THE COMMUNISTS

It has become commonplace among many whites in South Africa to lay the blame for current unrest on "the Communists." They point to neighboring Angola, where, a year after independence,

Cuban troops are still very much in evidence, where pictures of Lenin look down from buildings, and where the shelves of bookstores are heavy with volumes on Marxism. They point too to another former Portuguese territory, Mozambique, and its Marxist government. Rhodesia is the remaining buffer country on the north, but a commitment to majority rule has been made there. And South-West Africa, or Namibia, the former German colony controlled by South Africa since 1920—that is also pushing toward independence.

Suddenly South Africa stands fully exposed to those clichéd winds of change.

"I do not believe that South Africa can cope militarily or economically with concerted pressure from so many hostile neighbors. The liberation of Mozambique and Angola has had a great impact here."

Alan Paton scowled, causing his thick eyebrows to bunch and run together. The famed author of *Cry, the Beloved Country* was making it clear that the years—74 for him—have not made broth of his lavalike outspokenness. He remains a stern critic of apartheid and the Nationalist government.

As we sat in the study of his house atop Botha's Hill near Durban, he repeated some thoughts he had put down earlier on paper: "There is one future for South Africa over which we would have no control. That would be if the Soviet Union, Cuba, Mozambique, Angola, and the revolutionaries in South-West Africa attempted by force of arms to impose majority rule upon us. If the West did not intervene, that would be the end of the white tenure of South Africa."

His anger rose when he talked about the Afrikaner Nationalists and their attempts to ensure racial separation and white superiority through legislation. "It is quite clear that whatever else Mr. Vorster does, he will stick to separate development. For a white person to be too militant in demands for social justice means almost certain restriction under the Internal Security Act."

STIFLING DISSENT

He told me that many of his friends—40 at least—had been banned.

"Do you know what that means? It's kind of a living death, really. You're restricted in traveling. You can't enter a school or factory. You can't associate with more than two people at a time, meaning you can't even play a game of bridge. I was never banned. Why? I would say because I have too many friends in the outside world."

Of the many prophetic passages in his most famous book,

written almost thirty years ago, none is more haunting now to Alan Paton than this concern voiced to the Zulu parson who journeys to Johannesburg in search of his sister and his son. "I have one great fear in my heart, that one day when they [the whites] are turned to loving, they will find we are turned to hating."

I asked him if there would be a place for whites in a South Africa under majority rule.

"It will depend entirely on how majority rule is achieved," he said. "If it comes about by consultation, the threat will be minimized. But if the unitary state is imposed by war or revolution, it will result in grief and desolation. If the white army and white air force get wiped out, then obviously the power is gone, and you'd get a tremendous migration of white people out of the country. The poor whites will probably be absorbed, but you wouldn't have any way of lasting here as a rich white. None.

"As for me—well, if I came to the conclusion that the Nationalist government couldn't adapt itself to change, I wouldn't see much point in staying here to witness the desolation. I did my best to stop it and no one paid any attention. Is it my duty to stay here and see it out? I think I would say 'no.' That would be the first time in my life that I would have said that to myself. In all my years I have never given serious thought to leaving South Africa."

BLACK EXCLUSION = WHITE MAJORITY

If the Nationalists have their way there *will be* majority rule. The whites will be in the majority. The ultimate goal of apartheid, other than survival of Afrikaner tribalism, is for evolvement of a Republic of South Africa in which there are no black citizens. Rather, the millions of blacks—who are now considered only "subjects" of South Africa—would be assigned citizenship, according to tribal identification, in the ten areas called "homelands." Each homeland, according to the Nationalist plan, is to become an independent nation. The first, the Transkei, achieved independence late last year.

Therefore, if the homelands policy progresses as planned, there will be 11 nations—ten black and one white—within the present boundaries of the republic. The white slice will encompass something like 87 percent of the land. "But you must remember that our portion includes the desert," Prime Minister Vorster told me.

Critics of the government claim that the black nations are to be nothing more than labor pools for the whites. They also see the nations being set up as buffer-zone appendages dependent on Pretoria for economic survival. Finally, there is condemnation of the policy on the grounds of gross violation of human rights, for it is possible—indeed likely—that millions of blacks will be stripped of their South African identity in exchange for citizenship in a country in which they have no desire to live.

Black "Homelands"

Opposition to the plan is not confined to South Africa. In fact, no other country recognizes the Transkei as an independent country.

The denial of recognition draws a sharp reaction from Prime Minister Vorster. Leaning forward in his chair, cigarette cupped in hand, he said: "If you refuse to recognize the Transkei, then I can't understand how you can recognize any other country: (a) It has defined boundaries; (b) it is bigger than ever so many countries that are independent; (c) its per capita income is higher than about 20 or 30 members of the United Nations, its rate of literacy higher than 40, 50, or 60 members.

"The Transkei is independent in the true sense of the word, as independent as Britain or France or Germany or Ghana, or any other country for that matter. So on what grounds you refuse to recognize the Transkei, I wouldn't know. It would be sheer hypocrisy to refuse to recognize it and still recognize other countries that are far worse off from every angle that you look at it."

The Transkei is in southeastern South Africa, bounded by mountains and the sea. The earth there, while scarred by erosion, is rich and fertile, and the hills are green. The coast is jeweled with lagoons, and the white sands of the beaches spread so wide that they spill into the corridors of heavily treed woods. However it is received politically, the Transkei cannot be denied recognition of its beauty.

There are about two million people living in the Transkei, the great majority Xhosa-speaking blacks. Another two million members of the group (to be accurate, Xhosa is a name for a language, not a single tribe; however, it has come to be accepted as identification for a segment of the black population) live outside, and most of them, like it or not, are to be given Transkei citizenship.

The Prime Minister of the Transkei, Kaiser Matanzima, pursued independence. Gatsha Buthelezi, chief minister of KwaZulu, the Zulu homeland, vows that he will never agree to the emergence of an independent nation for his people under conditions laid down by the Nationalist government.

"I'm very distressed, you know, about the Transkei," he said. "Those people are my brothers and sisters, and for them to be cut out of the world that was theirs is a very tragic thing. That they should have, at the insistence of Pretoria, only crumbs of the world that they've built up is something I lament very, very much. They will become economic hostages of the white-minority regime, in that they will have to depend on financial transfusions from Pretoria.

"That, to me, limits their independence. So one asks whether such independence is worthwhile. I cannot see independence for KwaZulu under these conditions. No Zulu in his right mind would even look at it, would even touch that kind of independence."

CENTURY-OLD VILLAGE UPROOTED

But the mechanics of the homelands policy grind on. People are being moved from here to there in an effort to consolidate scattered settlements. "They're erasing the black spots," a non-Nationalist Afrikaner told me. "Sometimes the eraser grates like sandpaper.

"Our hearts are very sore."

THE PALESTINIAN MOVEMENT: AN INTERVIEW WITH YASIR ARAFAT

ORIANA FALLACI

From the moment the State of Israel was formally established by the United Nations in 1948, its Arab enemies vowed to overthrow it. The land designated as the Jewish state, traditionally known as Palestine, had been the home of millions of Arabs. Some of these people were relocated to other areas in the Middle East, while others remained in Israel. But regardless of where they lived, many Arabs felt that their own homeland had been wrongly taken to create Israel. Arab nations, including Egypt, Syria, Iraq, and Jordan, and various Arab guerrilla organizations warred with Israel, beginning with the Arab-Israeli War of 1948, in which Israel managed to gain even more Arab territory.

In 1964, several guerrilla groups banded together to form the Palestinian Liberation Organization, whose aim was to overthrow Israel and establish the nation of Palestine. The PLO was largely dominated by the radical al-Fatah faction, led by Yasir Arafat. In 1974, the Arab states and the United Nations recognized the PLO as a government in exile.

Despite more than five decades of fighting, little has been resolved. The Palestinians remain a displaced people, and the aging Arafat remains their best-known leader. The following article is excerpted from an interview with Arafat conducted by Italian journalist Oriana Fallaci in 1976 in which Arafat expresses the goals and feelings of the Palestinian people and the PLO.

Fallaci conducted many high-profile interviews and was known for her highly personal approach. Where most journalists remain bound by the idea of journalistic objectivity, Fallaci makes no pretense of doing so. In this interview she addresses Arafat as Abu Ammar, a name that is explained during the interview.

W hen he arrived, on the dot for the appointment, I remained for a moment uncertain, telling myself no, it couldn't be he. He seemed too young, too innocuous. At least at first glance, I noticed nothing in him that showed authority, or that mysterious fluid that always emanates from a leader to assail you like a perfume or a slap in the face. The only striking thing about him was his mustache, thick and identical with the mustaches worn by almost all Arabs, and the automatic rifle that he wore on his shoulder with the free-and-easy air of one who is never separated from it. Certainly he loved it very much, that rifle, to have wrapped the grip with adhesive tape the color of a green lizard: somehow amusing. He was short in height, five feet three, I'd say. And even his hands were small, even his feet. Too small, you thought, to sustain his fat legs and his massive trunk, with its huge hips and swollen, obese stomach.

All this was topped by a small head, the face framed by a kassiah [headdress], and only by observing this face were you convinced that yes, it was he, Yasir Arafat, the most famous guerrilla in the Middle East, the man about whom people talked so much, to the point of tedium. A very strange, unmistakable face that you would have recognized among a thousand in the dark. The face of an actor. Not only for the dark glasses that by now distinguished him like the eyepatch of his implacable enemy [Israeli General] Moshe Dayan, but for his mask, which resembles no one and recalls the profile of a bird of prey or an angry ram. In fact, he has almost no cheeks or forehead. Everything is summed up in a large mouth with red and fleshy lips, then in an aggressive nose, and two eyes that though screened by glass lenses hypnotize you: large, shining, and bulging. Two ink spots. With those eyes he was now looking at me, courteously and absentmindedly. Then in a soft, almost affectionate voice, he murmured in English, "Good evening, I'll be with you in two minutes." His voice had a kind of funny whistle in it. And something feminine. . . .

He was born in Jerusalem, sometime in the late twenties, that his family was noble and his youth spent in easy circumstances: his father owned an old fortune still largely unconfiscated. Such confiscation, which took place over the course of a century and a half, had been imposed by the Egyptians on certain land estates and on certain property in the center of Cairo. And then? Let's see. . . . Then in 1947 Yasir had fought against the Jews who were giving birth to Israel and had enrolled in Cairo University to study engineering. In those years he had also founded the Palestinian Student Association, the same from which the nucleus of Al Fatah was to emerge. Having obtained his degree, he had gone to work in Kuwait; here he had founded a newspaper in support of the nationalist struggle, and he had joined a group called the Muslim Brothers. In 1955 he had gone back to Egypt to take an officers' training course and specialize in explosives; in 1963 he had helped especially in the birth of Al Fatah and assumed the name of Abu Ammar. That is, He Who Builds, Father Builder. In 1967 he had been elected president of the PLO, the Palestinian Liberation Organization, a movement that now includes the members of Al Fatah, of the Popular Front, of Al Saiqa, and so forth; only recently he had been chosen as the spokesman of Al Fatah, its messenger. . . .

THE INTERVIEW

ORIANA FALLACI: Abu Ammar, people talk of you so much but almost nothing is known about you and . . .

YASIR ARAFAT: The only thing to say about me is that I'm a humble Palestinian fighter. I became one in 1947, along with the rest of my family. Yes, that was the year when my conscience was awakened and I understood what a barbarous invasion had taken place in my country. There had never been one like it in the history of the world.

O.F.: How old were you, Abu Ammar? I ask because there's some controversy about your age.

Y.A.: No personal questions.

O.F.: Abu Ammar, I'm only asking how old you are. You're not a woman. You can tell me.

Y.A.: I said, no personal questions.

O.F.: Abu Ammar, if you don't even want to tell your age, why do you always expose yourself to the attention of the world and let the world look on you as the head of the Palestinian resistance?

Y.A.: But I'm not the head of it! I don't want to be! Really, I swear it. I'm just a member of the Central Committee, one of many, and to be precise the one who has been ordered to be the spokesman. That is to report what others decide. It's a great misunderstanding to consider me the head—the Palestinian resistance doesn't have a head. We try in fact to apply the concept of collective leadership and obviously the matter presents difficulties, but we insist on it since we believe it's indispensable not to entrust the responsibility and prestige to one man alone. It's a modern concept and helps not to do wrong to the masses who are fighting, to our brothers who are dying. If I should die, your curiosity will be exhausted—you'll know everything about me. Until that moment, no.

O.F.: I wouldn't say your comrades could afford to let you die, Abu Ammar. And, to judge by your bodyguard, I'd say they think you're much more useful if you stay alive.

Y.A.: No. Probably instead I'd be much more useful dead than alive. Ah, yes, my death would do much to help the cause, as an incentive. Let me even add that I have many probabilities of dying—it could happen tonight, tomorrow. If I die, it's not a tragedy—someone else will go around in the world to represent Al Fatah, someone else will direct the battles. . . . I'm more than ready to die. I don't care about my safety as much as you think.

TRIPS OF THE FOX

O.F.: I understand. On the other hand, you cross the lines into Israel once in a while yourself, don't you, Abu Ammar? The Israelis are convinced that you've entered Israel twice, and just escaped being ambushed. And they add that anyone who succeeds in doing this must be very clever.

Y.A.: What you call Israel is my home. So I was not in Israel but in my home—with every right to go to my home. Yes, I've been there, but much more often than only twice. I go there continually, I go when I like. Of course, to exercise this right is fairly difficult—their machine guns are always ready. But it's less difficult than they think; it depends on circumstances, on the points chosen. You have to be shrewd about it, they're right about that. It's no accident that we call these trips "trips of the fox." But you can go ahead and inform them that our boys, the fedayeen, make these trips daily. And not always to attack the enemy. We accustom them to crossing the lines so they'll know their own land, and learn to move about there with ease. Often we get as far, because I've done it, as the Gaza Strip and the Sinai Desert. We even carry weapons there. The Gaza fighters don't receive their arms by sea—they receive them from us, from here.

O.F.: Abu Ammar, how long will all this go on? How long will you be able to resist?

Y.A.: We don't even go in for such calculations. We're only at the beginning of this war. We're only now beginning to prepare ourselves for what will be a long, a very long, war. Certainly a war destined to be prolonged for generations. Nor are we the first generation to fight. The world doesn't know or forgets that in the 1920s our fathers were already fighting the Zionist invader. They were weak then, because too much alone against adversaries who were too strong and were supported by the English, by the Americans, by the imperialists of the earth. But we are strong—since January 1965, that is since the day that Al Fatah was born, we're a very dangerous adversary for Israel. The fedayeen are acquiring experience, they're stepping up their attacks and improving their guerrilla tactics; their numbers are increasing at a tremendous rate. You ask how long we'll be able to resist—that's the wrong question. You should ask how long the Israelis will be able to resist. For we'll never stop until we've returned to our home and destroyed Israel. The unity of the Arab world will make this possible.

O.F.: Abu Ammar, you always invoke the unity of the Arab world. But you know very well that not all the Arab states are ready to go to war for Palestine and that, for those already at war, a peaceful agreement is possible, and can even be expected. Even Nasser said so. If such an agreement should take place, as Russia too expects, what will you do?

THE END OF ISRAEL IS THE GOAL

Y.A.: We won't accept it. Never! We will continue to make war on Israel by ourselves until we get Palestine back. The end of Israel is the goal of our struggle, and it allows for neither compromise nor mediation. The issues of this struggle, whether our friends like it or not, will always remain fixed by the principles that we enumerated in 1965 with the creation of Al Fatah. First: revolutionary violence is the only system for liberating the land of our fathers; second: the purpose of this violence is to liquidate Zionism in all its political, economic, and military forms, and to drive it out of Palestine forever; third: our revolutionary action must be independent of any control by party or state; fourth: this action will be of long duration. We know the intentions of certain Arab leaders: to resolve the conflict with a peaceful agreement. When this happens, we will oppose it.

O.F.: Conclusion: you don't at all want the peace that everyone is hoping for.

Y.A.: No! We don't want peace. We want war, victory. Peace for us means the destruction of Israel and nothing else. What you call peace is peace for Israel and the imperialists. For us it is injustice and shame. We will fight until victory. Decades if necessary, generations.

O.F.: Let's be practical, Abu Ammar. Almost all the fedayeen bases are in Jordan, others are in Lebanon. Lebanon has little wish to fight a war, and Jordan would very much like to get out of it.

Let's suppose that these two countries, having decided on a peaceful agreement, decide to prevent your attacks on Israel. In other words, they prevent the guerrillas from being guerrillas. It's already happened and will happen again. In the face of this, what do you do? Do you also declare war on Jordan and Lebanon?

ILLUMINATING THE ARAB NATION

Y.A.: We can't fight on the basis of "ifs." It's the right of any Arab state to decide what it wants, including a peaceful agreement with Israel; it's our right to want to return home without compromise. Among the Arab states, some are unconditionally with us. Others not. But the risk of remaining alone in fighting Israel is a risk that we've foreseen. It's enough to think of the insults they hurled at us in the beginning; we have been so maltreated that by now we don't pay any attention to maltreatment. Our very formation, I mean, is a miracle. The candle that was lighted in 1965 burned in the blackest darkness. But now we are many candles, and we illuminate the whole Arab nation. And beyond the Arab nation.

O.F.: That's a very poetic and very diplomatic answer, but it's not the answer to what I asked you, Abu Ammar. I asked you: If Jordan really doesn't want you any more, do you declare war on Jordan?

Y.A.: I'm a soldier and a military leader. As such I must keep my secrets—I won't be the one to reveal our future battlefields to you. If I did, Al Fatah would court-martial me. So draw your own conclusions from what I said before. I told you we'll continue our march for the liberation of Palestine to the end, whether the countries in which we find ourselves like it or not. Even now we are in Palestine.

O.F.: We're in Jordan, Abu Ammar. And I ask you: But what does Palestine mean? Even Palestine's national identity has been lost with time, and its geographical borders have also been lost. The Turks were here, before the British Mandate and Israel. So what are the geographical borders of Palestine?

Y.A.: We don't bring up the question of borders. We don't speak of borders in our constitution because those who set up borders were the Western colonialists who invaded us after the Turks. From an Arab point of view, one doesn't speak of borders; Palestine is a small dot in the great Arabic ocean. And our nation is the Arab one, it is a nation extending from the Atlantic to the Red Sea and beyond. What we want, ever since the catastrophe exploded in 1947, is to free our land and reconstruct the democratic Palestinian state.

O.F.: But when you talk of a state, you have to say too within what geographical limits this state is formed or will be formed! Abu Ammar, I ask you again: what are the geographical borders of Palestine?

Y.A.: As an indication, we may decide that the borders of Palestine are the ones established at the time of the British Mandate. If we take the Anglo-French agreement of 1918, Palestine means the territory that runs from Naqurah in the north to Aqaba in the south, and then from the Mediterranean coast that includes the Gaza Strip to the Jordan River and the Negev Desert.

O.F.: I see. But this also includes a good piece of land that today is part of Jordan, I mean the whole region west of the Jordan. Cisjordania.

ARAB UNITY IS SLOWLY COMING

Y.A.: Yes. But I repeat that borders have no importance. Arab unity is important, that's all.

O.F.: Borders have importance if they touch or overlap the territory of a country that already exists, like Jordan.

Y.A.: What you call Cisjordania is Palestine.

O.F.: Abu Ammar, how is it possible to talk of Arab unity if from now on such problems come up with certain Arab countries? Not only that, but even you Palestinians are not in agreement. There is even a great division between you of Al Fatah and the other movements. For example, with the Popular Front.

Y.A.: Every revolution has its private problems. In the Algerian revolution there was also more than one movement, and for all I know, even in Europe during the resistance to the Nazis. In Vietnam itself there exist several movements; the Vietcong are simply the overwhelming majority, like we of Al Fatah. But we of Al Fatah include ninety-seven percent of the fighters and are the ones who conduct the struggle inside the occupied territory. It was no accident that Moshe Dayan, when he decided to destroy the village of El Heul and mined 218 houses as a punitive measure, said, "We must make it clear who controls this village, we or Al Fatah." He mentioned Al Fatah, not the Popular Front. The Popular Front . . . In February 1969 the Popular Front split into five parts, and four of them have already joined Al Fatah. Therefore we're slowly being united. And if George Habash, the leader of the Popular Front, is not with us today, he soon will be. We've already asked him to join us; there's basically no difference in objectives between us and the Popular Front.

O.F.: The Popular Front is communist. You say that you're not set up that way.

Y.A.: There are fighters among us representing all ideas; you must have met them. Therefore among us there is also room for the Popular Front. Only certain methods of struggle distinguish us from the Popular Front. In fact we of Al Fatah have never hijacked an airplane, and we have never planted bombs or caused shooting in other countries. We prefer to conduct a purely military struggle. That doesn't mean, however, that we too don't have recourse to sabotage—inside the Palestine that you call Israel. For instance, it's almost always we who set off bombs in Tel Aviv, in Jerusalem, in Eilat.

O.F.: That involves civilians, however. It's not a purely military struggle.

ALL ISRAELIS ARE GUILTY

Y.A.: It is! Because, civilians or military, they're all equally guilty of wanting to destroy our people. Sixteen thousand Palestinians have been arrested for helping our commandos, eight thousand houses of Palestinians have been destroyed, without counting the tortures that our brothers undergo in their prisons, and napalm bombings of the unarmed population. We carry out certain operations, called sabotage, to show them that we're capable of keeping them in check by the same methods. This inevitably hits civilians, but civilians are the first accomplices of the gang that rules Israel. Because if the civilians don't approve of the methods of the gang in power, they have only to show it. We know very well that many don't approve. Those, for example, who lived in Palestine before the Jewish immigration, and even some of those who immigrated with the precise intention of robbing us of our land. Because they came here innocently, with the hope of forgetting their ancient sufferings. They had been promised Paradise, here on earth, and they came to take over Paradise. Too late they discovered that instead it was hell. . . .

Y.A.: . . . What we say is never believed by you Westerners, you listen to them and that's all, you believe them and that's all, you report what they say and that's all!

O.F.: Abu Ammar, you're an unfair man. I am here and I'm listening to you. And after this interview I'll report word for word what you've told me.

Y.A.: You Europeans are always for them. Maybe some of you are beginning to understand us—it's in the air, one can sense it. But essentially you're still for them.

O.F.: This is your war, Abu Ammar, not ours. And in this war of yours we are only spectators. But even as spectators you can't ask us to be against the Jews and you shouldn't be surprised if in Europe the Jews are often loved. We've seen them persecuted, we've persecuted them. We don't want it to happen again.

Y.A.: Sure, you have to pay your debts to them. And you want to pay them with our blood, with our land, rather than with your blood, your land. You go on ignoring the fact that we have nothing against the Jews, we have it against the Israelis. The Jews will be welcome in the democratic Palestinian state. We'll offer them the choice of staying in Palestine when the moment arrives.

O.F.: But, Abu Ammar, the Israelis are Jews. Not all Jews can identify themselves with Israel, but Israel can't help identifying itself with the Jews. And you can't ask the Jews of Israel to go wandering around the world once more and thereby end up in extermination camps. That's unreasonable.

Y.A.: So you want to send us wandering around the world.

O.F.: No. We don't want to send anybody. You least of all.

Y.A.: But wandering around is what we're doing now. And if you're so anxious to give a homeland to the Jews, give them yours—you have a lot of land in Europe, in America. Don't presume to give them ours. We've lived on this land for centuries and centuries; we won't give it up to pay your debts.

THE ANTIFEMINISM MOVEMENT

REBECCA E. KLATCH

The 1960s and 1970s were decades of great social activism in America, as well as of great division. Feminism, the movement to acquire equal rights for women, had as many opponents as proponents. Many opposed its principles on religious grounds—believing women's subservience to men was ordained; on economic grounds—believing women would usurp men as wage earners; and on social grounds—believing family structure would be undermined if women were not primarily raising children in the home.

Sociologist Rebecca E. Klatch interviewed many people who opposed feminists' views. The results of her interviews are explored in her book *Women of the New Right*, from which the following article is taken. In this excerpt, Klatch discusses the perspective of social conservatives who believe that female equality will threaten the family. They also believe that feminism encouraged selfish narcissism in women. Rebecca E. Klatch is a sociology professor at the University of California, San Diego. She is the author of *A Generation Divided: The New Left, the New Right, and the 1960s*.

From the early days of the women's movement, Feminism war perceived as a force actively working against the family. Social conservatives charge feminists with renouncing the family as a source of repression and enslavement, a tool used by men to entrap and oppress women. As one local pro-family activist puts it:

The libbers want to abolish the family. That's what Gloria Frie—I mean Steinem says. "Women will not be liberated until marriage is eliminated." Have you seen the "Declaration on Feminism"? They state quite clearly there that they want to eliminate the family. That's why, when I hear people say they support ERA, I say to them, "Do you know what that means? Do you know what they want to do?". . . The feminists want to abolish the family. But the family is the basis of everything. It is the foundation of our society; if that crumbles, everything else goes.

The national conference for International Women's Year (IWY) held in Houston in 1977 concretized the perception of Feminism as an anti-family force. Sponsored by the United Nations, the conference brought together women from all over the country to consider "women's issues." Social conservatives were shocked by the delegates' overwhelming support for such things as ERA, gay rights, federal funding of abortion, government-sponsored childcare, and contraception for minors without parental consent, all advocated in the name of "women's rights." Angry that the taxpayer's dollar was being used to fund a convention of feminists, the meeting in fact provoked activism by many women previously uninvolved in the political arena. One woman interviewed, now a Reagan administrator and national pro-family leader, explains her initial involvement in this way:

There was the international Women's Year meeting back in '76 or '77 and [actress] Jean Stapleton was on television and said here was this grassroots meeting for women to go and talk about their concerns. So I went. I mean I had voted in elections but that was it. So I went down to the IWY meeting and heard all sorts of talk about this issue and that issue and the other issue I didn't know anything about. I guess then the fate of the ERA was fast and furious and "ERA—what's that?" I just didn't know anything. And I noticed that these people were very upset—I shouldn't say upset, but concerned. There was a whole slew of issues that people were just really—I hate to use the word "violent"—very enthusiastic about. . . . There was one group of women taking A, B, C, and D position and another group of women were taking X, Y, and Z position and I thought, "Well, now, why all this discussion, why all this controversy?" So then I started doing some studying.

PRO-FAMILY MOVEMENT

IWY gave birth to a network of activists and organizations that called themselves the "pro-family movement." Rosemary Thomson, a leading figure of the movement, defines pro-family as a "person or group supporting legislation protecting traditional moral values, generally opposed to a range of issues, including ERA, abortion, gay rights, federal childcare, forced busing, etc." If IWY gave birth to the pro-family movement, President Carter's 1980 White House Conference on Families (WHCF) solidified the movement, deepening the wrath of pro-family activists and drawing in further supporters. Thomson, named national Eagle Forum coordinator for the WHCF by Phyllis Schlafly, declares: "IWY was our 'boot camp.' Now we're ready for the offensive in the battle for our families and our faith." Another activist, also a pro-family leader, explains:

> The excesses of the feminist movement activated a lot of people who otherwise wouldn't have noticed that anything was going on—the IWY, et cetera. The White House Conference on families activated a whole other group of people who had not been radicalized by IWY. . . . *Most* of the pro-family troops at the White House conference were new. That's fascinating because that got a whole new different segment of the population; those people are remaining active.

Social conservative critics charged that the conference was a sham, employing biased processes of delegate selection to stack the conference with "women's libbers" who sought to promote their own agenda. But clearly the chief criticism raised by critics of the conference centered on the definition of the family. The Reagan administrator initially drawn in through IWY explains what took place at the White House conference:

> There were two diametrically opposed definitions working at the family conference at the White House. One of them was the traditional family, that is, the family related by blood, marriage, or adoption. The other definition of the family is what I call the "groupie" or "roofers" definition of the family, those people that think that the family is anyone living under the same roof that provides support for each other *regardless* of blood, marriage, or adoption. These are two fundamentally different views that are in conflict. They're irreconcilable because the roofers, the groupie definition denies the existence of the traditional family. They don't recognize—they say *irregardless* of blood, marriage, and adoption. . . .

When I was a delegate in Virginia I found out that's the definition they were using. I found out that was the definition being put out by the American Home Economics Association. It's also the definition that NOW uses and a lot of the gay community uses. I hit the roof. . . . We've had this definition of the family for two thousand years. I don't know of any existing society that works on the other definition of the family. You need to have the biological connection.

A local pro-family activist expresses a similar reaction to the WHCF:

I went to the Conference on the Family in Washington. They couldn't even come up with a definition of the family. So it was changed to Conference on *Families.* But we should define what the family is. And then anything that doesn't fit into that is a broken home. The conference was biased from the start. You know, anytime someone with a particular view, my political view, was selected as delegates in a state, they reappoint them.

WHAT IS A FAMILY?

This battle over the definition of the family is a central focus of social conservative concern. The conflict centers on what constitutes a family, where the lines are drawn. On one side stand social conservatives, defining the family as persons related by blood, marriage, or adoption; this, they contend, is the traditional definition of the family. On the other side stand the feminists and humanists, who include more diverse forms in the definition of family. In fact, Phyllis Schlafly reports that Gloria Steinem worked for months to get the White House Conference changed from "Family" to "Families" in order to include alternative lifestyles. Social conservatives reject this acceptance of multiple family forms. In a debate held during the Family Forum conference between leftist Michael Lerner and New Right leader Paul Weyrich, Weyrich argued:

Where we disagree is in the effort to call a couple of lesbians who are bringing up a child a family, calling a couple of roommates a family, calling a couple of fornicators a family. These are families . . . under your definition—garbage!! . . . It is ludicrous to call acquaintances, neighbors, live-in types, and so on families. The problem of not defining the family is what leads to the kind of perversion of thinking which has resulted in people trying to pass off as legitimate families, illegitimate lifestyles.

This same opposition to diverse family forms, with particular animosity toward gay families, is echoed by Dr. Ronald Godwin, vice-president of the Moral Majority, who objects to the placement of "responsible, respectable kinds of families in with the homosexual families and the lesbian families and all the perverse pollutions of the definition." Yet Godwin also objects to what he calls the "pseudo-historical" approach to the family:

> You'll hear many, many feminists and anti-family spokesmen today talking about history. . . . They'll tell you that down on the Fiji Islands, somewhere down on an island of Uwunga-Bunga, there's a tribe of people who have never ever practiced family life as we know it. But they also have bones in their nose and file their front teeth. And they eat rat meat for breakfast. They're some fairly strange, non-representative people. But they'll tell you about all the strange aberrations that have popped up in the human family over the centuries in various strange geographical locations. They'll tell you that in the nineteenth century in the backside of Europe such and such a thing went on. They'll deal in what is called pseudo-history. They'll try to build a historical case for the proposition that the traditional family never really was traditional and never really was a dominant form in all civilized societies.

UPHOLDING TRADITIONAL VALUES

Once again, in upholding "traditional values" in this case regarding the definition of the family, social conservatives reject the acceptance of diverse cultural forms as equally valid and acceptable moral standards by which to live. Instead, they assert one absolute standard as the only legitimate code of behavior. Looking back on the White House conference, Thomson reflects:

> The pro-family movement was, indeed, engaged in a spiritual battle—a struggle between those who believe in Biblical principles and ungodly Humanism which rejects God's moral absolutes! . . .

> Somehow, it was to the organizers of the White House Conference on Families as if the Lord had never spoken in history. As if He had never declared that taking an innocent life was forbidden. That parents were to train up a child. That sexual activity outside of marriage was fornication, and that homosexuality was an abomination to Him—sin, not gay.

In this stark black and white world, Feminism is clearly intertwined with Secular Humanism. Both deny moral absolutes;
both undermine the family. Feminism, too, is intertwined with
Big Government. For it was the government-sponsored International Women's Year and White House conferences that allowed
feminists and humanists to promote anti-family policies. Hence,
in the battle to defend America, feminism is a threat because, like
the other forces of decay, it symbolizes an attack on the sacred
unit of the social conservative world.

FEMINISM AS THE NEW NARCISSISM

Inextricably bound to the association of Feminism as anti-family
is the perception of Feminism as an extension of the new narcissism, a symbol of the Me Decade. For in condemning the family,
social conservatives argue, the women's liberation movement ad-
vises women to pursue their *own* individual interest above all
else. Onalee McGraw explains: "The feminist movement issued
an appeal that rapidly spread through our culture urging women
to liberate themselves from the chains of family life and affirm
their own self-fulfillment as the primary good." McGraw argues
that the ultimate effect of such an appeal is the redefinition of the
family unit:

> The humanist-feminist view of the family is that it is a
> biological, sociological unit in which the individual
> happens to reside; it has no meaning and purpose be-
> yond that which each individual chooses to give it.
> Then, the autonomous self, freely choosing and acting,
> must satisfy its needs. When, by its very nature, the
> family exercises moral authority over its members, it
> thereby restricts the self in its pursuit of self-fulfillment
> and becomes an instrument of oppression and denial
> of individual rights.

Instead of the family's being bound together by a higher moral
authority, the family is reduced to a mere collection of individual interests.

Phyllis Schlafly reiterates this view of the feminist movement:

> Women's liberationists operate as Typhoid Marys car-
> rying a germ called lost identity. They try to persuade
> wives that they have missed something in life because
> they are known by their husband's name and play sec-
> ond fiddle to his career. . . . As a home-wrecker, women's
> liberation is far in the lead over "the other man," "the
> other woman," or "incompatability."

Schlafly illustrates the social destruction caused by women's liberation by quoting Albert Martin, who wrote a book discussing his own devastation when his wife of eighteen years walked out on him and their four sons, in search of her identity:

> An extraordinary emphasis on self is happening today across our nation, and this is why we continue to tear our marriages apart, splinter our families, and raise our divorce rates to new heights every year. The very core . . . is the enshrinement of individuality, the freedom of self, at the expense of marital union and social compromise.

FEMINISM AS THREAT TO FAMILY AND SOCIETY

Thus, in social conservative eyes, when individuality and freedom of self extend to women as well as to men, marriage, the family, and society itself are threatened. The ultimate result of such a development is what Connie Marshner labels "macho feminism":

> Feminism replaced the saccharine sentimentalizations of women and home life and projected instead a new image of women: a drab, macho feminism of hard-faced women who were bound and determined to serve their place in the world, no matter whose bodies they have to climb over to do it. This image provided the plot line for such cultural weathervanes as *Kramer vs. Kramer*. Macho feminism despises anything which seeks to interfere with the desires of Number One. A relationship which proves burdensome? Drop it! A husband whose needs cannot be conveniently met? Forget him! Children who may wake up in the middle of the night? No way! To this breed of thought, family interferes with self-fulfillment, and given the choice between family and self, the self is going to come out on top in their world. . . . Macho feminism has deceived women in that it convinced them that they would be happy only if they were treated like men, and that included treating themselves like men.

Marshner concludes: "Feminists praise self-centeredness and call it liberation."

Feminism is a threat, then, because, when women pursue self-interest, not only is the family neglected but also ultimately women become like men. Hence, "macho feminism" is destructive because if *everyone* pursues their own interest, no one is left to look out for the larger good, that is, to be altruistic, to be the nurturer, the caretaker, the mother. In short, the underlying fear expressed in this critique of Feminism is the fear of a total masculinization of the world.

Further, as "the most outrageous creation of the 'me-decade'" the women's movement is seen as one of the many groups ignited by the 1960s, greedily grabbing for their rights. Feminist claims of exploitation and oppression are perceived as illegitimate, as the overreaction to common problems by another self-pitying group jumping on the bandwagon of "minority rights." As part of this "craze for equal opportunity," according to one critic, Feminism is the "fight-for-your-right-to-do-anything-you-please-and-reject-all-obligations philosophy."

Carried to the extreme, this equation of Feminism with total self-gratification interprets abortion as the ultimate selfish act, the placement of a mother's desires above a baby's life. Ron Godwin, speaking at the Family Forum conference, portrays abortion in these terms:

> *Roe v. Wade* in 1973 gave mothers the right to rid themselves of unwanted children. Now as I speak this morning a recurring theme is going to occur . . . and that is that all of these changes that have occurred in the last few years are based on self-centeredness, on that which is convenient, on a principle of doing one's own thing, of doing that which is pleasurable and fulfilling to the individual.

He predicts the next step will be infanticide, in which a small group of people will decide which child shall live and which shall die. Hence, at the extreme Feminism represents callous self-interest, women's fulfillment at the price of human life.

ENVIRONMENTAL DISASTER: LOVE CANAL

MICHAEL H. BROWN

In 1962 Rachel Carson's book *Silent Spring* dramatically warned the world of the imminent dangers of environmental pollution. Her book was instrumental in inspiring the international environmental movement, which continues today.

All too soon after the book's publication, the kinds of events Carson warned about began to come to light. One highly publicized environmental disaster occurred near Niagara Falls, New York, in a little suburban area on the Love Canal. The canal had been built in the nineteenth century to connect the upper and lower Niagara River. Abandoned before it was completed, the canal was sold to be used as a municipal and chemical dump site. Hooker Chemical, a subsidiary of Occidental Petroleum, was the major user of the dump site, which was finally closed in 1953. At that time, the city took part of the land to be the site of an elementary school. Private homes were built elsewhere on the site and nearby.

In 1978 a newspaper article reported extensive chemical seepage from damaged waste barrels buried in the area, and a neighborhood woman named Lois Gibbs connected the information with health problems in her own family. Her young son had been frequently ill ever since they had moved to the neighborhood. In talking with other local residents, Gibbs discovered levels of serious illness and birth defects many times higher than normal. Through the work of Gibbs and others, the environmental catastrophe was exposed, and President Jimmy Carter declared Love

From "Love Canal and the Poisoning of America," by Michael H. Brown, *The Atlantic Monthly*, December 1979. Reprinted by permission of the author.

Canal a disaster area in 1978. Congress and the Justice Department investigated and began a campaign to root out similar dangerously polluted areas around the country. Eventually, most of the Love Canal residents were moved out of the area and cleanup began. Occidental Petroleum ended up paying more than $250 million toward cleanup costs and damages.

Michael H. Brown, a freelance writer and the author of *Laying Waste*, from which the following article was adapted, describes the early days of the Love Canal disaster. His series of newspaper articles at the time of the disaster's exposure earned him a nomination for a Pulitzer Prize in journalism.

N iagara Falls is a city of unmatched natural beauty; it is also a tired industrial work-horse, beaten often and with a hard hand. A magnificent river—a strait, really—connecting Lake Erie to Lake Ontario flows hurriedly north, at a pace of a half-million tons a minute, widening into a smooth expanse near the city before breaking into whitecaps and taking its famous 186-foot plunge. Then it cascades through a gorge of overhung shale and limestone to rapids higher and swifter than anywhere else on the continent.

The falls attract long lines of newlyweds and other tourists. At the same time, the river provides cheap electricity for industry; a good stretch of its shore is now filled with the spiraled pipes of distilleries, and the odors of chlorine and sulfides hang in the air.

Many who live in the city of Niagara Falls work in chemical plants, the largest of which is owned by the Hooker Chemical Company, a subsidiary of Occidental Petroleum since the 1960s. Timothy Schroeder did not. He was a cement technician by trade, dealing with the factories only if they needed a pathway poured, or a small foundation set. Tim and his wife, Karen, lived in a ranch-style home with a brick and wood exterior at 460 99th Street. They saved all the money they could to redecorate the inside and to make such additions as a cement patio, covered with an extended roof. One of the Schroeders' most cherished purchases was a Fiberglas pool, built into the ground and enclosed by a redwood fence.

Karen looked from a back window one morning in October 1974, noting with distress that the pool had suddenly risen two feet above the ground. She called Tim to tell him about it. Karen then had no way of knowing that this was the first sign of what would prove to be a punishing family and economic tragedy.

Mrs. Schroeder believed that the cause of the uplift was the unusual groundwater flow of the area. Twenty-one years before, an abandoned hydroelectric canal directly behind their house had been backfilled with industrial rubble. The underground breaches created by this disturbance, aided by the marshland nature of the region's surficial layer, collected large volumes of rainfall and undermined the back yard. The Schroeders allowed the pool to remain in its precarious position until the following summer and then pulled it from the ground, intending to pour a new pool, cast in cement. This they were unable to do, for the gaping excavation immediately filled with what Karen called "chemical water," rancid liquids of yellow and orchid and blue. These same chemicals had mixed with the groundwater and flooded the entire yard, attacking the redwood posts with such a caustic bite that one day the fence simply collapsed. When the chemicals receded in the dry weather, they left the gardens and shrubs withered and scorched, as if by a brush fire.

How the chemicals got there was no mystery. In the late 1930s, or perhaps early 1940s, the Hooker Company, whose many processes included the manufacture of pesticides, plasticizers, and caustic soda, began using the abandoned canal as a dump for at least 20,000 tons of waste residues—"still-bottoms," in the language of the trade.

Karen Schroeder's parents had been the first to experience problems with the canal's seepage. In 1959, her mother, Aileen Voorhees, encountered a strange black sludge bleeding through the basement walls. For the next twenty years, she and her husband, Edwin, tried various methods of halting the irritating intrusion, pasting the cinder-block wall with sealants and even constructing a gutter along the walls to intercept the inflow. Nothing could stop the chemical smell from permeating the entire household, and neighborhood calls to the city for help were fruitless. One day, when Edwin punched a hole in the wall to see what was happening, quantities of black liquid poured from the block. The cinder blocks were full of the stuff.

Although they later learned they were in imminent danger, Aileen and Edwin Voorhees had treated the problem as a mere nuisance. That it involved chemicals, industrial chemicals, was not particularly significant to them. All their lives, all of everyone's life in the city, malodorous fumes had been a normal ingredient of the ambient air.

More ominous than the Voorhees basement was an event that occurred at 11:12 P.M. on November 21, 1968, when Karen Schroeder gave birth to her third child, a seven-pound girl named Sheri. No sense of elation filled the delivery room. The child was born with a heart that beat irregularly and had a hole in it, bone blockages of the nose, partial deafness, deformed ear exteriors, and a cleft palate. Within two years, the Schroeders realized Sheri was also mentally retarded. When her teeth came in, a double row of them appeared on her lower jaw. And she developed an enlarged liver.

NO QUIRK OF NATURE

The Schroeders considered these health problems as well as illnesses among their other children, as acts of capricious genes—a vicious quirk of nature. Like Mrs. Schroeder's parents, they were concerned that the chemicals were devaluing their property. The crab apple tree and evergreens in the back were dead, and even the oak in front of the home was sick; one year, the leaves had fallen off on Father's Day.

The canal had been dug with much fanfare in the late nineteenth century by a flamboyant entrepreneur named William T. Love, who wanted to construct an industrial city with ready access to water power and major markets. The setting for Love's dream was to be a navigable power channel that would extend seven miles from the Upper Niagara before falling two hundred feet, circumventing the treacherous falls and at the same time providing cheap power. A city would be constructed near the point where the canal fed back into the river, and he promised it would accommodate half a million people.

So taken with his imagination were the state's leaders that they gave Love a free hand to condemn as much property as he liked, and to divert whatever amounts of water. Love's dream, however, proved grander than his resources, and he was eventually forced to abandon the project after a mile-long trench, ten to forty feet deep and generally twenty yards wide, had been scoured perpendicular to the Niagara River. Eventually, the trench was purchased by Hooker.

Few of those who, in 1977, lived in the numerous houses that had sprung up by the site were aware that the large and barren field behind them was a burial ground for toxic waste. That year, while working as a reporter for a local newspaper, the Niagara *Gazette,* I began to inquire regularly about the strange conditions reported by the Schroeders and other families in the Love Canal area. Both the Niagara County Health Department and the city said it was a nuisance condition, but no serious danger to the people. Officials of the Hooker Company refused comment, claiming only that they had no records of the chemical burials and that the problem was not their responsibility. Indeed, Hooker had deeded the land to the Niagara Falls Board of Education in 1953, for a token $1. With it the company issued no detailed warnings of the chemicals, only a brief paragraph in the quitclaim document that disclaimed company liability for any injuries or deaths which might occur at the site.

POISONED SCHOOL

The board's attorney, Ralph Boniello, says he received no phone calls or letters specifically relating the exact nature of the refuse and what it could do, nor did the board, as the company was later to claim, threaten condemnation of the property in order to secure the land. "We had no idea what was in there," Boniello said.

Though Hooker was undoubtedly relieved to rid itself of the contaminated land, the company was so vague about the hazards involved that one might have thought the wastes would cause harm only if touched, because they irritated the skin; otherwise, they were not of great concern. In reality, as the company must have known, the dangers of these wastes far exceeded those of acids or alkalines or inert salts. We now know that the drums Hooker had dumped in the canal contained a veritable witch's brew—compounds of truly remarkable toxicity. There were solvents that attacked the heart and liver, and residues from pesticides so dangerous that their commercial sale was shortly thereafter restricted outright by the government; some of them were already suspected of causing cancer.

Yet Hooker gave no hint of that. When the board of education, which wanted the parcel for a new school, approached Hooker, B. Klaussen, at the time Hooker's executive vice president, said in a letter to the board, "Our officers have carefully considered your request. We are very conscious of the need for new elementary schools and realize that the sites must be carefully selected so that they will best serve the area involved. We feel that the board of education has done a fine job in meeting the expanding demand for additional facilities and we are anxious to cooperate in any proper way. We have, therefore, come to the conclusion that since this location is the most desirable one for this purpose, we will be willing to donate the entire strip of property which we own between Colvin Boulevard and Frontier Avenue to be used for the erection of a school at a location to be determined. . . ."

The board built the school and playground at the canal's midsection. Construction progressed despite the contractor's hitting a drainage trench that gave off a strong chemical odor and the discovery of a waste pit nearby. Instead of halting the work, the authorities simply moved the school eighty feet away. Young families began to settle in increasing numbers alongside the dump, many of them having been told that the field was to be a park and recreation area for their children.

Children found the "playground" interesting, but at times

painful. They sneezed, and their eyes teared. In the days when the dumping was still in progress, they swam at the opposite end of the canal, occasionally arriving home with hard pimples all over their bodies. Hooker knew children were playing on its spoils. In 1958, three children were burned by exposed residues on the canal's surface, much of which, according to residents, had been covered with nothing more than fly ash and loose dirt. Because it wished to avoid legal repercussions, the company chose not to issue a public warning of the dangers it knew were there, nor to have its chemists explain to the people that their homes would have been better placed elsewhere.

UNFIT CHEMICAL CONTAINER

The Love Canal was simply unfit as a container for hazardous substances, poor even by the standards of the day, and now, in 1977, local authorities were belatedly finding that out. Several years of heavy snowfall and rain had filled the sparingly covered channel like a bathtub. The contents were overflowing at a frightening rate, sopping readily into the clay, silt, and sandy loam and finding their exit through old creekbeds and swales and into the neighborhood.

The city of Niagara Falls, I was assured, was planning a remedial drainage program to halt in some measure the chemical migration off the site. But no sense of urgency had been attached to the plan, and it was stalled in red tape. No one could agree on who should pay the bill—the city, Hooker, or the board of education—and engineers seemed confused over what exactly needed to be done.

Niagara Falls City Manager Donald O'Hara persisted in his view that, however displeasing to the eyes and nose, the Love Canal was not a crisis matter, mainly a question of aesthetics. O'Hara reminded me that Dr. Francis Clifford, county health commissioner, supported that opinion.

With the city, the board, and Hooker unwilling to commit themselves to a remedy, conditions degenerated in the area between 97th and 99th streets, until, by early 1978, the land was a quagmire of sludge that oozed from the canal's every pore. Melting snow drained the surface soot onto the private yards, while on the dump itself the ground had softened to the point of collapse, exposing the crushed tops of barrels. Beneath the surface, masses of sludge were finding their way out at a quickening rate, constantly forming springs of contaminated liquid. The Schroeder back yard, once featured in a local newspaper for its beauty, had reached the point where it was unfit even to walk upon. Of course, the Schroeders could not leave. No one would think of buying the property. They still owed on their mortgage and, with Tim's salary, could not afford to maintain the house while they moved into a safer setting. They and their four children were stuck.

Apprehension about large costs was not the only reason the city was reluctant to help the Schroeders and the one hundred or so other families whose properties abutted the covered trench. The city may also have feared distressing Hooker. To an economically depressed area, the company provided desperately needed employment—as many as 3000 blue-collar jobs in the general vicinity, at certain periods—and a substantial number of tax dollars. Perhaps more to the point, Hooker was speaking of building a $17 million headquarters in downtown Niagara Falls. So anxious were city officials to receive the new building that they and the state granted the company highly lucrative tax and loan incentives, and made available to the firm a prime parcel of property near the most popular tourist park on the American side, forcing a hotel owner to vacate the premises in the process.

SERIOUS PROBLEM

City Manager O'Hara and other authorities were aware of the nature of Hooker's chemicals. In fact, in the privacy of his office, O'Hara, after receiving a report on the chemical tests at the canal, had informed the people at Hooker that it was an extremely serious problem. Even earlier, in 1976, the New York State Department of Environmental Conservation had been made aware that dangerous compounds were present in the basement sump pump of at least one 97th Street home, and soon after, its own testing had revealed that highly injurious halogenated hydrocarbons were flowing from the canal into adjoining sewers. Among them were the notorious PCBs; quantities as low as one part PCBs to a million parts normal water were enough to create serious environmental concerns; in the sewers of Niagara Falls, the quantities of halogenated compounds were thousands of times higher. The other materials tracked, in sump pumps or sewers, were just as toxic as PCBs, or more so. Prime among the more hazardous ones was residue from hexachlorocyclopentadiene, or C-56, which was deployed as an intermediate in the manufacture of several pesticides. In certain dosages, the chemical could damage every organ in the body.

While the mere presence of C-56 should have been cause for alarm, government remained inactive. Not until early 1978—a full eighteen months after C-56 was first detected—was testing conducted in basements along 97th and 99th streets to see if the chemicals had vaporized off the sump pumps and walls and were present in the household air. The U.S. Environmental Protection Agency [EPA] conducted these tests at the urging of local Congressman John LaFalce, the only politician willing to approach the problem with the seriousness it deserved.

While the basement tests were in progress, the rains of spring arrived at the canal, further worsening the situation. Heavier fumes rose above the barrels. More than before, the residents were suffering from headaches, respiratory discomforts, and skin ailments. Many of them felt constantly fatigued and irritable and the children had reddened eyes. In the Schroeder home, Tim developed a rash along the backs of his legs. Karen could not rid herself of throbbing pains in her head. Their daughter, Laurie, seemed to be losing some of her hair.

BENZENE IS DISCOVERED

Three months passed before I was able to learn what the EPA testing had shown. When I did, the gravity of the situation became clear: benzene, a known cause of cancer in humans, had been readily detected in the household air up and down the streets. A widely used solvent, benzene was known in chronic-exposure cases to cause headaches, fatigue, loss of weight, and dizziness followed by pallor, nose-bleeds, and damage to the bone marrow.

No public announcement was made of the benzene hazard. Instead, officials appeared to shield the finding until they could agree among themselves on how to present it. Indeed, as early as October 18, 1977, Lawrence R. Moriarty, an EPA regional official in Rochester, had sent to the agency's toxic substances coordinator a lengthy memorandum stating that "serious thought should be given to the purchase of some or all of the homes affected. . . . This would minimize complaints and prevent further exposure to people." Concern was raised, he said, "for the safety of some 40 or 50 homeowners and their families. . . ."

Dr. Clifford, the county health commissioner, seemed unconcerned by the detection of benzene in the air. "We have no reason to believe the people are imperiled," he said. "For all we know, the federal limits could be six times too high. . . . I look at EPA's track record and notice they have to err on the right side." O'Hara, who spoke to me in his office about the situation, told me I was overreacting to the various findings. The chemicals in the air, he said, posed no more risk than smoking a couple of cigarettes a day.

Dr. Clifford's health department refused to conduct a formal study of the people's health, despite the air-montoring results. A worker from the department made a perfunctory call to the school, 99th Street Elementary, and when it was discovered that classroom attendance was normal, apparently the department ceased to worry about the situation. For this reason, and because of the resistance growing among the local authorities, I went to the southern end of 99th Street to take an informal health survey of my own. I arranged a meeting with six neighbors, all of them instructed beforehand to list the illnesses they were aware of on their block, with names and ages specified for presentation at the session.

UNNATURAL AFFLICTIONS

The residents' list was startling. Though unafflicted before they moved there, many people were now plagued with ear infections, nervous disorders, rashes, and headaches. One young man, James Gizzarelli, said he had missed four months of work owing to breathing troubles. His wife was suffering epileptic-like seizures which her doctor was unable to explain. Meanwhile, freshly applied paint was inexplicably peeling from the exterior of their house. Pets too were suffering, most seriously if they had been penned in the back yards nearest to the canal, constantly breathing air that smelled like mothballs and weedkiller. They lost their fur, exhibited skin lesions, and, while still quite young, developed internal tumors. A great many cases of cancer were reported among the women, along with much deafness. On both 97th and 99th streets, traffic signs warned passing motorists to watch for deaf children playing near the road.

Evidence continued to mount that a large group of people, perhaps all of the one hundred families immediately by the canal, perhaps many more, were in imminent danger. While watching television, while gardening or doing a wash, in their sleeping hours, they were inhaling a mixture of damaging chemicals. Their hours of exposure were far longer than those of a chemical factory worker, and they wore no respirators or goggles. Nor could they simply open a door and escape. Helplessness and despair were the main responses to the blackened craters and scattered cinders behind their back yards.

But public officials often characterized the residents as hypochondriacs. Timothy Schroeder would wander to his back land and shake his head. "They're not going to help us one damn bit," he said, throwing a rock into a puddle coated with a film of oily blue. "No way." His wife's calls to the city remained unanswered while his shrubs continued to die. Sheri needed expensive medical care and he was afraid the time would come when he could no longer afford to provide it. A heavy man with a round stomach and gentle voice, he had struck me as easygoing and calm, ready with a joke and a smile. That was disappearing now. His face—in the staring eyes, in the tightness of the lips and cheeks—candidly revealed his utter disgust. Every agent of government had been called on the phone or sent pleas for help, but none offered aid.

Commissioner Clifford expressed irritation at my printed reports of illness, and disagreement began to surface in the newsroom on how the stories should be printed. "There's a high rate of cancer among my friends," Dr. Clifford argued. "It doesn't mean anything." Mrs. Schroeder said that Dr. Clifford had not visited the homes at the canal, nor had he seen the black liquids collecting in the basements. Nor had the County Health Commissioner properly followed an order from the state commissioner to cover exposed chemicals, erect a fence around the site, and ventilate the contaminated basements. Instead, Dr. Clifford arranged for the installation of two $15 window fans in the two most polluted basements and a thin wood snow fence that was broken within days of its erection and did not cover the entire canal.

Partly as a result of the county's inadequate response, the state finally announced in May 1978 that it intended to conduct a health study at the dump site's southern end. Blood samples would be drawn to test for unusual enzyme levels showing liver destruction, and extensive medical questionnaires were to be answered by each of the families.

SHATTERING REVELATIONS

As interest in the small community increased, further revelations shook the neighborhood. In addition to the benzene, eighty or more other compounds were found in the makeshift dump, ten of them potential carcinogens. The physiological effects they could cause were profound and diverse. At least fourteen of them could impact on the brain and central nervous system. Two of them, carbon tetrachloride and chlorobenzene, could readily cause narcotic or anesthetic consequences. Many others were known to cause headaches, seizures, loss of hair, anemia, or skin rashes. Together, the compounds were capable of inflicting innumerable illnesses, and no one knew what new concoctions were being formulated by their mixture underground.

Edwin and Aileen Voorhees had the most to be concerned about. When a state biophysicist analyzed the air content of their basement, he determined that the safe exposure time there was less than 2.4 minutes—the toxicity in the basement was thousands of times the acceptable limit for twenty-four-hour breathing. This did not mean they would necessarily become permanently ill, but their chances of contracting cancer, for example, had been measurably increased. In July, I visited Mrs. Voorhees for further discussion of her problems, and as we sat in the kitchen, drinking coffee, the industrial odors were apparent. Aileen, usually chipper and feisty, was visibly anxious. She stared down at the table, talking only in a lowered voice. Everything now looked different to her. The home she and Edwin had built had become their jail cell. Their yard was but a pathway through which toxicants entered the cellar walls. The field out back, that prosed "park," seemed destined to be the ruin of their lives. I reached for her phone and called Robert Mathews, a city engineer who had been given the job of overseeing the situation. Was the remedial program, now in the talking stage for more than a year, ready to begin soon? No. Could he report any progress in deciding who would pay for it? No. Could Mr. and Mrs. Voorhees be evacuated? Probably not, he said—that would open up a can of worms, create a panic.

On July 14 I received a call from the state health department with some shocking news. The preliminary review of the health questionnaires was complete. And it showed that women living at the southern end had suffered a high rate of miscarriages and had given birth to an abnormally high number of children with birth defects. In one age group, 35.3 percent had records of spontaneous abortions. That was far in excess of the norm. The odds against it happening by chance were 250 to one. These tallies, it was stressed, were "conservative" figures. Four children in one small section of the neighborhood had documentable birth defects, club feet, retardation, and deafness. Those who lived there the longest suffered the highest rates.

"A GREAT AND IMMINENT PERIL"

The data on miscarriages and birth defects, coupled with the other accounts of illness, finally pushed the state's bureaucracy into motion. A meeting was scheduled for August 2, at which time the state health commissioner, Dr. Robert Whalen, would formally address the issue. The day before the meeting, Dr. Nicholas Vianna, a state epidemiologist, told me that residents were also incurring some degree of liver damage. Blood analyses had shown hepatitis-like symptoms in enzyme levels. Dozens if not hundreds of people, apparently, had been adversely affected.

In Albany, on August 2, Dr. Whalen read a lengthy statement in which he urged that pregnant women and children under two years of age leave the southern end of the dump site immediately. He declared the Love Canal an official emergency, citing it as a "great and imminent peril to the health of the general public."

THE AYATOLLAH KHOMEINI AND THE RISE OF A THEOCRACY

TIME

In January 1979, Iranians overthrew their leader, Shah Mohammed Reza Pahlavi, and established the world's only theocracy, under the leadership of the Ayatollah Ruhollah Khomeini, a highly respected, ascetic Muslim exile who preached that the shah's pro-Western decadence should be replaced by strict Muslim morality. The United States had supported the shah because of his anticommunist stance. But the Iranian people were tired of economic inequities and the interference of foreign nations in Iran's affairs. Inspired by Khomeini, the people took to the streets and forced the shah to flee.

The United States refused to grant the shah asylum, although he was allowed to receive medical treatment there, after which he moved to Panama and then to Egypt, where he died in 1980. Nevertheless, Iran blamed the United States for the shah's despotic and extravagant rule. In November 1979 a mob of students seized the American embassy and fifty-two hostages, demanding that the United States return the shah to Iran to face justice. U.S. president Jimmy Carter refused to force the shah's return, claiming that the United States would not negotiate with terrorists and aware of the threat of Soviet aggression in the region. In April 1980 Carter attempted a military rescue, which failed; Iran held the hostages for nearly fifteen months, but finally released them in January 1981 as Carter left office.

After the shah's overthrow, Khomeini retreated to a theological seminary, where he led the country from behind the scenes.

From "The Mystic Who Lit the Fires of Hatred," Man of the Year cover story, *Time*, January 7, 1980, pp. 9–21. Copyright © 1980 Time Inc. Reprinted with permission.

Khomeini's reign was marked by rigid religious orthodoxy and repression of opposition.

Time magazine named Khomeini its Man of the Year in January 1980 because of his impact on Iran, the United States, and the world. The following article, written while Iran still held the American hostages, is excerpted from *Time's* special section devoted to Khomeini and other important people and events of 1979.

The dour old man of 79 shuffles in his heel-less slippers to the rooftop and waves apathetically to crowds that surround his modest home in the holy city of Qum. The hooded eyes that glare out so balefully from beneath his black turban are often turned upward, as if seeking inspiration from on high—which, as a religious mystic, he indeed is. To Iran's Shi'ite Muslim laity, he is the Imam, an ascetic spiritual leader whose teachings are unquestioned. To hundreds of millions of others, he is a fanatic whose judgments are harsh, reasoning bizarre and conclusions surreal. He is learned in the ways of Shari'a (Islamic law) and Platonic philosophy, yet astonishingly ignorant of and indifferent to non-Muslim culture. Rarely has so improbable a leader shaken the world.

Yet in 1979 the lean figure of the Ayatullah Ruhollah Khomeini towered malignly over the globe. As the leader of Iran's revolution he gave the 20th century world a frightening lesson in the shattering power of irrationality, of the ease with which terrorism can be adopted as government policy. As the new year neared, 50 of the American hostages seized on Nov. 4 by a mob of students were still inside the captured U.S. embassy in Tehran, facing the prospect of being tried as spies by Khomeini's revolutionary courts. The Ayatullah, who gave his blessing to the capture, has made impossible and even insulting demands for the hostages' release: that the U.S. return deposed Shah Mohammed Reza Pahlavi to Iran for trial and no doubt execution, even though the Shah is now in Panama; that America submit to a trial of its "crimes" against Iran before an international "grand jury" picked by Khomeini's aides. He claimed that Iran had every legal and moral right to try America's hostage diplomats, an action that would defy a decision of the World Court, a vote of the U.N. Security Council and one of the most basic rules of accommodation between civilized nations. The Ayatullah even insisted, in an extraordinary interview with *Time*, that if Americans wish to have good relations with Iran they must vote Jimmy Carter out of office and elect instead a President that Khomeini would find "suitable."

Unified by an Unknown Cleric

Unifying a nation behind such extremist positions is a remarkable achievement for an austere theologian who little more than a year ago was totally unknown in the West he now menaces. But Khomeini's carefully cultivated air of mystic detachment cloaks an iron will, an inflexible devotion to simple ideas that he has preached for decades, and a finely tuned instinct of articulating the passions and rages of his people. Khomeini is no politician in the Western sense, yet he possesses the most awesome—and ominous—of political gifts: the ability to rouse millions to both adulation and fury.

Khomeini's importance far transcends the nightmare of the embassy seizure, transcends indeed the overthrow of the Shah of Iran. The revolution that he led to triumph threatens to upset the world balance of power more than any political event since Hitler's conquest of Europe. It was unique in several respects: a successful, mostly nonviolent revolt against a seemingly entrenched dictator, it owed nothing to outside help or even to any Western ideology. The danger exists that the Iranian revolution could become a model for future uprisings throughout the Third World—and not only its Islamic portion. Non-Muslim nations too are likely to be attracted by the spectacle of a rebellion aimed at expelling all foreign influence in the name of xenophobic nationalism.

Already the flames of anti-Western fanaticism that Khomeini fanned in Iran threaten to spread through the volatile Soviet Union, from the Indian subcontinent to Turkey and southward through the Arabian Peninsula to the Horn of Africa. Most particularly, the revolution that turned Iran into an Islamic republic whose supreme law is the Koran is undermining the stability of the Middle East, a region that supplies more than half of the Western world's imported oil, a region that stands at the strategic crossroads of super-power competition.

As an immediate result, the U.S., Western Europe and Japan face continuing inflation and rising unemployment, brought on, in part, by a disruption of the oil trade. Beyond that looms the danger of U.S.-Soviet confrontation. Washington policymakers, uncertain about the leftist impulses of Iran's ubiquitous "students"—and perhaps some members of Iran's ruling Revolutionary Council—fear that the country may become a new target of opportunity for Soviet adventurism. The Kremlin leaders in turn must contend with the danger that the U.S.S.R.'s 50 million Muslims could be aroused by Khomeini's incendiary Islamic nationalism. Yet if the Soviets chose to take advantage of the turmoil in Iran as they have intervened in neighboring Afghanistan, the

U.S. would have to find some way of countering such aggression.

Khomeini thus poses to the U.S. a supreme test of both will and strategy. So far his hostage blackmail has produced a result he certainly did not intend: a surge of patriotism that has made the American people more united than they have been on any issue in two decades. The shock of seeing the U.S. flag burned on the streets of Tehran, or misused by embassy attackers to carry trash, has jolted the nation out of its self-doubting "Viet Nam syndrome." Worries about America's ability to influence events abroad are giving way to anger about impotence; the country now seems willing to exert its power. But how can that power be brought to bear against an opponent immune to the usual forms of diplomatic, economic and even military pressure, and how can it be refined to deal with others in the Third World who might rise to follow Khomeini's example? That may be the central problem for U.S. foreign policy throughout the 1980s.

CHANGING THE NEWS

The outcome of the present turmoil in Iran is almost totally unpredictable. It is unclear how much authority Khomeini, or Iran's ever changing government, exerts over day-to-day events. Much as Khomeini has capitalized on it, the seizure of the U.S. embassy tilted the balance in Iran's murky revolutionary politics from relative moderates to extremists who sometimes seem to listen to no one; the militants at the embassy openly sneer at government ministers, who regularly contradict one another. The death of Khomeini, who has no obvious successor, could plunge the country into anarchy.

But one thing is certain: the world will not again look quite the way it did before Feb. 1, 1979, the day on which Khomeini flew back to a tumultuous welcome in Tehran after 15 years in exile. He thus joins a handful of other world figures whose deeds are debatable—or worse—but who nonetheless branded a year as their own. In 1979 the Ayatullah Ruhollah Khomeini met *Time*'s definition of Man of the Year: he was the one who "has done the most to change the news, for better or for worse.". . .

A year ago, in its cover story on 1978's Man of the Year, Chinese Vice Premier Deng Xiaoping, *Time* noted that "the Shah of Iran's 37-year reign was shaken by week upon week of riots." Shortly thereafter, the Shah fell in one of the greatest political upheavals of the post–World War II era, one that raised troubling questions about the ability of the U.S. to guide or even understand the seething passions of the Third World.

Almost to the very end, the conventional wisdom of Western diplomats and journalists was that the Shah would survive; after all, he had come through earlier troubles seemingly strengthened. In 1953 the Shah had actually fled the country. But he was restored to power by a CIA-inspired coup that ousted Mohammed Mossadegh, the nationalist Prime Minister who had been *Time*'s Man of the Year for 1951 because he had "oiled the wheels of chaos." In 1963 Iran had been swept by riots stirred up by the powerful Islamic clergy against the Shah's White Revolution. Among other things, this well-meant reform abolished the feudal landlord-peasant system. Two consequences: the reform broke up properties administered by the Shi'ite clergy and reduced their income, some of which consisted of donations from large landholders. The White Revolution also gave the vote to women. The Shah suppressed those disturbances without outside help, in part by jailing one of the instigators—an ascetic theologian named Ruhollah Khomeini, who had recently attained the title of Ayatullah* and drawn crowds to fiery sermons in which he denounced the land reform as a fraud and the Shah as a traitor to Islam. In 1964 Khomeini was arrested and exiled, first to Turkey, then to Iraq, where he continued to preach against the idolatrous Shah and to promulgate his vision of Iran as an "Islamic republic."

The preachments seemed to have little effect, as the Shah set about building the most thoroughly Westernized nation in all of the Muslim world. The progress achieved in a deeply backward country was stunning. Petroleum revenues built steel mills, nuclear power plants, telecommunication systems and a formidable military machine, complete with U.S. supersonic fighters and missiles. Dissent was ruthlessly suppressed, in part by the use of torture in the dungeons of SAVAK, the secret police. It is still not clear how widespread the tortures and political executions were; but the Shah did not heed U.S. advice to liberalize his regime, and repression inflamed rather than quieted dissent.

By 1978 the Shah had alienated almost all elements of Iranian society. Westernized intellectuals were infuriated by rampant corruption and repression; workers and peasants by the selective prosperity that raised glittering apartments for the rich while the poor remained in mud hovels; bazaar merchants by the Shah-supported businessmen who monopolized bank credits, supply contracts and imports; the clergy and their pious Muslim followers by the gambling casinos, bars and discothèques that seemed the most visible result of Westernization. (One of the

---

*An appellation that means "sign of God." There is no formal procedure for bestowing it; a religious leader is called ayatullah by a large number of reverent followers and is accepted as such by the rest of the Iranian clergy. At present, Iran has perhaps 50 to 60 mullahs generally regarded as ayatullahs.

Shah's last prime ministers also stopped annual government subsidies to the mullahs.) Almost everybody hated the police terror and sneered in private at the Shah's Ozymandian megalomania, symbolized by a $100 million fete he staged at Persepolis in 1971 to celebrate the 2,500 years of the Persian Empire. In fact, the Shah's father was a colonel in the army when he overthrew the Qajar dynasty in 1925, and as Khomeini pointed out angrily from exile at the time of the Persepolis festival, famine was raging in that part of the country.

STABLE AND VALUABLE ALLY?

But the U.S. saw the Shah as a stable and valuable ally. Washington was annoyed by the Shah's insistence on raising oil prices at every OPEC meeting, yet that irritation was outweighed by the fact that the Shah was staunchly anti-Communist and a valuable balance wheel in Middle East politics. Eager to build up Iran as a "regional influential" that could act as America's surrogate policeman of the Persian Gulf, the U.S. lent the Shah its all-out support. President Richard Nixon and Secretary of State Henry Kissinger allowed him to buy all the modern weapons he wanted. Washington also gave its blessing to a flood of American business investment in Iran and dispatched an army of technocrats there.

The depth of its commitment to the Shah apparently blinded Washington to the growing discontent. U.S. policymakers wanted to believe that their investment was buying stability and friendship; they trusted what they heard from the monarch, who dismissed all opposition as "the blah-blahs of armchair critics." Even after the revolution began, U.S. officials were convinced that "there is no alternative to the Shah." Carter took time out from the Camp David summit in September 1978 to phone the Iranian monarch and assure him of Washington's continued support.

By then it was too late. Demonstrations and protest marches that started as a genuine popular outbreak grew by a kind of spontaneous combustion. The first parades drew fire from the Shah's troops, who killed scores and started a deadly cycle: marches to mourn the victims of the first riot, more shooting, more martyrs, crowds swelling into the hundreds of thousands and eventually millions in Tehran. Khomeini at this point was primarily a symbol of the revolution, which at the outset had no visible leaders. But even in exile the Ayatullah was well known inside Iran for his uncompromising insistence that the Shah must go. When demonstrators began waving the Ayatullah's picture, the frightened Shah pressured Iraq to boot Khomeini out. It was a fatal blunder; in October 1978 the Ayatullah settled in Neauphlele-Château, outside Paris, where he gathered a circle of exiles and for the first time publicized his views through the Western press.

Khomeini now became the active head of the revolution. Cassettes of his anti-Shah sermons sold like pop records in the bazaars and were played in crowded mosques throughout the country. When he called for strikes, his followers shut down the banks, the postal service, the factories, the food stores and, most important, the oil wells, bringing the country close to paralysis. The Shah imposed martial law, but to no avail. On Jan. 16, after weeks of daily protest parades, the Shah and his Empress flew off to exile, leaving a "regency council" that included Prime Minister Shahpour Bakhtiar, a moderate who had spent time in the Shah's prisons. But Khomeini announced that no one ruling in the Shah's name would be acceptable, and Iran was torn by the largest riots of the entire revolution. The Ayatullah returned from Paris to a tumultuous welcome and Bakhtiar fled. "The holy one has come!" the crowds greeting Khomeini shouted triumphantly. "He is the light of our lives!" The crush stalled the Ayatullah's motorcade, so that he had to be lifted out of the crowds, over the heads of his adulators, by helicopter. He was flown to a cemetery, where he prayed at the graves of those who had died during the revolution.

Khomeini withdrew to the holy city of Qum, appointed a government headed by Mehdi Bazargan, an engineer by training and veteran of Mossadegh's Cabinet, and announced that he would confine his own role during "the one or two years left to me" to making sure that Iran followed "in the image of Muhammad." It quickly became apparent that real power resided in the revolutionary *komitehs* that sprang up all over the country, and the *komitehs* took orders only from the 15-man Revolutionary Council headed by Khomeini (the names of its other members were long kept secret). Bazargan and his Cabinet had to trek to Qum for weekly lunches with Khomeini to find out what the Ayatullah would or would not allow.

DUAL REVOLUTION

Some observers distinguish two stages in the entire upheaval: the first a popular revolt that overthrew the Shah, then a "Khomeini coup" that concentrated all power in the clergy. The Ayatullah's main instrument was a stream of *elamiehs* (directives) from Qum, many issued without consulting Bazargan's nominal government. Banks and heavy industry were nationalized and turned over to government managers. Many of the *elamiehs* were concerned with imposing a strict Islamic way of life on all Iranians. Alcohol was forbidden. Women were segregated from men in schools below the university level, at swimming pools, beaches and other public facilities. Khomeini even banned most music from radio and TV. Marches were acceptable, he told Italian Journalist Oriana Fallaci, but other Western music "dulls the mind, because it involves pleasure and ecstasy, similar to drugs." Fallaci: "Even the music of Bach, Beethoven, Verdi?" Khomeini: "I do not know those names."

In power, Khomeini and his followers displayed a retaliatory streak. Islamic revolutionary courts condemned more than 650 Iranians to death, after trials at which defense lawyers were rarely, if ever, present, and spectators stepped forward to add their own accusations to those of the prosecutors; death sentences were generally carried out immediately by firing squad. An unknown but apparently large number of other Iranians were sentenced to life imprisonment. Khomeini preaches the mercy of God but showed little of his own to those executed, who were, he said, torturers and killers of the Shah's who got what they deserved. Some were, including the generals and highest-ranking politicians, but the victims also included at least seven prostitutes, 15 men accused of homosexual rape, and a Jewish businessman alleged to be spying for Israel. Defenders of Khomeini's regime argue with some justification that far fewer people were condemned by the revolutionary courts than were tortured to death by the Shah's SAVAK, and that the swift trials were necessary to defuse public anger against the minions of the deposed monarch.

As usually happens in revolutions, the forces of dissolution, once let loose, are not so easily tamed. Iran's economy suffered deeply, and unrest in at least three ethnic areas—those of the Kurds, the Azerbaijanis and the Baluchis—presented continuing threats to Tehran's, or Qum's, control. Many Western experts believe Khomeini shrewdly seized upon the students' attack on the U.S. embassy, which he applauded but claims he did not order, as a way of directing popular attention away from the country's increasing problems. It gave him once again a means of presenting all difficulties as having been caused by the U.S., to brand all his opponents—believers in parliamentary government, ethnic separatists, Muslims who questioned his interpretations of Islamic law—tools of the CIA. When the United Nations and the World Court condemned the seizure, he labeled these bodies stooges of the enemy. It was Iran against the world—indeed, all Islam against the "infidels."

When Bazargan resigned to protest the capture of the hostages, the Ayatullah made the Revolutionary Council the government in name as well as fact. Then, during the holy month known as Muharram, with popular emotion at a frenzied height as a result of the confrontation with the U.S., Khomeini expertly managed a vote on a new constitution that turned Iran into a theocracy. Approved overwhelmingly in a Dec. 2–3 referendum, the constitution provided for an elected President and parliament, but placed above them a "guardian council" of devout Muslims to make sure that nothing the elected bodies do violates Islamic law. Atop the structure is a *faqih* (literally, jurisprudent), the leading theologian of Iran, who must approve of the President, holds veto power over virtually every act of government, and even commands the armed forces. Though the constitution does not name him, when it goes fully into effect after elections this month and in February, Khomeini obviously will become the *faqih*.

WHY KHOMEINI WON

How did the Ayatullah capture a revolution that started out as a leaderless explosion of resentment and hate? Primarily by playing adroitly to, and in part embodying, some of the psychological elements that made the revolt possible. There was, for example, a widespread egalitarian yearning to end the extremes of wealth and poverty that existed under the Shah—and the rich could easily be tarred as clients of the "U.S. imperialists." Partly because of the long history of Soviet, British and then American meddling in their affairs, Iranians were and are basically xenophobic, and thus susceptible to the Ayatullah's charges that the U.S. (and, of course, the CIA) was responsible for the country's ills. Iranians could also easily accept that kind of falsehood since they had grown used to living off gossip and rumor mills during the reign of the Shah, when the heavily censored press played down even nonpolitical bad news about Iran. When Khomeini declared that the Americans and Israelis were responsible for the November attack by Muslim fanatics in Mecca's Sacred Mosque, this deliberate lie was given instant credence by multitudes of Iranians.

By far the most powerful influence that cemented Khomeini's hold on his country is the spirit of Shi'ism—the branch of Islam to which 93% of Iran's 35.2 million people belong. In contrast to the dominant Sunni wing of Islam, Shi'ism emphasizes martyrdom; thus many Iranians are receptive to Khomeini's speeches about what a "joy" and "honor" it would be to die in a war with the U.S. Beyond that, Shi'ism allows for the presence of an intermediary between God and man. Originally, the mediators were twelve imams, who Shi'ites believe were the rightful successors of the Prophet Muhammad; the twelfth disappeared in A.D. 940. He supposedly is in hiding, but will return some day to purify the religion and institute God's reign of justice on earth. This belief gives Shi'ism a strong messianic cast, to which Khomeini appeals when he promises to expel Western influence and to turn Iran into a pure Islamic society. The Ayatullah has never claimed the title of Imam for himself, but he has done nothing to discourage its use by his followers, a fact that annoys some of his peers among the Iranian clergy. Ayatullah Seyed Kazem Sharietmadari, Khomeini's most potent rival for popular reverence, has acidly observed that the Hidden Imam will indeed return, "but not in a Boeing 747"— a reference to the plane that carried Khomeini from France to Iran.

Iran and Iraq are the main Muslim states where the majority of the population is Shi'ite; but there are substantial Shi'ite minorities in the Gulf states, Lebanon, Turkey and Saudi Arabia. Khomeini's followers have been sending these Shi'ites messages urging them to join in an uprising against Western influence. The power of Khomeini's appeal for a "struggle between Islam and the infidels" must not be underestimated. In these and many other Islamic countries, Western technology and education have strained the social structure and brought with them trends that seem like paganism to devout Muslims. In addition, Muslims have bitter memories of a century or more of Western colonialism that kept most Islamic countries in servitude until a generation ago, and they tend to see U.S. support of Israel as a continuation of this "imperialist" tradition.

With Khomeini's encouragement, Muslims—not all of them Shi'ites—have staged anti-American riots in Libya, India and Bangladesh. In Islamabad, the capital of Pakistan, a mob burned the U.S embassy and killed two U.S. servicemen; the Ayatullah's reaction was "great joy." In Saudi Arabia, possessor of the world's largest oil reserves, the vulnerability of the royal family was made starkly apparent when a band of 200 to 300 well-armed raiders in November seized the Sacred Mosque in Mecca, the holiest of all Islamic shrines, which is under the protection of King Khalid. The raiders appeared to have mixed religious and political motives: they seemingly were armed and trained in Marxist South Yemen, but were fundamentalists opposed to all modernism, led by a zealot who had proclaimed the revolution in Iran to be a "new dawn" for Islam. It took the Saudi army more than a week to root them out from the catacomb-like basements of the mosque, and 156 died in the fighting—82 raiders and 74 Saudi troopers. In addition, demonstrators waving Khomeini's picture last month paraded in the oil towns of Saudi Arabia's Eastern Province. Saudi troops apparently opened fire on the protestors and at least 15 people are said to have died.

IMPACT ON THE WORLD

Such rumblings have deeply shaken the nerves, if not yet undermined the stability, of governments throughout the Middle

East. Leaders of the House of Saud regard Khomeini as an outright menace. Egypt's President Anwar Sadat denounced Khomeini as a man who is trying to play God and whose actions are a "crime against Islam [and] an insult to humanity." Nonetheless, the Ayatullah's appeal to Muslims, Sunni as well as Shi'ite, is so strong the even pro-Western Islamic leaders have been reluctant to give the U.S. more than minimal support in the hostage crisis. They have explicitly warned Washington that any U.S. military strike on Iran, even one undertaken in retaliation for the killing of the hostages, would so enrage their people as to threaten the security of every government in the area.

The appeal of Khomeini's Islamic fundamentalism to non-Muslim nations in the Third World is limited. Not so the wave of nationalism he unleashed in Iran. Warns William Quandt, senior fellow at the Brookings Institution: "People in the Third World were promised great gains upon independence [from colonialism], and yet they still find their lives and societies in a mess." Historically, such unfulfilled expectations prepare the ground for revolution, and the outbreak in Iran offers an example of an uprising that embodies a kind of nose-thumbing national pride.

Selig Harrison, senior associate at the Carnegie Endowment for International Peace, says the overthrow of Iran's Shah "is appealing to the Third World as a nationalist revolution that has stood up to superpower influence. At the rational level, Third World people know that you cannot behave like Khomeini and they do not condone violation of diplomatic immunity. But at the emotional level, mass public opinion in many Third World countries is not unfriendly to what Khomeini has done. There is an undercurrent of satisfaction in seeing a country stand up to superpower influence."

CHRONOLOGY

1945

U.S. president Franklin Roosevelt, British prime minister Winston Churchill, and Soviet leader Joseph Stalin meet at Yalta in the Ukraine to discuss postwar settlements. Adolf Hitler commits suicide. United Nations is formed. Atomic bomb is dropped on Japan, effectively ending the war in the Pacific. World War II ends. Allied leaders meet at Potsdam, Germany, to discuss peace terms. Abstract expressionist painting—often dominated by large patches and streaks of color—begins its rule of the art world.

1946

The Nuremburg international war crimes trials try Nazi war criminals. Churchill gives his "Iron Curtain" speech at Fulton, Missouri. President Harry S. Truman establishes the Truman Doctrine, pledging to aid countries threatened by an aggressor. Vietnamese nationalists battle France for independence. French actor Marcel Marceau begins his career as the world's most famous mime.

1947

The European Recovery Plan (also known as the Marshall Plan) is instituted, providing U.S. financial aid to war-damaged European countries. India gains independence from Great Britain but is split into two rival nations—India (Hindu) and Pakistan (Muslim)—that battle over the state of Kashmir, which was granted to India in the separation. *The Diary of Anne Frank* is published. The Dead Sea Scrolls are discovered. Flying saucers are reported in the United States. Jackie Robinson is the first black player to sign a contract with a major league baseball team.

1948

Israel becomes a nation. Communist forces invade Czechslo-
vakia, making it a Soviet satellite and sparking Western nations' anxiety about Communist expansionism. Mahatma
Gandhi is assassinated. The Soviet Union creates a blockade around West Berlin; the allies bring in supplies by air.
Korea splits into two nations—North Korea (Communist)
and South Korea. Bell Labs invents the transistor.

1949

South Africa officially adopts apartheid. NATO is formed;
Communist nations form a similar mutual-support organization, COMECON. Germany is divided into East Germany (managed by the Soviet Union) and West Germany
(managed by the Western allies). Jerusalem is partitioned
into two parts—one owned by Jordan, the other by Israel.
Alan Paton's novel of Africa, *Cry, the Beloved Country,* is
published. England allows most of Ireland to become an independent nation—the Republic of Eire. Chinese Communists take over mainland China and establish the People's
Republic of China; nationalists flee to the island of Formosa, where they remain the officially recognized Chinese
government in the eyes of the United States and some other
nations. George Orwell's *1984* is published. Rogers and
Hammerstein musical *South Pacific* hits Broadway.

1950

The red scare (fear of Communists) sweeps the United States.
The McCarran Act requires all Communists to register
with the government and imposes other restrictions on
them. President Truman instructs the Atomic Energy Commission to develop a hydrogen bomb. Communist China
invades Tibet. The United States becomes involved in the
Korean War. The musical *Guys and Dolls* is a Broadway hit.

1951

The United States sentences Julius and Ethel Rosenberg to
death for being Communist spies. J.D. Salinger's *Catcher in
the Rye* is pubished. Color television begins to appear in
U.S. homes.

1952

Norman Vincent Peale publishes *The Power of Positive Thinking.*

1953

Elizabeth II is crowned queen of England. New Zealander Edmund Hillary and Sherpa Tenzing Norgay climb Mount Everest. Researchers report the correlation between cigarette smoking and lung cancer.

1954

Vietnam is divided into North (Communist) and South; the division heightens rather than eliminates conflict. SEATO is founded to prevent Communist expansion in Asian nations. Argentine president Juan Peron is overthrown. The U.S. Supreme Court rules in *Brown v. Board of Education of Topeka* that school segregation is unconstitutional. J.R.R. Tolkein's *Lord of the Rings* is published. Roger Bannister is the first runner to break the four-minute mile.

1955

International Geneva conference explores the peaceful use of the atom. Communists sign Warsaw Pact pledging mutual assistance. Black Alabaman Rosa Parks refuses to give up her bus seat to a white man and sparks the Selma bus boycotts and other civil rights activism.

1956

Cuban guerrilla activity against U.S.-supported dictator Fulgencio Batista begins. Egypt nationalizes the Suez Canal (formerly owned by a French-British coalition), an important shipping zone; British and Israeli troops attack Egypt, and the United States intervenes at the UN to try to end the conflict; the canal is closed for more than a year. Hungarians revolt against Communist repression, but Soviet troops quickly quell the rebellion. Lerner and Lowe's musical *My Fair Lady* is a hit. Elvis Presley makes teenage girls swoon.

1957

International Atomic Energy Commission is established. Britain explodes a nuclear bomb in the Pacific. "Eisenhower doctrine" pledges to protect the Middle East from communism. Russia launches *Sputnik I*—and the space race. Jack Kerouac's *On the Road* is published, as is Dr. Seuss's *Cat in the Hat*. Leonard Bernstein's Broadway musical *West Side Story* transfers *Romeo and Juliet* to gang-ridden New York.

1958

Egypt and Syria form the United Arab Republic. Belgian Congo rebels. President Eisenhower sends federal troops to Little Rock, Arkansas, to prevent violence over school desegregation. NASA is established.

1959

Cuban guerrillas overthrow their goverment and install Fidel Castro as premier. The European Common Market is formed. *The Sound of Music* is a Broadway hit.

1960

European colonial powers grant independence to several African nations: The age of colonialism is rapidly drawing to a close as most European nations are forced to let their colonies go. U.S. pilot Gary Powers is shot down in his U-2 spy plane over the USSR. Harper Lee's *To Kill a Mockingbird* is published. The laser is developed. W.F. Libby wins the Nobel Prize for chemistry for developing the carbon 14 method for dating archaeological artifacts. Chubby Checker has teens twisting and shouting on the dance floor.

1961

The United States unsuccessfully supports an invasion of Cuba near the Bay of Pigs. The Berlin Wall is erected. Israel puts former Nazi Gestapo chief Adolf Eichmann on trial for Holocaust crimes and sentences him to death. Russian astronaut Yuri Gagarin orbits Earth in a satellite and becomes the first man in space. Black and white American Freedom Riders try to force integration in the South and face violent resistance.

1962

The first international nuclear disarmament conference is held in Geneva, Switzerland. The Cuban missile crisis brings the United States and the USSR to the brink of nuclear war. President John F. Kennedy establishes the Peace Corps. Algeria gains its independence from France after an eight-year war. *Lawrence of Arabia* sweeps away moviegoers, and *Dr. No* introduces superspy James Bond. Rachel Carson's *Silent Spring* warns the world of the dangers of pollution. Thalidomide, a drug given to pregnant women to stop nausea, is discovered to have caused numerous cases of birth defects.

1963

The United States, USSR, and United Kingdom sign a nuclear test ban treaty. British spy Kim Philby flees to the USSR. President Kennedy calls out three thousand federal troops to quell civil rights riots in Birmingham, Alabama. The United Arab Republic, Syria, and Iraq establish a cooperative union. The United States and the USSR set up a "hot line" from the White House to the Kremlin to deal with emergencies such as the accidental launch of a nuclear missile. John LeCarre's *The Spy Who Came in from the Cold* is published. New York's Guggenheim Museum hosts a show of pop art. Folk and protest music gain popularity through such artists as Bob Dylan, Joan Baez, and Peter, Paul, and Mary. The Beatles record their first hits in England. The first female astronaut, Russian Valentina Tereshkova, flies in space. U.S. president John F. Kennedy is assassinated, and his assassin is killed by another gunman on national television.

1964

Congress passes the Civil Rights Act. Yasir Arafat takes over leadership of Palestinian organization El Fatah. Greece, Cyprus, and Turkey suffer ongoing conflict. Gang fights in England—the Mods and the Rockers—disrupt British seaside resorts. Cassius Clay wins the world heavyweight boxing championship.

1965

The first U.S. Marines land in Vietnam. The antiwar protest movement sweeps the United States. Malcolm X is assassinated. Rhodesia declares independence from Britain, sparking a conflict that lasts several years. The Watts (Los Angeles) riots terrify the United States and express black rage against racist U.S. society. England abolishes the death penalty.

1966

China's Cultural Revolution begins. Indira Gandhi becomes India's prime minister. Truman Capote writes the first "nonfiction novel," *In Cold Blood,* chronicling the events surrounding a brutal Kansas murder. The miniskirt hits the fashion runways.

1967

The Israel-Syria conflict heats up. Israel wins the Six-Day War against Egypt, Jordan, and Syria. South Africa's Dr. Christiaan Barnard performs the first heart transplant. The Greek military overthrows the king and establishes a dictatorship. The United States is wracked by both pro- and anti-Vietnam protests. Boxer Muhammed Ali refuses to be inducted into military service, and the World Boxing Association takes away his world heavyweight champion title. The year's major art exhibitions include the works of Pablo Picasso and the treasures of Tutenkhamen. Communist China sets off its first hydrogen bomb. The Boston Strangler is sentenced to life in prison. The Broadway musical *Hair* announces the "dawning of the Age of Aquarius."

1968

The United States suffers a wave of domestic terrorism never before seen in the country. Martin Luther King Jr. is assassinated, as is popular U.S. attorney general Robert Kennedy. When liberal Communist leader Alexander Dubcek institutes reforms, the USSR invades and clamps down once again. The modern crisis in Northern Ireland begins, violently pitting Catholics against Protestants. A new political party, Parti Québécois, forms in Quebec to promote Quebec's secession from Canada. Black activist Eldridge Cleaver's *Soul on Ice* is published.

1969

Americans are stunned when U.S. soldiers are convicted of wantonly slaying civilians at My Lai, Vietnam. The United States begins withdrawing troops from Vietnam. England sends troops into Northern Ireland. Mario Puzo's *The Godfather* is published. The United States lands men on the moon. Pope Paul VI eliminates two hundred saints from the Catholic pantheon. More than four hundred thousand rock music fans crowd a music festival at Woodstock, New York, for three days of peace, love, and music. The Charles Manson murders shock the United States.

1970

The United States invades Cambodia. A rash of airplane hijackings make air travelers nervous. Soviet novelist Alexandr Solzhenitsyn wins the Nobel Prize for his fiction depicting the ugliness of the Soviet system.

1971

Against U.S. protest, Communist China joins the UN and the Republic of China is forced out. The United States and the USSR ban nuclear arms on the ocean floor. Britain clamps down in Northern Ireland, imprisoning terrorist suspects without trials, but violence escalates anyway.

1972

U.S. president Richard Nixon visits Red China, the first time in two decades that the United States has acknowledged the Communist nation. Arab terrorists place Olympic Village under siege, taking hostages and killing two athletes.

1973

The Watergate scandal breaks, bringing to the public eye revelations about dirty politics in the previous presidential election campaign. A military coup ousts Chilean president Salvador Allende. The American Indian Movement holds off the FBI at Wounded Knee, South Dakota. An energy crisis—fueled by the Arab oil embargo against nations that aided Israel—strikes western Europe, the United States, and Japan. The U.S. Supreme Court rules in *Roe v. Wade* that a woman has the right to choose an abortion.

1974

The Watergate scandal leads to the impeachment and resignation of President Nixon. Famine threatens millions in Africa. Little League baseball agrees to let girls join the teams. Russian ballet dancer Mikhail Baryshnikov defects to the West. Stephen King publishes his first novel, *Carrie.*

1975

The United States officially ends two decades of involvement in Vietnam. Christians and Muslims fight in Lebanon. The Canadian Anglican Church begins ordaining female priests. Six thousand third-century B.C. lifesize terra cotta figures are discovered in northwestern China. *Jaws* scares summer moviegoers. In an unusual collaboration, U.S. and Soviet spacecraft link up in space. Domestic terrorism in South America, Europe, Africa, and the United States keeps the world on edge.

1976

South African riots protest apartheid. The first South African black homeland, Transkei, is given independence. North and South Vietnam reunite. Researchers announce that the gases emitted from spray cans are harming Earth's ozone layer. U.S. spacecraft *Viking I* and *Viking II* land on Mars, transmit photos of the surface, and bring Martian soil samples back to Earth. The Concorde jets in London and Paris inaugurate supersonic transatlantic air service to Washington, D.C. The previously unknown Legionnaires' Disease kills twenty-nine American Legion convention attendees and leaves more than 150 seriously ill. Punk rock and disco invade the popular music scene.

1977

U.S. president Jimmy Carter pardons Vietnam draft evaders. Palestinians call for a Palestinian nation to be created from parts of Israel and Jordan.

1978

The United States and the People's Republic of China establish diplomatic relations, and the United States breaks off relations with its former favorite, Nationalist China. U.S. president Carter helps facilitate peace negotiations between Israel and Egypt. Leftist guerillas begin a violent campaign to overthrow Nicaraguan dictator Antonio Somoza. The Honduran government is overthrown by a military coup. Bolivia undergoes its two-hundredth coup since gaining its independence 158 years ago. The first test tube baby, conceived through in vitro fertilization, is born in England. A Japanese explorer, Naomi Uemura, becomes the first person to travel alone to the North Pole.

1979

Marxists win the bloody Nicaraguan civil war. The shah of Iran is deposed, and the Ayatollah Khomeini gains power, establishing a theocracy. Iran takes fifty-two American embassy workers hostage. A military coup overthrows El Salvador's government. The Soviet army invades Afghanistan. The nuclear reactor in the energy plant at Three Mile Island, Pennsylvania, melts down, but it avoids the widespread nuclear disaster many people have feared.

1980

Poland's Solidarity Union brings about a massive strike of 500,000 shipyard workers, who stop work and demand civil rights. Iran and Iraq battle over borderlands. The United States allows the immigration of 120,000 anti-Castro Cubans. Musician John Lennon is murdered in New York. Smallpox is eradicated. The sunken *Titanic* is discovered. Scientists discover evidence that a meteorite wiped out the dinosaurs. More than fifty nations boycott the Olympics, hosted in Moscow, to protest the Soviet invasion of Afghanistan.

FOR FURTHER RESEARCH

AFRICA

John W. DeGruchy, "Sharpeville Revisited," *Christian Century*, April 26, 1995.

William S. Ellis, "South Africa's Lonely Ordeal," *National Geographic*, June 1977.

William Galvéz, *Che in Africa: Che Guevara's Congo Diary*. Melbourne, Australia: Ocean, 1999.

Jonathan E. Helmreich, *United States Relations with Belgium and the Congo, 1940–1960*. Newark: University of Delaware Press, 1998.

International Defense and Aid Fund for Southern Africa, in Co-Operation with the United Nations Centre Against Apartheid, *Apartheid: The Facts*. London: International Defense and Aid Fund, 1983.

Madelaine G. Kalb, "The C.I.A. and Lumumba," *New York Times Magazine*, August 2, 1981.

Sean Kelly, *America's Tyrant: The CIA and Mobutu of Zaire*. Washington, DC: American University Press, 1993.

Alex La Guma, ed., *Apartheid*. New York: International, 1971.

David Lamb, *The Africans*. New York: Vintage, 1987.

Brian Lapping, *Apartheid: A History*. New York: George Braziller, 1986.

Colin Legum, *Congo Disaster*. Gloucester, MA: Peter Smith, 1972.

David Mermelstein, ed., *The Anti-Apartheid Reader: The Struggle Against White Racist Rule in South Africa*. New York: Grove, 1987.

Dan O'Meara, *Forty Lost Years: The Apartheid State and the Politics of the National Party, 1948–1994.* Athens: Ohio University Press, 1996.

John W. Turner, *Continent Ablaze: The Insurgency Wars in Africa, 1960 to the Present.* London: Arms and Armour, 1998.

Desmond Tutu, *Hope and Suffering.* Grand Rapids, MI: William B. Eerdmans, 1983.

Nigel Worden, *The Making of Modern South Africa: Conquest, Segregation, and Apartheid.* Cambridge, MA: Blackwell, 1994.

THE ATOM BOMB

Gar Alperovitz and Kai Bird, "The Centrality of the Bomb," *Foreign Policy,* Spring 1994.

George R. Caron and Charlotte E. Meares, *Fire of a Thousand Suns,* Westminster, CO: Web, 1995.

John Hersey, *Hiroshima.* New York: Alfred A. Knopf, 1946.

Toyofumi Ogura, *A Firsthand Account of the Bombing of Hiroshima.* Tokyo: Kodansha International, 1997.

Apata Osada, comp., *Children of Hiroshima.* London: Publishing Committee for *Children of Hiroshima,* 1980.

J. Siemes, *The Day the Bomb Fell: Hiroshima, 6 August 1945: An Eyewitness Account.* London: Catholic Truth Society, 1984.

Lequita Vance-Watkins and Aratani Mariko, eds. and trans., *White Flash, Black Rain: Women of Japan Relive the Bomb.* Minneapolis: Milkweed Editions, 1995.

THE BEAT GENERATION

James Campbell, *This Is the Beat Generation.* New York: Secker & Warburg, 1999.

Bruce Cook, *The Beat Generation: The Tumultuous '50s Movement and Its Impact on Today.* New York: William Morrow, 1994.

Edward Halsey Foster, *Understanding the Beats.* Columbia: University of South Carolina Press, 1992.

Jack Kerouac, *The Portable Kerouac.* New York: Viking, 1995.

China

Yuan-tsung Chen, *The Dragon's Village: An Autobiographical View of Revolutionary China.* New York: Peng, 1980.

Yue Daiyun and Carolyn Wakem, *To the Storm: The Odyssey of a Revolutionary Chinese Woman.* Berkeley and Los Angeles: University of California Press, 1985.

Henry Harding, *China's Second Revolution: Reform After Mao.* Washington, DC: Brookings Institution, 1987.

Liang Heng and Judith Shapiro, *Son of the Revolution.* New York: Vintage, 1983.

Yan Jiaqi and Gao Gao, *Turbulent Decade: A History of the Cultural Revolution,* trans. and ed. by D.W.Y. Kwok. Honolulu: University of Hawaii Press, 1986.

Robert Jay Lifton, *Revolutionary Immortality: Mao Tse-Tung and the Chinese Cultural Revolution.* New York: Vintage, 1968.

Zi-Ping Luo, *A Generation Lost: China Under the Cultural Revolution.* New York: Henry Holt, 1990.

David Milton et al, eds., *People's China.* Harmondsworth, England: Penguin, 1977.

Teresa Poole, "Mao's Frenzy of Mass Violence," *London Independent on Monday,* May 12, 1996.

Hung Tsin-ta and Nan Hsueh-lin, "Salesmen of Reactionary Western Culture," *Chinese Literature,* no. 11, 1968.

U.S. News & World Report, "'Holy War' in Tibet—What It Is All About," April 13, 1959.

Ching-chi Yi-ling Wong, *Thirty Years in Deep Freeze: My Life in Communist China.* Santa Barbara, CA: Fithian, 2000.

Jan Wong, *Red China Blues: My Long March from Mao to Now.* New York: Doubleday/Anchor, 1997.

Gao Yuan, *Born Red: A Chronicle of the Cultural Revolution.* Stanford, CA: Stanford University Press, 1987.

The Civil Rights and Black Power Movements

Clayborne Carson, *The Eyes on the Prize Civil Rights Reader.* New York: Penguin, 1991.

E. Culpepper Clark, *The Schoolhouse Door: Segregation's Last Stand at the University of Alabama*. New York: Oxford University Press, 1993.

Archie Epps, ed., *Malcolm X: Speeches at Harvard*. New York: Paragon House, 1991.

Alex Haley, *The Autobiography of Malcolm X*. New York: Ballantine, 1964.

Henry Hampton and Steve Fayer, eds., *Voices of Freedom: An Oral History of the Civil Rights Movement from the 1950s Through the 1980s*. New York: Vintage, 1988.

James Jackson Kilpatrick, *The Southern Case for School Segregation*. Springfield, OH: Crowell-Collier, 1962.

Martin Luther King Jr., "I Have a Dream," *Negro History Bulletin*, May 1968.

———, *Where Do We Go from Here—Chaos or Community?* New York: Harper & Row, 1967.

Elijah Muhammed, *Message to the Blackman in America*. Newport News, VA: United Brothers Communications Systems, 1992.

Rosa Parks and Jim Haskins, *Rosa Parks, My Story*. New York: Puffin Books/Penguin, 1999.

Roberta Hughes Wright, *The Birth of the Montgomery Bus Boycott*. Southfield, MI: Charro, 1992.

THE COLD WAR

Graham Allison and Philip Zelikow, *Essence of Decision: Explaining the Cuban Missile Crisis*. New York: Longman, 1999.

David Cannadine, ed., *Blood, Toil, Tears, and Sweat: The Speeches of Winston Churchill*. Boston: Houghton Mifflin, 1989.

CQ Researcher, "Superpower Battleground," November 27, 1992.

John Foster Dulles, Nikita Khrushchev, Bertrand Russell, exchange of letters on peaceful coexistence, *New Statesman*, November 23, 1957; December 21, 1957; February 8, 1958; March 14, 1958.

John F. Kennedy, radio and television report to the American people on the Soviet arms buildup in Cuba, October 22,

1962, in *Public Papers of the Presidents of the United States: John F. Kennedy, 1962.*

Nikita S. Khrushchev, *On Peaceful Co-Existence: A Collection.* Moscow: Foreign Languages Publishing House, 1961.

Melvin P. Leffler and David S. Painter, eds., *Origins of the Cold War: An International History.* New York: Routledge, 1994.

Joseph McCarthy, speech presented at the Ohio County Republican Women's Club, Wheeling, West Virginia, February 9, 1950, *Congressional Record,* 81st Cong., 2nd sess., February 20, 1950.

David S. Painter, *The Cold War: An International History.* New York: Routledge, 1999.

Gabriel Partos, *The World That Came in from the Cold: Perspectives from East and West on the Cold War.* London: Royal Institute of International Affairs, 1993.

Harry S. Truman, speech to Congress, February 21, 1947, in *Congressional Record,* 80th Cong., 1st sess.

EASTERN EUROPE

Ivo Banac, ed., *Eastern Europe in Revolution.* Ithaca, NY: Cornell University Press, 1992.

J.F. Brown, *Surge of Freedom: The End of Communist Rule in Eastern Europe.* Durham, NC: Duke University Press, 1991.

R.J. Crampton, *Eastern Europe in the Twentieth Century—and After,* 2nd ed. New York: Routledge, 1994.

Christopher Cviic, *Remaking the Balkans.* London: Royal Institute of International Affairs, 1991.

Stephen Fischer-Galati, *Eastern Europe and the Cold War: Perceptions and Perspectives.* New York: Columbia University Press, 1994.

Timothy Foote, "'But If Enough of Us Get Killed Something May Happen,'" *Smithsonian,* November 1986.

Joseph Held, *The Columbia History of Eastern Europe in the Twentieth Century.* New York: Columbia University Press, 1992.

THE MIDDLE EAST AND NEAR EAST

J.J. Akbar, *India: The Siege Within—Challenges to a Nation's Unity.* New Delhi: UBSPD, 1985.

Leonard Binder, ed., *Ethnic Conflict and International Politics in the Middle East.* Gainesville: University Press of Florida, 1999.

Kamal Boullata, *Faithful Witness: Palestinian Children Recreate Their World.* New York: Olive Branch, 1990.

James Ciment, *Palestine/Israel: The Long Conflict.* New York: Facts On File, 1997.

Catherine Clement, *Gandhi: The Power of Pacifism.* New York: Henry N. Abrams, 1989.

John L. Esposito, ed., *The Iranian Revolution: Its Global Impact.* Gainesville: University of Florida Press, 1990.

Oriana Fallaci, "Yasir Arafat," in *Interview with History,* Trans. John Shepley. Boston: Houghton Mifflin, 1976.

Elizabeth Warnock Fernea and Mary Evelyn Hocking, eds., *The Struggle for Peace: Israelis and Palestinians.* Austin: University of Texas Press, 1992.

Aloysius Fonseca, "Gandhi and Nonviolence," *America,* October 4, 1969.

Prebhudas Gandhi, *My Childhood with Gandhi.* Ahmedabad, India: Navajivan Publishing House, 1957.

Haig Khatchadourian, *The Quest for Peace Between Israel and the Palestinians.* New York: Peter Lang, 2000.

Walter Laqueur and Barry Rubin, eds., *The Israel-Arab Reader: A Documentary History of the Middle-East Conflict,* 5th ed. New York: Penguin, 1995.

Yehuda Lukacs and Abdalla M. Battah, eds., *The Arab-Israeli Conflict: Two Decades of Change.* Boulder, CO: Westview, 1988.

Staughton Lynd, Sam Bahour, and Alice Lynd, eds., *Homeland: Oral Histories of Palestine and Palestinians.* New York: Olive Branch, 1994.

David McDowell, *The Palestinians: The Road to Nationhood.* London: Minority Rights, 1994.

Newsweek, "'Oh Lovely Dawn,'" August 25, 1947.

Rinna Samuel, *A History of Israel: The Birth, Growth, and Development of Today's Jewish State.* London: Weidenfeld and Nicolson, 1989.

Tom Segev, *1949: The First Israelis*. New York: Free, 1986.

Shashi Tharoor, *India: From Midnight to the Millennium*. New York: Arcade, 1998.

Time, "The Mystic Who Lit the Fires of Hatred," January 7, 1980.

Pop Art

Thomas Crow, *The Rise of the Sixties*. New York: Henry N. Abrams, 1996.

Allan Kaprow, "Pop Art: Past, Present, and Future," *The Malahat Review*, July 1967.

Steven Henry Madoff, *Pop Art: A Critical History*. Berkeley and Los Angeles: University of California Press, 1997.

Carol Anne Mahsun, ed., *Pop Art: The Critical Dialogue*. Ann Arbor, MI: UMI Research Press, 1989.

Tilman Osterwold, *Pop Art*. Köln, Germany: Taschen, 1999.

John Russell, "Pop Reappraised," *Art in America*, July/August 1969.

Tony Scherman, "When Pop Art Turned the World Upside Down," *American Heritage*, February 2001.

Popular Music

Michael T. Bertrand, *Race, Rock, and Elvis*. Urbana: University of Illinois Press, 2000.

Kevin Chappell, "How Blacks Invented Rock and Roll," *Ebony*, January 1997.

Reebee Garofalo, ed., *Rockin' the Boat: Mass Music and Mass Movements*. Boston: South End, 1992.

David Gates, "The Roots of Rock," *Newsweek*, June 2, 1997.

Tony Scherman, "Little Richard's Big Noise," *Smithsonian*, February/March 1995.

Ed Ward, Geoffrey Stokes, and Ken Tucker, *Rock of Ages: The "Rolling Stone" History of Rock and Roll*. Englewood Cliffs, NJ: Rolling Stone Press/Prentice-Hall, 1986.

GENERAL

Robert Aldrich and John Connell, *The Last Colonies.* New York: Cambridge University Press, 1998.

Franz Ansprenger, *The Dissolution of the Colonial Empires.* New York: Routledge, 1989.

Glen St. J. Barclay, *Twentieth Century Revolutions of Our Time: Nationalism.* London: Weidenfeld and Nicolson, 1971.

Carlton Beals, *Great Guerrilla Warriors.* Englewood Cliffs, NJ: Prentice-Hall, 1970.

Sharon Begley, "The Transistor," *Newsweek,* Winter 1997.

David V.J. Bell, *Resistance and Revolution.* Boston: Houghton Mifflin, 1973.

James and Grace Lee Boggs, *Revolution and Evolution in the Twentieth Century.* New York: Monthly Review, 1974.

Michael H. Brown, "Love Canal and the Poisoning of America," *Atlantic,* December 1979.

William H. Chafe and Harvard Sitkoff, *A History of Our Time: Readings on Postwar America,* 3rd ed. New York: Oxford University Press, 1991.

Anthony R. DeLuca, *Gandhi, Mao, Mandela, and Gorbachev: Studies in Personality, Power, and Politics.* Westport, CT: Praeger, 2000.

Edwin Diamond and Stephen Bates, "Sputnik," *American Heritage,* October 1997.

Oriana Fallaci, *Interview with History.* Boston: Houghton Mifflin, 1976.

Michael Farrell, *Northern Ireland: The Orange State.* London: Pluto, 1986.

Ronald Fernandez, *Cruising the Caribbean: U.S. Influence and Intervention in the Twentieth Century.* Monroe, ME: Common Courage, 1994.

Betty Friedan, *It Changed My Life.* New York: Random House, 1976.

L.H. Gann and Peter Duignan, *Contemporary Europe and the Atlantic Alliance.* Oxford, England: Blackwell, 1998.

Paul A. Hanle, "The Beeping Ball That Started a Dash into Outer Space," *Smithsonian*, October 1982.

Rajan Harshè, *Twentieth-Century Imperialism: Shifting Contours and Changing Conceptions*. Thousand Oaks, CA: Sage, 1997.

C.R. Hensman, *The Polemics of Revolt: From Gandhi to Guevara*. London: Allen Lane, 1969.

Lyndon B. Johnson, "Pattern for Peace in Southeast Asia," *Department of State Bulletin*, April 26, 1965.

John F. Kennedy, inaugural address, in *Public Papers of the Presidents: John F. Kennedy, 1961*, Washington, DC: US Government Printing Office, 1962.

Rebecca E. Klatch, *Women of the New Right*. Philadelphia: Temple University Press, 1987.

Brian Lapping, *End of Empire*. New York: St. Martin's, 1985.

Jon E. Lewis, ed., *The Permanent Book of the Twentieth Century: Eye-Witness Accounts of the Moments That Shaped Our Century*. New York: Carroll & Graf, 1994.

Geir Lundestad, *East, West, North, South: Major Developments in International Politics, 1945–1996*. Trans. Gail Adams Kvam. Oslo: Scandinavian, 1986.

George C. Marshall, speech at Harvard University, June 5, 1947, in *Congressional Record*, 80th Cong., 1st sess., Appendix.

Robert J. McMahon, *The Limits of Empire: The United States and Southeast Asia Since World War II*. New York: Columbia University Press, 1999.

James E. Miller, "A Short History of NATO," *Department of State Bulletin*, August 1989.

Paul Romer, "In the Beginning Was the Transistor," *Forbes*, December 2, 1996.

Steven L. Spiegel and Kenneth N. Waltz, eds., *Conflict in World Politics*. Cambridge, MA: Winthrop, 1971.

Raymond Tanter, *Rogue Regimes: Terrorism and Proliferation*. New York: St. Martin's, 1998.

Derek W. Urwin, *Western Europe Since 1945, a Political History*. 4th ed. New York: Longman Group, 1989.

INDEX